TWAYNE'S WORLD AUTHORS SERIES

A Survey of the World's Literature

Sylvia E. Bowman, Indiana University

GENERAL EDITOR

Ulrich Weisstein, Indiana University

EDITOR

Arnold Zweig

TWAS 361

Arnold Zweig

Arnold Zweig

By GEORGE SALAMON

TWAYNE PUBLISHERS

A DIVISION OF G. K. HALL & CO., BOSTON

Library of Congress Cataloging in Publication Data

Salamon, George.
  Arnold Zweig.

  (Twayne's world authors series ; TWAS 361)
  Bibliography: pp. 193 - 97.
  Includes index.
  1. Zweig, Arnold, 1887 - 1968.
PT2653.W4Z84   833'.9'12   75-12736
ISBN 0-8057-6212-4

MANUFACTURED IN THE UNITED STATES OF AMERICA

Contents

About the Author

George Salamon was born in Vienna, Austria, and owes his child-hood residence in Switzerland to the Third Reich. He received his B.A. from Brandeis University and his Ph.D. from Harvard. He has taught German language and literature at Haverford, Duke, Dart-mouth, and Smith, and held a Fellowship for Younger Humanists from the National Endowment for the Humanities. His work in-cludes an edition of Max Frisch's play *Graf Öderland*, an anthology of German history, and a comparative article on E. T. A. Hoffmann and I. B. Singer. The relations between German history and literature, especially in Wilhelminian Germany, are his main in-terests, and he is currently at work on a study of German fiction about the First World War.

Preface

When *The Case of Sergeant Grischa* was published in 1927, Arnold
Zweig was universally praised for one of the most moving and
perceptive books about World War I and about war in general. Yet
when his cycle of novels about the war was finally completed in
1957, both historical events and a shift of emphasis in his work had
deprived the author of wide critical recognition and public response.
An erudite man, solidly rooted in the German philosophical tradition
of the nineteenth century, Zweig interpreted upheavals in European
history and German society within the framework of intellectual
history, and therefore his fiction appeals as much to the mind as it
does to the emotions. Thus the six novels Zweig devoted to prewar
Germany and to Germany at war provide a chronicle of the social
history and the history of ideas of Wilhelminian Germany.

But Zweig's prolific output was not restricted to the war. His early
work records the tensions he experienced as an artist and a Jew in a
society suspicious of both, and his period of exile in Palestine and last
years in the German Democratic Republic reflect successive disillusionment with one credo and endorsement of another. The present study, the first in English about Arnold Zweig, attempts to assess
his literary achievements and record his shifting allegiances to the
ideologies of our century. A biographical chapter has not been included, because his work was his life, and the chronological order of
his publications, generally followed here, gives us the man as well as
his work. Because his long life as a professional writer resulted in
prolific production of varying quality, some stories and many essays
are not discussed at all or mentioned only peripherally.

Minor deviations from a strict chronological order occur in chapter
3, which treats exclusively and extensively the major novels of the
cycle Zweig called "The Great War of the White Man." These
novels are discussed in the order in which Zweig wrote them rather

than in order of temporal occurrence for reasons outlined in that chapter. In chapter 5 the two novels added to the cycle after his return to the German Democratic Republic are also treated in chronological order. In the interest of economy, the frequent quotations from these works are identified simply by a parenthetical page number, referring to the first edition. Chapters 1, 2, and 4 deal broadly with significant segments of Zweig's life and his development as a writer. Since numerous works are discussed in each of these chapters, each citation includes the volume quoted from, according to the table of abbreviations appended below. Except in the cases noted, quotations are drawn from the first editions, as listed in the bibliography.

I wish to thank Beatrice Zweig, who, shortly before her death in 1971, generously allowed me to quote and translate from all of her husband's work. My thanks go also to Ilse Lange, longtime companion to the Zweigs and Keeper of the Archive in Berlin today, to the Aufbau-Verlag for permission to cite and translate any works of Zweig published by them, to Eberhard Hilscher for his suggestions and good wishes, and to Eric Sutton, whose translations of Zweig's major novels served as a basis for my own.

These are the abbreviations used:

B   = *Die Beste.*
BJ   = *Bilanz der deutschen Judenheit 1933.*
C   = *Caliban oder Politik und Leidenschaft.*
D   = *Dramen* (Volume XIII of *Ausgewählte Werke.*)
DE   = *Drei Erzählungen.*
DV   = *De Vriendt kehrt heim.*
E,I = *Essays;* Erster Band. (Volume XV of *Ausgewählte Werke.*)
E,II = *Essays;* Zweiter Band. (Volume XVI of *Ausgewählte Werke.*)
FF   = *Frühe Fährten.*
Fk   = *Der Früchtekorb; Jüngste Ernte. Aufsätze.*
G   = *Der Streit um den Sergeanten Grischa.*
J   = *Jahresringe; Gedichte und Spiele.* (Volume XIV of *Ausgewählte Werke.*)
KM   = *Knaben und Männer.*
MF   = *Mädchen und Frauen.*
N   = *Über den Nebeln.*
NC   = *Die Novellen um Claudia.*
OA   = *Das ostjüdische Antlitz.* (In *Herkunft und Zukunft; Zwei Essays zum Schicksal eines Volkes.*)

Preface

PA = *Pont und Anna.* (Published separately in 1928.)
SZ = *Spielzeuge der Zeit.*
ÜS = *Über Schriftsteller.*
VT = *Versunkene Tage.*
W   = *Das Beil von Wandsbek.*

GEORGE SALAMON

Chronology

1887   Arnold Zweig born to Adolf Zweig and Bianca van Spandow Zweig on November 10 in Groß -Glogau, Silesia.

1896   A decree forbidding Jews from dealing with the Prussian army forces Adolf Zweig to give up his grain and feed business and move to Kattowitz, where he resumes the craft of saddlery. Arnold attends schools there for ten years.

1907 - Zweig attends five German universities — Breslau, Munich,
1915   Berlin, Göttingen, and Rostock — where he studies modern languages and literatures, philosophy, psychology, and art history. First literary efforts while a student in Breslau in 1907. Acquaintance with the work of Freud.

1909   Coeditor of the bimonthly student magazine *Die Gäste*, in which his short story "Vorfrühling" and the verse drama *Abigail und Nabal* are published.

1911   *Aufzeichnungen über eine Familie Klopfer* published.

1912   Zweig's first success, *Die Novellen um Claudia*, published.

1914   Collection of war stories, *Die Bestie,* published.

1915   Zweig recipient of the Kleist Prize for the drama *Ritualmord in Ungarn*, written in 1913 and published in 1914. Produced after the war by Max Reinhardt.

1915 - Service in the German army at the front in Belgium, Hun-
1918   gary, Serbia, and during the battle of Verdun, and then as clerk in the headquarters of the eastern front in Lithuania and Russia.

1916   Marriage to his cousin Beatrice Zweig on July 5 in Berlin.

1918 - Demobilization and return to Berlin, followed by one
1919   semester of studies in literature and sociology at the University of Tübingen. Move to Starnberg, Bavaria, where the Zweigs live until 1923; early attempts at free-lance-writing career.

1920 Son Michael born on July 25 in Starnberg.

1921 Completion of the play about Sergeant Grischa, which is not performed until 1930.

1921 - 1924 Appearance of numerous novellas and Zionist essays. Zweig supports himself and his family primarily through journalism.

1924 - 1927 Move to Berlin. Birth of second son, Adam, on October 14, 1924. Many essays for the Zionist journal *Jüdische Rundschau*, of which Zweig was briefly an editor, and for the leftist *Die Weltbühne*, where he knew Kurt Tucholsky. In 1925 publication of his collected novellas, including *Pont und Anna*.

1927 *Der Streit um den Sergeanten Grischa* published to rapid international acclaim and financial success. Twelve-year correspondence with Freud begun.

1931 *Junge Frau von 1914* published.

1932 Exploratory trip to Palestine, where Zweig learns the truth about the de Haan case. Writing and publication of *De Vriendt kehrt heim*.

1933 - 1948 Flight from Berlin in March, 1933. Via Prague, Vienna, and Switzerland he reaches Sanary-sur-Mer in southern France, a center for German literary refugees. *Bilanz der deutschen Judenheit 1933* begun. In December, 1933, the Zweigs move to Palestine and settle in Haifa, where they reside until 1948. English-language essays published in Jerusalem and London.

1935 *Erziehung vor Verdun* published in Amsterdam. Zweig deprived of his German citizenship by the National Socialist government.

1936 - 1939 Annual trips to Europe. Treatment of failing eyesight in Vienna. In 1937 Zweig hears of the events narrated in *Das Beil von Wandsbek*.

1939 Attendance at the PEN-Club meeting in New York, where he meets Albert Einstein and Thomas Mann. Received by President Roosevelt in the White House.

1940 Zweig studies the basic works of Marx and Engels, requested from German exiles in Moscow. He coedits the journal *Orient* and works for the pro-Soviet V-Liga ("Victory League").

1943 The Hebrew translation of *Das Beil von Wandsbek* published. An English version appears in 1947, the German original in 1948.

1948   Zweig returns to East Germany and settles in Berlin.

1949   Election to the Volkskammer, the Parliament of the newly created German Democratic Republic. Member of the World Peace Council and delegate at the World Peace Congress in Paris.

1950   Recipient of the National Prize for Literature.

1950 - President of the German Academy of the Arts.
1953

1952   First visit to the Soviet Union.

1954   *Die Feuerpause* published.

1957   *Die Zeit ist reif* published. The Aufbau-Verlag begins publication of his collected works.

1958   Recipient of the Lenin Peace Prize in Moscow.

1962   *Traum ist teuer* published.

1967   Involvement in a controversy with West Germany's conservative press over his stance in the Arab-Israeli war.

1968   Arnold Zweig dies on November 26 in Berlin; his home becomes a memorial archive.

CHAPTER 1

Early Sensibilities

ARNOLD ZWEIG suggested a Goethean dictum as model for the *modus operandi* of the creative artist: "Everything that man strives to achieve must engage his united powers acting in concert; anything fragmentary is in vain."[1] But Zweig's own career, beginning amid the perplexity of literary and political isms at the turn of the century, and ending in the safety and security of one of those isms half a century later, represents a characteristically German and modern oscillation between ideals and ideologies rather than Goethe's call to total commitment at all times. Zweig's work moves from self to society, from the unraveling of private egos in his early stories to the exploration of social consciousness and societal morality in his mature novels. Regarded as a whole, Zweig's career does not form the "fragments of a great confession," which would require an independent organic growth or development of artistic sensibilities at the center of his work, but rather a series of reactions to Germany's intellectual and political fortunes in this century. In addition, Zweig's responses were those of an outsider, for he was a Jew among Germans, an artist in a middle-class culture, and after World War I, a pacifist in a militantly nationalist and increasingly militarized society. Zweig's work, therefore, can be divided quite readily into periods which correspond both to political eras in German history and to extraliterary influences in European culture.

What forms a common thread in the career of Arnold Zweig, setting him apart from most modern novelists, is not the range of literary experimentation, since Zweig remained loyal to the narrative techniques of the realistic novel of the nineteenth century, but a steady and stubborn quest for the realization of philosophical truth in his fiction. In an essay he commented on this search: "I had always taken the problem of the philosophical certainty of human knowledge very seriously. . . . Philosophy was supposed to provide answers to all questions of human existence."[2] The answers Zweig found in each period of his career are phases in the formation of his critical consciousness. They reflect German life transmuted into fiction, with the emphasis shifting from the artistic and cultural spheres to the social and political ones. Kenneth Keniston has recently pointed out that "every individual is in [a] sense his society writ small. . . . A man's life history includes so intimate a factor as his childhood fantasies and so global a force as the intellectual tradition of his culture."[3] It is rather striking that Zweig's search for "philosophical certainty" follows Keniston's formulation so closely. Zweig began his literary career as a Freudian and concluded it as a Marxist. Or, to come closer to Keniston, his early work deals with the intimate world of private fantasy and its youthful expressions, while his later work presents a global indictment of Germany's intellectual tradition and its devastating explosions.

That Zweig's intellectual orientation should shift from Freud to Marx is not surprising. The common ground for both thinkers has been explored by Erich Fromm: "While for Marx truth was a weapon to induce social change, for Freud it was the weapon to induce individual change. . . . Freud was a liberal reformer; Marx, a radical revolutionist. Different as they were, they have in common an uncompromising will to liberate man, an equally uncompromising faith in truth as the instrument of liberation and the belief that the condition for this liberation lies in man's capacity to break the chain of illusion."[4] Like many of his contemporaries, the young Zweig hoped to find such liberation from the dishonest and oppressive social morality of Wilhelminian Germany by accepting the Freudian awareness of the libidinal organization of each individual. In a society in which strict pedantry and abstract philosophy were the intellectual ideals, and rigid manners and hollow customs the social standards, Freud's attempt to discover the logic of unreason, to communicate the irrational metaphysical assumptions inherent in man's nature, was received with great enthusiasm and relief by honest and sensitive young men and women. When Zweig read Freud in 1906, his sense of relief, coupled with anxiety and anticipation about coping with man's hitherto "dark nature," was felt in a personal as well as an intellectual way: "We had looked for eternal truths about humanity; Freud unearthed animal instincts in man. . . . Thus I was confronted with 'my' Freud. The most modern opposition to the old authorities had spoken."[5] Zweig's seven-year-long philosophical quest at six universities came to a sudden if temporary end. It was to be a most profitable interruption, for Freud's new method of self-understanding paved the way for Zweig's breakthrough as a writer. The new psychology helped him bridge the gap between motive and action, allowed him to approach problems from within, and thereby give voice to the texture of inner experience and the quality of personal life. The short stories he wrote between 1907 and 1912 are attempts to see through to the psychic reality hidden by the behavioral reality of self and society.

Such a trend toward inwardness and introspection, already a much lamented and lauded tradition in German literature by Zweig's time, did not, however, survive intact the social and moral shock waves caused by World War I. In the words of Barbara Tuchman, "The Great War of 1914 - 18 lies like a band of scorched earth dividing that time from ours. In wiping out so many lives, . . . in destroying beliefs, changing ideas, and leaving incurable wounds of disillusion, it created a physical as well as psychological grief between two epochs."[6] The use of psychoanalytic insights in literature had become a permanent part of modern literature, and did not lose its bearing on thought and fiction in the 1920s. But after the war the emphasis at the core of German novels gradually shifted from the purely psychological to a wider social perspective. In part this transition was due to the vitality and variety of political and cultural life in the Weimar Republic, in part it was a consequence of the war: there was a widely felt need for a social philosophy, both to account for the enormous upheavals brought about by the war and to project some kind of social progress and order for the future. In these two areas Freud's somewhat mechanistic theories were found wanting, and his skepticism about the possibility of an open and fair society held out little hope to idealistic intellectuals and artists. It is no wonder that amid economic chaos and under the threat of fascism many European intellectuals turned to the promise of Marxism. For Zweig this turn came only after Hitler's rise to power in Germany and a severe disappointment with Zionism during his period of exile in Palestine.

Because of such intellectual changes in orientation, critics have had difficulty in attaching any label to Zweig. He has been called a "Prussian Jew,"[7] his intellectual evolution has been portrayed as leading from Zionism to Marxism,[8] and his concerns have been described as essentially and always psychological.[9] Taken together these interpretations of Zweig's history give an accurate view of his interests and the dominant influences on his career. It would be unfair, looking at the succession of these influences, to interpret his changes of allegiance as a game of philosophical or ideological chairs. It is not a case of one ideology replacing the other; Zweig never renounced the previous for the present one. He never turned his back on his Jewish heritage, he refused to denounce Freud under official pressure after his return to East Berlin, and he did not allow the use of his name for an anti-Israeli declaration during the Six-Day War in 1967. Zweig, rather than exchanging one set of ideas for another, attempted to absorb and integrate them all: German philosophical idealism, Jewish ethical and ethnic values, Freudian insight, and Marxist determinism. In an autobiographical sketch he described his role as a writer in a three-part composition: "Jew and Zionist, European intellectual, and German author" (BJ, 140). The only one of these three characters open to Zweig after the triumph of nazism in Germany and his disillusion with Zionism in Palestine was that of European intellectual. It was therefore natural for him to join the move toward the left made by so many European intellectuals in the early 1930s.

It is to Zweig's credit that he did not allow the clash between the three elements so deep in his heritage and vision to fragment or prejudice his work. Instead, he tried to combine the best each tradition had to offer. At his best, as in *Der Streit um den Sergeanten Grischa* (The Case of Sergeant Grischa, 1927) such a synthesis produced the most comprehensive and penetrating fictional insight into the causes of World War I in particular and the nature of war in general. In describing the contributions of Freud, Marx, and Einstein, Erik H. Erikson has noted the triune nature of their drive to change their respective fields radically: "These thinkers climaxed the cultural and scientific crisis of Europe not because they were Jews, but because they were Jews *and* Germans *and* Europeans."[10] In a much more modest way Zweig, too, operates within these parameters, and the inner tension caused by his struggle to draw from all three traditions — and still to judge them — gives his work its special excitement and fascination.

I   *Aesthetes and other Outcasts*

Arnold Zweig was first and foremost a writer of prose narratives. Although he did write ten dramas and a volume of poetry, his plays deal almost exclusively with Jewish themes, whereas his poetry was very personal and derivative in his youth and overly political and tendentious in his last years. His fiction rightly established his reputation.

Until the appearance of Theodor Fontane's novels in the last decade of the nineteenth century, there were no first-rate German works of fiction within the main current of European realism. It was Fontane who "guided the novel away from metaphysics toward a concern with society, from romanticism toward realism. Along with various non-German writers — especially Tolstoy, Dostoevsky, Flaubert, and Zola — he laid the foundations of the modern German novel."[11] In the first decade of this century, the publication of Thomas Mann's *Buddenbrooks* (1901) seemed to insure the continuation of realism, with its emphasis on the public life of bourgeois society, in Germany. But the German notion of the special character of the artist opposed the realistic tradition. Although Mann's novel does portray the German middle class against the social background of the period, still the enervated artist Hanno defies middle-class ambitiousness. Thus "the theme of decadence clearly predominates."[12]

From the publication of Zweig's first story in 1909 until the outbreak of the war, he followed Mann's earlier, almost obsessive concern with the theme realized in Hanno: the conflict of bustling life with art or "spirit," the triumph of one signifying the decay or abandonment of the other. Zweig's preoccupation with this theme, like Mann's, was part of a personal catharsis. A severe psychological adjustment was required to be an artist in a society which had accepted the material values of capitalism but pretended to live by the spiritual values of national tradition. The artist, dedicated to the higher things in life, had to assume a contemptuous attitude toward the basic and ordinary things, and this scorn usually meant alienation from the artist's own bourgeois background. In addition, the cultural criticism directed against Wilhelminian Germany by Nietzsche and others was almost purely negative. No new morality was offered to replace the old, and certainly none which could be reconciled with the demands of a highly industrialized and politically ambitious nation. A tragic consequence of the discrepancy between material reality and idealized morality was that the "Germans needed to be sheltered from the winds of change and from the outside world."[13]

The hero of Zweig's first story, "Vorfrühling" (Early Spring),[14] has forsaken worldly life for the life of the mind. Karl Magnus, whose name implies ambition and achievement, is a young psychologist whose twenty-two years have been "purely intellectual, joyless . . . without the experience of youthfulness and fulfillment, and above all, without love" (FF, 160). Karl doubts that he "ever even could love, and certainly never expect love; for thinking and love rarely go together" (FF, 161). On a trip to the Austrian Alps he manages to overcome an attack of useless *Grübelei* ("pondering") about the proper approach and introduces himself straightforwardly to the pretty young woman who is the only fellow passenger in his railroad car. A long stroll to their mountain lodging gives Karl the opportunity to reveal the pseudophilosophy behind his "lovelessness" and Zweig the chance to develop his theme fully.

The simplicity and openness of human congeniality must, naturally, be inimical to the tortuous mental processes Karl despises in himself and yet values as deep and somehow holy. It does not really matter that Eva Marer, who tempts him to engagement in life, is not shallow but perceptive, not dull but quick-witted, not insensitive but responsive, for in his scheme of things she "must be stronger than he, closer to nature, simpler, less inhibited; but then he hoped to even things by drawing on his mind, his spirituality, his inclination to analysis" (FF, 156). With a delightfully ironic touch, Zweig turns Karl's antithetical manner of thinking upside down. It is Eva's perception which correctly analyzes Karl's inhibitions about life and love, whereas Karl's untried feelings mistake her pity for romantic interest. Encouraged by the personal nature of their conversation, Karl kisses Eva. After she explains to Karl that she is engaged and will marry soon, she gently returns his kiss, thereby "giving life and warmth to a repressed human being" (FF, 174). Not unlike a patient's first session with his analyst, "Early Spring" is the author's semiautobiographical unburdening, a fictionalized version of the "talking cure" made famous by Freud's first case. Karl has been released from his anxiety, relieved of his intellectual superiority complex, and set free to experience the pleasures of youth and the senses. For the first time in his life he now can take pleasure in nature "without nature's demand that he must [approach nature] as an artist or burgher, but as a man" (FF, 175).

Zweig's treatment of so pat a theme is surprisingly deft and free of pathos. Karl's pretensions to powers of analysis are gently mocked — "Well, I am a psychologist after all" (FF, 148) — and the Alpine scenes are depicted with cheery delight, not romantic sighing. Although the story begins *in medias res*, like so much fiction at the turn of the century,[15] Zweig returns to a calmer, more old-fashioned and chroniclelike setting of the scene in the second paragraph: "It took place on that train which departs from Innsbruck at 9:25 in the morning, puffing white clouds of steam" (FF, 145). In short, a topic usually treated with ardent subjectivity is viewed here from a distance, coupling sympathy with irony.

Significantly, the "new Karl" is envisioned only in his own dream at the story's conclusion. For Zweig, too, the light tone and humane resolution of "Early Spring" remained a dream for some time to come. The acceptance of so simple and serene a solution required the experience and maturity the twenty-year-old Zweig simply did not possess. Personal recollections of unhappiness as well as dreary visions of the future caused him not to resolve the problem of the artist in his first major publication, "Aufzeichnungen über eine Familie Klopfer" (Notes about a Family Named Klopfer), but to push the antagonists of engagement with life into extreme isolation.

"Notes . . . ," written in 1909, was strongly influenced by Zweig's reading of *Buddenbrooks*.[16] It, too, deals with four generations of one family, but what Mann skillfully develops in over seven hundred pages, Zweig forcibly condenses into sixty-five. The novella, therefore, moves along too rapidly, with too many names, dates, and anecdotal versions of family scandals crushing the many sharp observations on the hardships of German-Jewish life in Bismarck's Germany. Only the introductory pages and the final two chapters glow with the languid fever of world-weary decadence newly discovered.

The history of the Klopfer family, German Jews of Russian origin, is told by Heinrich Klopfer, self-exiled to the shores of Lake Tiberias at the age of thirty-two with his sister Miriam "with whom I live and who replaces all women in my life" (DE, 9). The intention of Mann's novel was to portray "the psychology of those grown weary of life . . . which is an accompaniment of biological decay."[17] Similarly, the concern of "Notes . . ." is to give "the history of my disease traced through four generations," and to penetrate the "heritage of blood . . . which produced me" (DE, 10).

The first half of the story recounts rather breathlessly the few successes and frequent misfortunes of the Klopfer tribe. The sympathy Heinrich extends to them as victims of anti-Semitism is erased by his petty and malicious descriptions of physical characteristics: "He grew into a tall, pale man with narrow eyes, his red nose drooped down over a very small chin, not unlike a rabbit" (DE, 20). Zweig does not really warm to his topic until Heinrich reaches the story of his father Peter, an alter ego for Zweig himself, told in the form of Peter's diary. Heinrich's purpose in exposing his father through the diary is to destroy the myth created around his father.

Peter was a well-known writer on German-Jewish subjects, admired for the personal flair in his life and the psychological vision in his work; and Heinrich wants to deflate his father's reputation in both spheres. Yet at this point of the story Heinrich's motivation is deliberately ridiculed. His admission that his hatred of his father stems from envy because "I am unproductive," both physically and aesthetically, jars the reader's expectations and Heinrich's justification. Peter's life may have been filled with the lies and contradictions that a lust for life united with aesthetic overrefinement is bound to produce, but the tension between the two was responsible for all that was vital and brave as well as false and cowardly in his life, for his ability to endure as well as his suicide. Heinrich has inherited only the wish for the latter.

Indeed, Heinrich has an artist's neurosis without artistic ability or sensibility. The artist, Freud writes, "turns away from reality and transfers all his interest, and all his libido too, on to the creation of his wishes in the life of phantasy, from which the way might readily lead to neurosis."[18] The trouble with Heinrich is that he has created the life of his wishes in the real world. These wishes all represent failures to meet normal adult demands. The sexual form such a failure takes is the infantile incest fantasy. Heinrich has never "had a friend, a lover, or a wife, for I had my sister" (DE, 62). The world Heinrich and Miriam have created for themselves is described in a pastiche of slogans from Nietzsche: "We live for ourselves and follow our strange longings and commit our deeds as our will dictates. . . . Morality is a deception, education merely a notion, religion, fatherland, the people [Volk] themselves only prejudices, love is subject to change even hate wears off" (DE, 63). Such total hopelessness about the possibility of European civilization and human relations might have some validity if it were based on disillusion by experience, but Heinrich and Miriam have forsaken humanity because they were unable to participate in human ways. They are guilty of a sin Nietzsche condemns more than any other: resentment.

It is only Peter Klopfer's diary that offers a feeling for the joys of life as a protective wall against his children's whining *Weltschmerz.* Peter bore up under his isolation, both from the philistine masses and from the Jewish community, and his art was both prize and penalty for it. His children have chosen to live by the symptoms of their inherited decadence. Unable to transform these symptoms into art and unwilling to engage a hostile world in defense of them, they merely analyze them, and each other. As a result, their "philosophy" only parrots Nietzsche's criticism of culture without accepting his affirmation of life, and their "psychoanalysis is the disease of which it pretends to be the cure."[19]

Even if Zweig, in the person of Peter Klopfer, could view the equation that art equals decadence, and conversely that life equals health, with some irony and detachment, the outcast heroes of the stories Zweig wrote between 1907 and 1912 take this arbitrary antithesis in dead earnest. In "Abreise" (Departure) Hubert von Muhr and his beloved Lenore reenact the suicide of the playwright Heinrich von Kleist,[20] complete with a visit to Kleist's grave and a nocturnal swim in the Wannsee. Hubert's novel has been rejected by three publishers, and Lenore's parents have refused her permission to marry him. Their final hours are spent in an agitated state filled with ardent passion and irritable restlessness: "In the desperate desire of overheated caresses and ecstatic abandonment they sought protection from the fear threatening them everywhere. . . . They remained lying in the grass as long as possible . . . but the horrid restlessness did not even grant them this last refuge; they had to get dressed and go" (MF, 19). Although the reader can well understand the couple's decision to commit suicide, the pleasures they share in the last days of their lives provide enough reasons to go on living. Lenore senses this only too well, but too late: "It seemed to her useless and groundless to die. She had forgotten the restrictions of bourgeois life; all rules and habits had been robbed of their reality and buried during those last days. A new world of joy had opened itself to them. . . . Why should it not be possible to live in it?" (MF, 22). But the dialectic is not to be denied. Hubert reads Lenore's desire to live in her eyes, and, as she exclaims "Let us live, somehow," he shoots her. He then douses her body with gasoline, burns it, and fires two bullets into his mouth. The lovers have died not because they could not have lived happily together, but because death, too, in the dualism of Hubert's thinking, must be the romantic and beautiful counterpart to brutal and ugly life. Ironically, their death represents the ugliness they sought to avoid. It is nobler to be a martyr of love than to wrest love, tinged and tainted by daily struggle, from the impure world outside. For Hubert there can only be the "either-or," never an "as well as."

Occasionally, as in "Revanchen" (Revenge), Zweig mocks the art-life battle, pokes fun at the positions of both sides, and comes close to achieving the kind of parody Thomas Mann brought off so

brilliantly in his novella *Tristan*. Egon Hoon, a middle-class
merchant, and Gustav Trällermann, a would-be singer, vie for the
love of Kitty Sperlich, daughter of a wealthy banker and patron of
the arts. In a delightful reversal of the usual order, we learn that it
was the merchant who "bought books, not to give away as presents,
but for his own enjoyment! In addition, he subscribed to a monthly
filled with literature, fine reproductions, also read the critical
weeklies at his coffee-house and regularly attended the finer
theaters," whereas the tragedy of the physically repulsive artist was
that he did not possess "the treasured voice of a tenor, but only a
booming bass" (MF, 219), and therefore he had to be satisfied with
playing unsympathetic villains and scoundrels. Nonetheless, Kitty
follows the terms of Zweig's dialectic and rejects Egon in favor of
Gustav.

Egon's turn at revenge comes first. He sends Gustav a letter in
which he informs him that he has slept with Kitty, citing the
birthmark under Kitty's bosom as evidence. Gustav is enraged, in
Zweig's mordantly humorous phrase, "denn der Künstler hielt auf
relative Reinheit" ("because the artist put much stock in relative
purity," MF, 222). Gustav feels himself betrayed and mails his entire
correspondence with Kitty, disclosing the intimacy of their
relationship, to her mother. The adolescent pettiness and emotional
immaturity exhibited by both men is shown as the consequence of
their silly enmity, a hostility based entirely on the superficialities of
appearance and profession, rather than the realities of affection or
even sexual attraction. Zweig ridicules the outcome of their rivalry
with keen psychological insight and in an appropriately breezy style
in the final paragraph: "Lie down, Trällermann, and give yourself
snoringly into the arms of Morpheus . . . tomorrow you will have
forgotten everything; then you will have dark premonitions, feel
fretfully restless, sit straight up in your bed . . . and then, quite
suddenly, you will understand everything and will be tormented
with remorse — for at least three days" (MF, 228). This devastating
phrase, with which the story closes, reduces the level of combat
between "art" and "life" to personal feuds and adolescent pouts.
The stance of both sides, when no genuine feelings are involved or
when no artistic achievement is attained through the loss of private
happiness, is exposed as a pose.

The opposition of self-conscious aestheticism and unreflective
normality was taken seriously by many German writers and intellectuals in the decade before World War I. Thomas Mann treats the

theme with humor and irony, but Zweig's intellectual intensity did not yet allow him to distinguish easily or often between genuine alienation and poseur exclusiveness. He was too charmed with his artistic existence to see art's roots in life, too involved in his philosophical quest to understand philosophy's relation to reality. Only after "the political consequences of the unpolitical German"[21] did Zweig realize that spirituality untouched and uncompromised by political and social reality will turn into narrower and narrower self-interpretations and really become decadent, while politics and public life are abandoned to the brute and the bully.

The greater part of Zweig's fiction prior to the war deals seriously with the same theme. The few historical tales he wrote (the setting is usually ancient Israel or revolutionary France) are exercises in the art of the short story, pleasant but slight imitations of de Maupassant. Most of the stories set in contemporary Germany deal with unsuccessful attempts to accommodate the self to life, with youthful idealism, or with artistic ambition succumbing to the world. But Zweig never really shows us the world. Everything is seen through the eyes of the protagonist, and his defeat, taking place in a kind of social vacuum, loses any authenticity and significance.

The final and major work Zweig devoted to the topic of *Künstlertum* and *Bürgerlichkeit* is also the one in which he finds a way out of sterile aestheticism and resolves the problem of the artist by allowing him to become just another human being. *Die Novellen um Claudia* (Claudia) is a novel in the form of seven novellas. The story of the love and marriage of Walter Rohme and Claudia Eggeling holds the plot together, while self-revelatory discussions about art and life thematically connect all seven novellas and provide the center for Zweig's structure of the book. Zweig has taken the introspection and self-consciousness of an intellectual — Walter is an impoverished university assistant and budding author — and around his inwardness has drawn in the series of novellas an ever-widening concentric circle until "the centre cannot hold,"[22] and the circle breaks. Walter and Claudia can then begin to live as human beings. Their spirituality is not lost but directed toward the world of persons and things.

A close examination of the seven novellas reveals that Zweig has expanded the possibilities for a union of inner life and outer reality with each succeeding novella. The topic of each story may serve to illustrate the expansion of the perimeters: the awkwardness of a self-conscious artist; art sacrificed for success; life forsaken for art; the emotional ties of family life; the pleasures and pains of sensuality; the artistic *and* moral potential of the common people; the self-conscious artist's breakthrough to the outer world. The pattern of expanding circles does not fit perfectly. The first three novellas proceed from private inhibition to the choice between art and life. The growth of an artistic soul is traced, although the examples change, and the implications of the career in art as opposed to success in life are shown. But at this point, after three novellas, Zweig sensed that he had exhausted the topic, and that art and life are neither inimical nor exclusive. He then turns in the opposite direction, into the sphere from which the artist had considered himself excluded, the world of instincts and of the senses. In conquering the idea that his intellect stands in opposition to love, the artist liberates his being from imprisonment within itself. The procedure may seem very tortuous and typically Teutonic to English or American readers, but it was Zweig's personal response and humanistic answer to the dangerous heritage of the "purity" of intellectual life in Germany.

Only five characters appear in the book. In addition to Walter and Claudia there are Claudia's mother and two artist friends, the painter Klaus Manth, and the composer Oswald Saach. There are only a few excursions from the dimly lit world of the book's drawing rooms into the sunlit and noisy world outside.

The opening novella "Postpaket" (Parcel) examines once more the young intellectual who "always thinks of what might happen" (NC, 20). Walter Rohme is charmingly clumsy and touchingly nervous; behind his formidable mind there is a young boy straining to become a man. Blocking the way, as in "Early Spring," is his intelligence, which divides life into higher and lower regions. The mind, in this scheme, constructs soaring abstractions, whereas the body is a slave to its instincts. This hierarchy applies to male-female relationships: feminine instinctiveness must be subservient to male intellectuality. Walter suffers internally from its rigid constraints, as well. "My intellect is greater than yours but it is housed in the body of a slave; because I see many possible solutions for every problem . . . because I reflect and am therefore overwhelmed by life. Because I smile a little contemptuously at decisions and deeds, because these people full of pompous energy and lacking in intelligence seem grotesque in their simplicity. . . . They have more strength and greater success — but since when do success and strength count for anything in the region of the spirit? . . . I am the higher type,

weaker, subtler, and more spiritual" (NC, 33 - 34). Walter's intellectual boasting is in fact an emotional plea for help. The story of the
parcel, absurdly silly and seemingly pointless, tells Claudia exactly
that. Walter's tale describes in great detail his inability to decide
whether to send a package of books by rail freight or through the
mails. The story, which depicts innumerable trips to the offices of
both shipping agents, is a declaration of weakness and affection.
Claudia at first responds with the expected puzzlement, but then she
understands: "Why had he told her such a futile story? . . . Why did
he display himself today as so feckless and weak? There he sat, with
his head bent, like a condemned man, and did not budge. . . . And
then she knew. A sudden flash illuminated everything" (NC, 52).
Walter's confession is the first groping attempt to scale the barrier he
has erected between his mind and his feelings.

The two following novellas, "Das dreizehnte Blatt" (The
Thirteenth Etching) and "Der Stern" (The Star), are intensified
variations on the first. In "The Thirteenth Etching" the painter
Klaus Manth had "placed his art where my affection had been, and I
served art and art alone in stern austerity" (NC, 89). But to gain
public showing for his etchings, he altered the thirteenth in a series
and replaced the figure of Jesus with that of Aphrodite, for the
bourgeois audience would have been offended by a Jesus experiencing passion. Since then Klaus has found no joy in his art, which he
feels he has betrayed, and nothing to replace the affection he
renounced for art. "I was Judas, allowed to live, and worked ten
times more zealously than Paul, who fought against his Lord but
never betrayed him" (NC, 89). The simple exchange, just like the
choice between art and life, affords happiness in neither. The reverse
choice teaches the same lesson to the composer Oswald Saach in
"The Star." He gives up his mistress whom he loves deeply, when a
flashing star signals to him "a consuming desire, for whose fulfillment the falling star was a propitious sign. What then was the ever-
present desire of a man who was fighting to keep the first human being that had ever loved him for himself? That unspoken word was
Fame" (NC, 140). Klaus gives up artistic integrity for public success;
Oswald gives up personal happiness for wider fame. Both artists now
live divided lives, tormented by the emptiness they have created by
submitting to their one-sided but total commitments.

Here Zweig arrived at a *cul-de-sac* in his development of a theme.
Success has not sweetened the austere demands of art, and fame has
not replaced the loss of genuine affection. In the fourth piece, "Das

Album," Zweig departs from the usual dualism and depicts only one thing, the deep sense of loss Claudia's mother experiences after Walter and his bride have departed on their honeymoon. The chapter is pure emotion, undiluted by any form of intellectual analysis. Zweig uses this outpouring of parental grief to bridge the gap between the instinctual and the spiritual. It signals a return to one of the most basic human emotions, and its insertion into the novel at this juncture is significant. The three chapters which follow resume the depiction of the possibilities of a full life, but this time with a difference. "The Album" has placed emotion at the center of life, and it is viewed for the first time as neither base nor anti-intellectual.

In the next novella, Zweig moves from motherly affection to romantic love. The young couple's wedding night is described with great delicacy and tenderness. Walter is nervous and has thought too much about the procedures of sex, and Claudia is fastidious and has heard too much about its pains. Now Walter cannot draw on his great intellect or refined spirit, and "this was the vengeance of culture which forced its way even in here, where the soul could do nothing, and was merely a hindrance, a burden, and a torture. After all, it was a simple situation to describe: she got into bed, he climbed in beside her, and the deed was done. . . . Here alone true innocence could help, pure shameless Nature, and the finer feelings, self-consciousness . . . become an agony that devours the spirit like a chemical acid" (NC, 101 - 2). Very slowly and uncertainly Walter and Claudia accept their bodies' desires as natural equals to the sensibilities of their souls. The next novella, "Die Passion" (The Matthew Passion), proves that the experience of love has not damaged the mind's faculty to enjoy "the higher things." What's more, Walter makes the startling discovery that even a small-town audience of common people can react with proper awe and appreciation to great music. This insight has an electrifying effect on Walter: "I do not of course want to feel as they do, or share their life and happiness; that would be beneath me. On the other hand, they are richer than I in a certain area of sensation, and that fills me with awe. They are united by one feeling, their feeling for God, and thus they grow into a single being with a common pulse of life. This whole source of experience is closed to people like us. . . . A man only completes his life when he has shared an emotion with his fellow men. . . . As individuals they are no doubt dull and ordinary; but together, as a community, they were magnificent" (NC, 255 - 56).

Walter has not given up his airy aestheticism ("that would be beneath me"), but it has been joined by the experience of sensual pleasure and a community spirit. The last of the three remains theory; it is an intellectual love for people that requires great distance from them. The test of experience might convert it into social commitment or political action. Walter is at least ready to enter the outside world without feeling that he is entering totally alien territory.

Claudia's decision to face social reality must come from another source. As a woman she has been trained to think with her feelings, and her feelings must be touched to change her thoughts. In the final novella, "Die Sonatine" (The Sonatina), Walter's childhood memories are stirred by playing a composition he often practiced on the violin as a boy. Caught up in the recollection of those days he confesses to youthful homoerotic experiences, the type of sadomasochistic games often played by boys in puberty. Claudia's shock exceeds the nature of Walter's disclosure. It is precisely the comprehension of her overreaction as a result of excessive protection from the outside world that leads to her recovery and a change in her outlook: "I *was* leading a false and artificial life. I knew what the world was like, but I had never seen it before my very eyes as I see you now, my dearest. It is wicked to turn one's back on unhappiness and not to see the evil that exists" (NC, 302).

An American critic wrote of the novel that "there are novels like *Claudia* that are finished performances, molded into beautiful forms by artistic hands; but such novels have no great vitality, no sweep, no close relationship to the pervasive problems of modern life. Then there are novels that are full of life, intimately related to our daily problems, thrilling in their portrayal of events that affect us all; but they lack form, and that is simply to say they lack meaning. They leave those vital materials in the chaos in which we find them in the daily paper. . . . Cannot the two qualities be reconciled?"[23] *Claudia* does not yet achieve such a combination. But after half a decade of painful introspection the ending of *Claudia* opens a window to the world and projects the possibility of that combination in the future. Walter and his author no longer put art above everything else, and both can now turn their attention to public life in Germany. The winds of change, however chauvinistic, have blown down the artificial barriers of art. Zweig was ready to fashion fiction out of life's daily problems and to reflect the public mood of pre-World War Germany.

II *Jewish Identities*

The only social concern Zweig treats repeatedly before the outbreak of the war is anti-Semitism. In a few stories and in two of three plays written prior to 1914, the possibility of Jewish identity in a Christian society and the sociopsychological roots of anti-Semitism are sensitively considered, but the author's own stance fluctuates between personal outrage and patriotic confusion. Zweig was a "good German" and nonreligious Jew, and he sought a formula for Jewish assimilation which would, somehow, integrate his Jewish consciousness with his German soul. Before Jew and Christian became irreparably separated by postwar concepts of race, Zweig hoped to find a basis for a German-Jewish union in the irrational and mystical heritage of both peoples. His prewar writings reflect the youthful torment of these divided loyalties: awareness of anti-Semitism and identification with the German national character.

As a child, Zweig had personally experienced the depth of anti-Semitic feeling in his native Silesia. "This entire province was seething with hatred of Jews. The hopeless predicament of the middle class and the farmer had whipped up in them a suppressed rage, and in order to deflect this fury from the landowners and industrialists, an ancient custom was used; it was directed against the Silesian Jews, who had been in the area for five or six centuries and had given it countless scholars, doctors, and artists" (SZ, 230). Zweig's own father was forced to give up his grain and feed business in the 1890s when a regulation forbade Jews to deliver agricultural products to the army. However, on the eve of World War I in Germany, "in economic terms, the wealth of Jews had now reached its high point but had not caused any considerable conflict. In all cultural fields, Jewish progress was remarkable; and assimilation remained the basis still for all creative work."[24]

To Zweig the period of virulent anti-Semitism in Germany seemed over at the end of the first decade of the century; yet he saw that, although "the German prejudice against commercial occupations may have favoured the economic rise of the German Jews, it largely thwarted their social recognition."[25] As a result, two distinct types of socioeconomic anti-Semitism flourished in Germany: the Junkers' aristocratic disdain for the Jew as the archetype of the new commercial man, and the lower middle class's jealousy of the Jews' success in commerce and trade. The first type is rejection based on norms of social behavior, and it desires to create distance, whereas the latter is resentment based on an economic envy that seeks to destroy or eliminate the imagined obstacles in its own path to financial better-ment. However, Zweig preferred to scant the social reality and seek a psychological rationale for hate; he subscribed to the theory that "Anti-Semites project on to the Jew all their more or less un-conscious evil instincts; longing for bloodshed, riches, depravity, sensuality. Thus, by transferring these burdens to the Jew, they themselves are washed clean and seem to become radiantly pure. In this way the Jew serves as an admirable foil on which to project the Devil who, as it were, is only dragged from hell the better to live on earth."[26] Zweig employs such psychological projection as the basis for the ominous union of the two types of anti-Semitic expression in his most impressive early drama, *Ritualmord in Ungarn* (Ritual Murder in Hungary). When the distaste of the powerful and the violence of the weak are combined, all levels of society — the land-owners and industrialists and the workers and peasants, as well as the officials in the state's bureaucracy, which serves the wealthy — become involved in translating anti-Semitic feelings into action. Anti-Semitism, as Zweig anticipates it, was to become "an obvious assumption as a social norm,"[27] and thus could easily develop into mob rule or state policy.

Ritual Murder, completed in 1913 and published a year later, was banned by the wartime censor. A new version, called *Die Sendung Semaels* (Semael's Mission) was published in 1918 and performed in 1919. The play is based on a famous trial in Hungary in 1882 - 83, called the Tisza-Eszlar affair after the town where it occurred.[28] A fourteen-year-old peasant girl, Esther Solymossi, disappeared from the home of her widowed mother early in April, 1882. Two members in the House of Deputies, Von Onody and Von Istoczy, raised the traditional accusation against the Jewish community of having slaughtered Esther to use her blood in the Passover service. Spurred on by these fiercely anti-Semitic speeches, on the fourth of May Esther's mother formally charged the Jews of the town with abduc-tion and murder. A politically ambitious attorney, Bary, was dis-patched to the village as the examining judge. In league with the two deputies, he tortured an "eye witness" confession out of Moritz Scharf, the fourteen-year-old son of the synagogue caretaker. During the drawn-out trial, which stirred up much comment and controver-sy in Europe, Bary's machinations were finally exposed; and the twenty-nine men on trial were acquitted on August 3, 1883.

Zweig's dramatization of this case reveals his overwhelmingly philosophical approach to a social problem. The subject requires no

cosmic framework, yet in an attempt to emulate Goethe's *Faust*,
Zweig provides a celestial "outer drama," reducing the folly of prejudice and the terror of its brutality to the whims of destiny. In a work
of the breadth and scope of *Faust*, the outer drama makes an appropriate moral background to man's quest for knowledge, but in a
tightly focused study of inhumanity caused by ignorance, divine
guidance merely turns both the oppressor and his victims into
playthings of heaven. In attempting to universalize the nature of
prejudice through a dramatization of anti-Semitism, Zweig should
have allowed his example to make his case. Instead, Zweig placed
the origin of the affair in the will of God, and its significance within
God's — not man's — relationship to man. In *The Mission*, Semael,
the legendary Satan in Jewish mythology, is to "bring the defama-
tion of blood over the heads of the people of Israel," so that they
shall cry out for the Messiah in times of despair. With the help of
Stupidity, whose role is merely "just to be there, men will do the
rest" (D, 80), the task is as effortless as it seems pointless to Semael.
His coolly rational refutation of God's assertion that "man is on earth
to choose between you and me" (D, 72) is borne out by the ending of
the play. Moritz, disgraced by the betrayal of his people and broken
by the torture of his captors, commits suicide in his father's synagogue. Like Faust he, too, is sneaked into heaven because "man's
soul strives heavenward" (D, 150). Faust's striving can be interpreted as the restless drive of Western man — a drive both ruthless
and grandiose. The suffering of a fourteen-year-old boy, however, is
only pathetic and pitiable. His salvation comes about neither
through his nature, which is the undeveloped one of a child, nor
through any deeds, since he suffers passively and submits weakly.
Moritz must be saved because "in him is all of Israel" (D, 98), and
God will not abandon His people.

Just as Moritz is idealized out of all reality by his pure innocence,
so Von Onody is debased by his pure evil. The evidence of the trial
suggests that Esther's death was accidental, but Zweig concludes his
case by turning the architect of evil into its chief instrument as well:
Onody's attempt to seduce Esther, whom Zweig depicts at seven-
teen, results in her death by strangulation in the 1913 version, by
drowning while escaping from Onody's clutches in the revisions of
1918. The militant anti-Semitism of the actual Onody, in part
sincere conviction and in part a politically convenient vehicle for advancement, renders him a murderer as well. Zweig changes his
group hatred into private villainy and reduces the level of dramatic

confrontation to that of melodramatic murder-mystery.

If the portrayal of Onody is unconvincing because of Zweig's reliance on the psychological projection of all "evil instincts" as motivation, and Moritz is a cardboard figure because his fate is truly not his character, how does the play come to grips with anti-Semitism? A few glimpses into Jewish life and Christian reaction to it, unfortunately not at the center of the play, provide some insight into the problems Zweig largely chose to avoid. The Jews of Tisza-Eszlar are not ideally good; their moral behavior is not beyond reproach. In a scene in the synagogue during the Passover service, the Jewish men confess to their sins: "our greed for money, our coldness toward the poor, our exploitation of orphans, our lending of money at high interest rates" (D, 128). But Zweig never shows, through either exposition or dramatic action, why or how such behavior is either characteristic or exceptional, traditional or avoidable for the Jewish population. No social or economic details about daily life permit any interpretation or judgment of the Jewish situation, whether sympathetic or critical. Similarly, the Christian reaction is restricted to the rantings of an Onody or the resentment of a farmer, who is all too willing to testify falsely against his Jewish moneylender. At this point, however, Zweig was too much under the influence of his philosophical training and Freudian theory to see truth on the surface of daily life. As *The Mission* clearly shows, he sought his answers in the realms of heaven or in the depths of the subconscious. Yet there is, however small, a concern for the nature of social justice, so central in Zweig's future work. The terse, vivid interrogation and trial scenes and the electric force of the crowd gatherings endow the play with tension and authenticity in the tradition of Büchner's *Woyzeck* and Hauptmann's *Die Weber*. Only the content, which Zweig was to find in the war, is missing.

Perhaps Zweig's judgment of his dramas, "I write plays which nobody performs" (Fk, 156), shows resignation to the role of playwrighting within his *oeuvre*. His plays as well as his poetry serve as a testing ground for ideas and themes, as a rehearsal for the final fictional form which these concepts and topics were to take. Two plays in his prewar period, *Abigail und Nabal* in 1909 and *Die Umkehr* (The Return) in 1914, reveal once more the two chief interests of the young Zweig. *Abigail* is a psychological study of male-female relationships with a biblical background. Taken from I Samuel 25, the tragedy dissects the foolishness of passivity, that stubborn and fatal urge which should elevate man above his fellow creatures but usually only casts him aside. Nabal, whose name means "dunce" in Hebrew, refuses to give food and drink to David and his warriors for the protection of Nabal's herd against hostile tribes. To save the peasants and servants of her husband's estate, Nabal's wife, Abigail, visits David's camp at night. Her bravery prevents the shedding of blood except that of Nabal, who melodramatically commits suicide after hearing of his wife's effort. Nabal is akin to the artist-aesthete hero of so many of Zweig's early stories. The aim of his life is to "preserve my lonely soul" (D, 54), and to achieve this goal he neglects all material matters. He has not spoken to Abigail for months, he is incapable of deeds or decisions, his desires strain for the impossible. As a result, his human relationships are pale imitations, mere charades. Abigail's lament that "he intended to attach me to his life like a piece of jewelry, and oh woe, I brought him a human being" (D, 34) is but another comment on the artist's inability to engage himself with real life.

Zweig wanted to stage psychological insights and validate them by giving them the timelessness of biblical settings. Within this play, as is the case in *The Return*, there are therefore many perceptive observations on subjects ranging from capital punishment to sensual rewards. But they are never integrated into the play, the characters, or the period. Each character carries with him one tag, one particular line or attitude. At given moments, generally during a dialogue at the center of an act, a character releases his speech. *The Return* suffers as much from prolixity as *Abigail*, but in the later play, composed in July and August, 1914, all the talk is intellectual. Zweig takes the story of a Jew's return to his religion from a tale he found in the works of Martin Buber, where it is filled with the glow of mystical wonder and awe. Zweig's attempt to translate this radiance into drama fails, not because he did not understand the meaning of the story, but because Hasidic wisdom should induce a knowing nod of the head and a sad smile of understanding, not a dramatic catharsis. Zweig's dramatic efforts suffer from the author's own reflective nature, which is much better suited to the exploratory potentials of prose than the relentless forward movement of events in drama. Moreover, his attempt to dramatize Judaism failed: in the later two plays it is mere background or color, with no direct effect upon the characters, just as in *Semael* it became celestial vision. Jewish life in Europe was much too earthy to be treated in the stately manner of German classicism; the problems of German Jews were firmly rooted in social and economic affairs. To deal with the actual feelings of being a Jew in Germany Zweig required the narrowed and personal focus of the short story.

Zweig is at his best when he deals with concrete matters in straightforward prose. Three short stories about one family written between 1909 and 1914,[29] "Episode," "Die Krähe" (The Crow), and "Quartettsatz von Schönberg" (Schönberg Quartet) tell more about the consequences of anti-Semitism than could any heavenly interpretation or intellectual debate. Two brothers experience successively the physical brutality of a pogrom in which their father dies, an ambiguous response to the act of revenge committed by one brother, and the bittersweetness of departure for Palestine by the other. "Episode" is a short and stark depiction of a pogrom in a small Russian city. Eli Saamen awakens on the eve of Easter Sunday to the sound of shots and the crackling of fire. Eli's fearful response includes an accurately observed insider's note of joy: he gleefully anticipates the comeuppance of the orthodox Jewish boys who have teased him as a violator of the Sabbath rules. But as he and his father, who is an inspector at a factory, make their way to the Jewish quarter to help, violence suddenly meets them, and it does not distinguish between assimilated and orthodox Jew. Three thugs pursue a woman and her two children, stab her nine-year-old boy and kill Eli's father as he attempts to come to her aid. Eli escapes with scalp injuries. As suddenly as the cold violence appeared, so it evaporates into the night. The pogrom — merely another case of "beating the godless Jews" (B, 74) — is over. The next day is Easter Sunday and everyone will be in Church. Zweig has not tried to enhance his journalistic vignette with descriptions of mood or the evocation of horror; its matter-of-fact grimness and objectivity make it far more harrowing.

In the second story of this trio Eli's brother, Leo, hears of his father's death and decides he must find a way to avenge it. His hatred of Russia, directly across the river from the German city he lives in, compels him to spend many afternoons on the banks of the Przemsa, staring across with glazed eyes. Suddenly his plans for revenge crystallize. He sees a Russian soldier, posted to prevent smuggling operations. Although he knows that this man is not his father's murderer in the literal sense, he convinces himself of the solder's psychological guilt. A sudden movement by Leo draws the soldier's attention. To frighten Leo, he shoots a crow. The dead bird falls into the grass beside Leo; at this moment he decides to kill the guard. A few nights later Leo swims across the river, ambushes the soldier, and stabs him. The dead crow is draped over the man's neck, and Leo returns to Germany. Weeks later, when the recuperated Eli has joined him, Leo tells him the story of the murder. Suddenly the brothers are separated by decades rather than eighteen months. Eli's loathing for the senselessness of revenge is tinged by envy for Leo's liberation through action, for there is a physical and psychological sense of freedom to be obtained in striking back at one's enemy or oppressor. But to Eli, opposed to violence ethically and conditioned against it ethnically, violence is an endless treadmill, physically repulsive and intellectually unjustifiable. Eli cannot reconcile Leo's psychological freedom with his own mental anguish. The Jewish response to anti-Semitic brute force is thus utterly ambiguous: Leo's action negates the Jewish heritage, since it destroys life as indiscriminately as the bloodthirsty Cossacks, but organized resistance is as unthinkable as meek subjugation is unsatisfactory. Eli's sadness is rooted precisely in understanding this conflict. His own solution is emigration to Palestine, the subject matter of the third story, "Schönberg Quartet." During his last day in Germany, Eli attends a concert. While listening to a quartet by Schönberg, he reviews with painful pleasure the cultural glory that is Western Europe in general, and the musical achievements that characterize Germany in particular. With a masochistic bent for philosophical reflection he asks himself if anti-Semitism may not be the inevitable other side of the coin to such grandeur. There is, of course, no answer. His departure promises relief from physical danger, but regret for intellectual loss. As he sits in his compartment, the rhythm of the train's wheels beat out a melancholy "I shall return . . . I shall return . . ."

The three stories build a kind of pyramid of Zweig's German-Jewishness and his struggle to come to terms with it. Each story represents one dimension of that relationship: physical, psychological, and intellectual. While the first is simply description, the latter two represent dilemmas. Both conclude in a peculiarly German *Haßliebe* (love and hatred directed at the same object). Zweig's Freudian insights dictate Leo's aggressive response (it is he who can sleep well at night after his act of murder, whereas Eli's sleep is disturbed and restless) and Eli's escape from danger, but Zweig's intellectual training and heritage, Jewish and German, condemn violence and bemoan the loss of roots and reasonable compromise. Eli Saamen will never really leave Germany, just as Zweig never left the ideas and ideals of German nineteenth-century philosophy. In each story, as if to escape this insoluble problem, the crux of the matter is placed closer to the ending. Successively more of each story is left to introductory matter, to unwelcome preparation for facing the problem. The physical violence enters "Episode" shortly after its beginning; the decision to avenge the murder is made in the middle of "The Crow"; in "Schönberg Quartet" Eli's release and remorse through Schönberg occur only shortly before the tale ends. It is as if Zweig shied further and further away from coming to terms with being both German and Jew.

An extraordinary essay Zweig wrote in 1913, "Die Demokratie und die Seele des Juden" (Democracy and the Jewish Soul),[30] provides insight into the intellectual and academic climate of prewar Germany, which inspired both Zweig's vitality and his confusion. Essentially the essay argues that the spirit of Judaism is inimical to the theory and practice of democracy, because democracy "perverts the Jewish spirit, reverses the Jew's system of values, which is based on intensity of devotion to the divine will" (214). Zweig wishes to disengage Jews in Germany from the accusations of materialism and lack of soul. To accomplish this he employs the terminology and ideas popular with German *völkisch* thinkers and hopes to establish the similarities of Judaism and *Deutschtum* ("German-ness"): rootedness in the soil, hierarchy of spirit or soul, and the primacy of order in social conduct. Not only the Jewish merchants and industrialists but the entire petite bourgeoisie, Zweig suggests, have been converted to "American worship of money" (218) in the last few decades. In fact, the Jew, by his Oriental heritage, is inclined to a hierarchy based on nobility of soul and birth rather than the Occidental and democratic notion of "the same for all" (228). Zweig's confusion of democracy and socialism leads him to the current German notion that individualism will, somehow, be realized only when the individual is absorbed into the *Volk*. To attain this goal Zweig justifies Germany's rejection of democracy and her aims in the war: "To become one's authentic self means to overcome democracy. Who ever has understood his own integrity, his incomparable singularness, how could he believe in equality?" (233). The language of philosophical idealism and personal self-realization was used by Zweig, and so many German intellectuals of the time, to elevate the nation's political and economic ambitions. For the young Zweig, who had, after all, studied at German universities for seven years, the ideas of his famous professors were central to his view of the world; Max Scheler's "ladder of ethical values, like a Gothic cathedral, culminating in a mystical and spiritual union," and Edmund Husserl's "abstract thinking"[31] were not conducive to the discovery of truths in social reality.

The clash of aesthete and bourgeois, as depicted in *Claudia* and many stories, and the conflict of German and Jew in the early plays both had to be resolved in a higher truth or overcome in a mystical union. When the war came Zweig saw, for the first time, a united Germany. All distinctions and differences, those of class and profession, religion and party, seemed to disappear in the nation's effort to assert itself, to defend its soul and safety. The men who were Zweig's professors hailed the war as glorious and holy, and their pupil hoped to find in it the manhood that comes through unity with the people and thereby overcome the nagging uncertainty of Jewish identity in German society. Zweig wanted his aesthetic sensibilities and his Jewish consciousness to be transformed into German values by the war. In 1914 he believed that war was not a reflection or continuation of the society from which it sprang, but a state or condition all its own. His enthusiastic welcome of the war had its valuable aspect — Zweig had everything to learn from it.

CHAPTER 2

From War to Weimar

THE outbreak of World War I on August 1, 1914, was greeted not only in Germany but throughout Europe with bursts of patriotic enthusiasm. The special factor in the German response to the news was an internalized sense of national identity. "Each individual experienced an exaltation of his ego, he was no longer the isolated person of former times. He had been incorporated into the mass, was part of the people, and his own person, hitherto unnoticed, had been given meaning."[1] The absorption of the individual into the communal whole was treated with almost religious reverence in the writings of Zweig's teachers Max Scheler and Georg Simmel, was celebrated in the poetry of Rilke and Dehmel, and received the unequivocal support of a majority of Germany's intellectuals and writers.

The basis for their support was not love of war but a fervor for national unity, a perceived need for psychological liberation, and a wish for moral regeneration. The austere, almost antiseptic self-abnegation of such drives was antimaterialistic and thus antibourgeois. Scheler cites Dostoevsky to support his claim that a new European man might emerge from the war: "It is a proven fact that the bourgeois is driven to war through long peace, as a sad, frantic flight from himself."[2] To the German intellectuals this flight would bring more than personal freedom or individual happiness: "The war of 1870/71 brought us national unity; this one is to bring us moral unity."[3] The prospect of war, with its reality of communal life at the front, was expected to break through the petrification of German class structure and weld together a society whose members had become alienated by barriers of class and suffocated by psychological limitations. The vision of the postwar future, as expressed by supporters of the war, offered a synthesis of these two aims: "Personal freedom must be allowed to grow only in the same measure as our increasing social cohesion grows."[4]

Arnold Zweig's work before 1914 dealt with two types of alienation which displayed just the symptoms that the newly gained
national solidarity seemed to cure, the artist's psychological isolation
and the Jew's social exclusion. The young Zweig could therefore
accept the necessity for war without personally investigating its
historical roots or possible effects; he endorsed Germany's world-
historical mission in the war as an idealistic abstraction without understanding war's material origins in the spheres of economics and
politics. The fictional representations that he produced over more
than a decade — about three dozen novellas, attempts at drama including his first treatment of the true-life story of Sergeant Grischa, a
small body of verse, and finally in 1925 his second novel — all record
either directly or tangentially his changing view of World War I, as it
happened at the front and in retrospect. Eventually he came to understand the need for a political and economic grasp of the war,
although he realized its horrors first through the sympathy of common humanity, and although his mature vision continued to insist
upon a grasp of the German psyche, expressed in individuals, as well
as a critique of German society, expressed through a socialist outlook. His work moves from intellectualized stories of violent
patriotism, through awareness of the universal suffering in war and
growing acquaintance with the special vulnerability of the working
class, to a clearly Marxist rejection of aristocracy and elitism in the
play about Grischa and the novellas of the twenties, and to a Freudian insight into the forces of repression in German bourgeois life in
"Helbret Friedebringer" and *Pont and Anna*. The dozen years from
1914 to 1926, in short, provided Zweig not only with the experience
to discover his ideal fictional form, but with a revolutionary political
education and an enduring theme.

Neither the artistic advance nor the deepening wisdom attained in
these turbulent years, however, could have been predicted from the
youthful Zweig's fervid, intellectual nationalism at the outbreak of
the war. His immediate response was to echo that combination of
hardheaded *Realpolitik* and lofty idealism employed by German intellectuals and statesmen to justify and ennoble their country's
military aggression. Zweig wrote a bubblingly favorable review of
Scheler's book on war, accepting the professor's opinion that the
roots of war can be found "in the nature of organic life itself" and
"in the metaphysical sense of the world."[5] In the essay "Kriegsziele"
(War Aims) Zweig argues that the war must be viewed on only one
level, that of what he calls "the given political reality."[6] On this level

"the preservation of our own state by the means war permits is our only aim in this war. Foreign interests are not to concern us now. When weapons speak, then God has taken over the decision-making between nations; those to whom He grants Power must use it." That the German navy was a product of German industry and not a gift of God did not yet occur to a young man caught up in the spirit of 1914.

Zweig's acceptance of the spiritual and predestined basis of Germany's imperialistic push for world power had the candor of simplistic chauvinism. But when he attempted to transform his views into the complex world of human relationships in fiction, he could only translate the slogans into caricatures. Prior to his induction in the spring of 1915, Zweig wrote a collection of battle stories, *Die Bestie* (The Beast), in which he mouths patriotic slogans and fictionalizes the atrocity propaganda according to his government's official line.[7] He based his tales on bulletins in the German press; although they are set on the battlefield, the reader can neither smell the smoke nor taste the soil. Indeed, there is — metaphorically, if not literally — no blood in these sketches. They do, however, reveal a change in Zweig's view of war even before he experienced its horrors firsthand. Ill at ease with the caricatures his flag-waving forced him to create, the artist in him revolted against patriotic dismissal of the individual, and artistic concern won out over nationalist fervor. Zweig simply could not validate the received theories in the flesh-and-blood world of persons and things. The fiction he produced between 1914 and 1916 is evidence both of this failure and of Zweig's turn toward new formal and political horizons. The manner of his awakening is typical of his rather circuitous approach to the world and the word.

I *Propaganda*

"Blick auf Deutschland" (Glance at Germany) is a prelude to the combat stories, a depiction of the transformation of an apolitical German private person into a political German citizen. Lilly Ebert, a twenty-year-old schoolteacher from Rostock, travels to London in July, 1914, to improve her English. She witnesses an anti-German, specifically anti-Wilhelm II, demonstration, during which twenty men hold aloft photos of the Kaiser, captioned "The Man Who Has Gone Mad" (B, 68). Sickened and frightened by this experience, she decides to return home on the next boat. The journey serves as a vehicle for her dramatic exposure to international politics and national hatreds: "As a German girl she knew nothing of politics —

the *Reich* had always been a presence to her, mightier, friendlier, even more natural than her own mother, and she never thought about the *Reich's* existence or nature" (B, 71). Now she must confront her relationship to the state for the first time, and the consequences of an uncritical and uninterested past manifest themselves in the ideological extremes and hypocritical pieties which Zweig enthusiastically endorsed at this time. Quite suddenly Zweig makes Lilly see the English with the anglophobia of Scheler and Werner Sombart, and her thoughts even echo the title of Sombart's hate-filled diatribe against England, *Händler und Helden* (Hawkers and Heroes)[8]: "All these nonthinking and unmusical people, this mass of merchants and hawkers, these idiots who live only by external standards, whose world is limited by what they can touch and made valid by what they can pay" (B, 71 - 72). Once the enemy is identified with the calculating attitude of bourgeois commercialism, then Germany has to assume the noble spirit of heroism and become the savior of human civilization. When Lilly arrives in her homeland, the German soldiers in their field-gray uniforms seem not only far removed from the butchers and barbarians of British propaganda but are elevated into a volunteer army fighting in the just cause of peace and sovereignty.

That Lilly can see through the propaganda of the British, and look at German soldiers as human beings and not demons in uniform, is natural. But the lack of political education and the feverish spirit of the summer of 1914 were not conducive to balance or objectivity. If the Germans are not the devils, then surely the British must be. Germany is no longer a modern and industrial country, but "Germany stood there, and majesty emanated from her as from an ancient god" (B, 75). The Kaiser is no longer head of state and chief of government but priest to the new national deity: "The soul of the whole population streamed to him like the wind, and the eyes of the people sought out the Kaiser, who today is but the will of the united nation" (B, 76). After the shock of an incomprehensible attack on her casually accepted nationality, Lilly's religious vision of "*Ein Volk, ein Reich, ein Kaiser*" is naturally the first refuge of a politically naive girl in troubled times, but the tone and language of her sense of oneness foreshadows the really ominous "*Ein Volk, ein Reich, ein Führer*" cries of Germany's next *Reich*. The basis for both visions requires the loss of individual selfhood, and Lilly is now only too willing to give that up; "She had always considered only her own role, her feelings, her sufferings and sacrifices, her joys and devotions — herself and always herself, never an abstract subject or achievement, always only her little Ego" (B, 80). From now on she vows to renounce the strivings of her soul, and instead "do my duty" (B, 80), because "I know where I belong" (B, 81).

Lilly, although a schoolteacher, is devoid of any ideas or convictions; her doubts about Germany's role and conduct in the war are as easily dispelled as her newfound passions are instilled. She is propelled, without the benefit of experience, from innocence to knowledge — or rather blind faith. Since fatherland and Kaiser have become holy land and savior in this credo, the enemy will have to become hell and Satan.

In his most blatantly propagandistic story, "The Beast," Zweig turns his attention to an equally one-dimensional but garishly gruesome portrait of the enemy as bloodthirsty barbarian. Labrousse, a Belgian farmer, permits three German cavalry soldiers to spend the night in his barn. The German invaders are perfect gentlemen; they offer to pay for bed and board, they behave like tourists, not conquerors. But Labrousse's fierce hatred, neither explained by wounded national pride nor analyzed as a personal obsession, permits him to see the Germans only as pigs. After a cordial supper with the soldiers, he doctors their dessert and wine with liquor, and when they have fallen into heavy sleep, sneaks into the barn and, "inwardly glowing" (B, 16), cuts their throats with a straight razor. He then strips them like slaughtered pigs, hangs them up "like any dressed animal" (B, 16 - 17), and feeds their intestines to his own pigs. The following day a German search party comes to his house but only discovers what has happened when the dead men's horses gallop across the field in perfect formation as the trumpeter gives the signal for assembly. Labrousse is shot, and his house is burned.

There was, of course, much material of this horrific nature printed and distributed by both sides during the early days of the war. Zweig's tale of Belgian bestiality could have been invented to counteract British propaganda stories in *The Times* of London claiming that the Germans in Belgium were using corpses to produce "lubricating oils, and everything is ground down in the bone mill into a powder which is used for mixing with pigs' food and as manure — nothing can be permitted to go to waste."[9] Only the similarity between the English newspaper dispatches and Labrousse's bestiality can explain Zweig's use of such material. His story lacks all the elements characteristic of his fiction before the ·

war: careful attention to psychological motivation, a personal
narrative point of view, parodistic asides to create a sense of distance, and intellectual delight at the intricacies and contradictions of
thought and feeling. Here Labrousse's burning hatred is not
directed against Germans as nationals or against the three soldiers as
human beings but almost against the human body itself. His ghastly
plan occurs to him not at the soldiers' arrival, but only when he
watches them strip to wash and their bodies appear to him "rosy as
those of pigs" (B, 13). That Zweig sensed the portent of Labrousse's
twisted vision seems unlikely. Nowhere does he expand on the
physical and anatomical expression of Labrousse's violent loathing as
a pathological phenomenon. Only the words of the German officer,
as the house is burning, place the events in a possible perspective:
"There is no retribution possible here, only judgment, not even
judgment, only extermination" (B, 21). Zweig had followed the
national phobias, so fierce in 1914, to a final and logical conclusion.
This step also marked the end of a fortunately brief phase of his
thinking and writing: as a human being and a creator of human
characters he had plummeted to a point from which creation as an
act of empathy was impossible. His next works are a second beginning.

Since all stories in the collection *The Beast* were written prior to
1914,[10] there is no precise indication of when or how a change occurred in Zweig. It seems unfair, and chronologically questionable,
to ascribe a change of mind wholly to his induction in the spring of
1915. Before that date, Zweig had begun to observe the war and the
men caught in it on both sides from a new point of view. His first
steps toward such a new balance in characterization and ideology
were tentative. Three anecdotes announce that their author no
longer banishes the enemy into the sphere of devils and butchers but
is ready to come to terms with the normal vagaries of human conduct
in a new setting. Just as his very first stories delicately probed the
outsider's relationship with his society, so "Der Kaffee," "Die Quit-
tung" (The Receipt), and "Der Schieβplatz" (The Firing Range)
hesitantly explore man's role in war. In the first anecdote German
soldiers give a pot of coffee to a French lieutenant whose men in the
trench two-hundred meters across from them have been without
supplies for five days. The afternoon of the same day, the Germans
overrun the French position, and see the Lieutenant once again —
dead in his foxhole. The exchange with the officer had been pleasant in a comradely way, and now there is nothing left to be done;

"we had our pot back and buried the dead" (B, 28). A melancholy sense of loss imbues Zweig's understated little sketch; it records — without embellishment or exegesis — that speechless astonishment at, and acceptance of, death at the front. In the other two anecdotes the self-sacrifice of individual heroism and the horror of mass sacrifice are recorded with quiet humor and loud screams respectively. Zweig has found human voices again, and they speak of war in a language very different from the idealistic justification of Germany's aims and heroic glorification of German conduct in the summer of 1914.

"Der Feind" (The Enemy) records Zweig's resolution of his alternation between hypnotic patriotism and a human outlook. With a clarified and intensified vision, the story rejects division into hostile camps, destruction, and killing as the inevitable *donnés* of human social conduct. Zweig's developing antiwar views, as this story shows, were not the intellectual property of others which he merely adopted like his prewar enthusiasm. The opening paragraph, remarkably similar to the beginning passages of his later war novels, signals a resumption of Zweig's characteristic attempt to place his narrative into a cosmic setting, to give it philosophical truth by gazing at it from a universal perspective: "Many an individual's fate is chosen purely according to the law of his own nature, and any event which seems to overtake him from the outside, be it even a deadly bullet, was also called forth by the daemon of his self. In such a way the Silesian Sergeant Paul Paschke died unavoidably at the very start of the last European War" (SZ, 157). This angle of vision may appear shrouded in the mysteries of Fate to a modern reader, but it does return responsibility for oneself to oneself, demonic or benign, and it places the phenomenon of war into a human framework. Moreover, while the opening passage serves to universalize one life, the story itself fuses a number of lives — and by doing so returns to each life the individual value which mass euphoria had absorbed.

In "The Enemy", Paul Paschke, the son of a Silesian carpenter, joins the army with a feeling of patriotic pride. Only "mothers sensed something of the reality of war at that time" (SZ, 159). But whenever instincts are suppressed, be it for artistic dedication as in Zweig's earlier stories or for national goals, a heavy price must be paid. While Paschke recovers from a wound in a field hospital, he observes two dying men — a Prussian carpenter and a Russian POW, who may also be a craftsman, farmer, or vagabond, but most of all also "a man, a human being" (SZ, 164). Suddenly, before Paschke drops off to sleep, he realizes drowsily but deeply that "enmity was not worth much any more, when external affairs were so sticky and internal things always remained the same" (SZ, 164). From this moment on, Paschke is drawn into a confusing current of emotions, enigmas, and doubts. Since both men die so like each other, Paschke cannot but ask himself if perhaps "the enemy lived just like himself, like Paul Paschke? If so, how could one shoot him, with pride, with honor, in fulfillment of duty? Apparently the enemy could be a man like himself — and at the same time a kind of human target. That didn't seem to fit. And yet it did" (SZ, 170). These doubts do indeed seal Paschke's fate, because they have formed his character. It has become his nature now to doubt the mission of his army, to question his army chaplain's reminder that God is on Germany's side. On a night reconnaissance patrol he comes face to face with a Russian soldier, a Jewish bookbinder from Lithuania. All his questions and doubts determine his conduct: he understands that the Russian is as little prepared to kill as he is, he comprehends that as Socialists and workers they are both "oppressed by society" (SZ, 178), and he feels that his Christian charity takes precedence over his military obligation — he cannot shoot. His inner sense of duty to himself proves stronger than army discipline, and he cries to the enemy to surrender and escape death. A shot rings out, Paschke is mortally wounded, and one of his men bayonets the Russian. Paschke's squad moves on, secure in the knowledge that "the company, the regiment, the entire corps, the whole marching army was behind them" (SZ, 181).

Like Paschke, Zweig has stepped out of the ranks of marching armies. For him this new comprehension came very early in the war, without the disillusionment of front experience or the bitterness of military defeats. It was, essentially, an act of empathy, an identification with common humanity, not in order to seek personal security or share in folksy pleasures, not to gain artistic insight or trace social roots, but simply to renounce an ideological structure that made a lie out of reality. Zweig's choice of a carpenter as the subject for his first realistic war story does not signify that the truth about the war was revealed only to the workers. But it does reveal the author's need to give his picture of a world in violent change a broader base than that of a lonely artist, an obedient *Bürger*, or a Jew with his divided loyalties. "The Enemy" shows that in 1914 Zweig was ready to begin raising the same questions about the world of society that he had asked about the world of the soul in the first decade of the century. To this task he could now apply his philosophical training, his psychological insight, and his artistic skills. In 1915 he received his notice of induction and was soon to add the dimension of personal experience to the examination of a large and chaotic world.

II *Encounter with Reality*

From April, 1915, until June, 1917, Zweig served in a supply unit in the north of France, Hungary, and Serbia, and for thirteen months he participated in the battle of Verdun. In the summer of 1917 a few friends at headquarters on the eastern front in Bialystok rescued him from the hell of Verdun and arranged a job in the public information office for him, first in Bialystok and then in Kovno. Once Zweig had experienced the European war from the mud of the trenches to the paperwork of headquarters, its economic, political, and social origins and effects began to take on the shape and significance that were to occupy him for the rest of his life. But the first two years of military duty seem, at first, to have yielded no striking response in artistic production. To be sure, there was little time for writing or reflection, although Zweig was stationed well behind the combat zones. Nonetheless, three stories written during this period tend to contradict the contention that "at this period — 1916/17 — it is impossible to determine what sort of positive effects the war experience and Zweig's own illusions about it would have on his life and particularly on his work."[11]

Zweig's portrait of Paschke's renunciation of war was based, after all, on what Zweig assumed to be a proletarian's enlightened and human revulsion to senseless killing. That Zweig was capable of creating such a study, without acquaintance with workers or personal knowledge of combat, may be remarkable. But he was not a worker; his own endorsement of the war had intellectual underpinnings, which could be destroyed or replaced only by an intellectual reaction against the war. In November, 1915, he published a story called "Wespen" (Wasps) in the *Simplicissimus*, and in this novella he delineates his own road from chauvinism to pacifism. "Wasps" is a densely complex story, alternating autobiographical confession with philosophical digression and personal narrative with military history. Like a set of Chinese boxes, the story comprises the small fable of the title, placed within the hero's letter to a younger brother recuperating at a field hospital, which is itself included in a long letter to a Husserl-like former philosophy professor to whom the hero is writing from London some years after the war. The opening sentence alone of this convoluted document takes up twenty-five

lines and is reminiscent of the famous sentence on Gustav Aschenbach's works and life in Thomas Mann's "Death in Venice." It is a
grotesquely labyrinthine construction, but it is an accurate reflection
of Zweig's struggle to rescue something of his intellectual past as a
stay against the present. The overly complicated structure of the
whole story is clothed in a baroque style, filled with the fiery images
of youthful anger and confusion. The professor's philosophical
system is dismissed as "neither wise nor able to grasp the world, and
it shall never encompass the world. For the world, Sir, is becoming
more spiritual, more spiritual through life, and your realm will melt
like a snowflake touched by the breath of the fire of life" (KM, 210).
So violent a reaction to seminars on Kant and Hegel by a twenty-
seven year old exposed to the slaughter of war for the first time is understandable. Zweig now felt himself betrayed by the uses to which
German philosophical idealism had been put by both his professors
and his government. Neither the Hegelian world spirit nor the Kantian maxim of duty could make sense of the war, and surely neither
justified its effects. Zweig felt it incumbent upon himself, upon his
own vision as a human being and writer, to comprehend the course
of events.

As the letter to the professor expresses Zweig's anguish in confronting the irrational war with rational philosophy, so the inner
letter — based on a human, not an intellectual, relationship —
adumbrates the solution that he was beginning to find. Philosophy
and sociology are caught in the systems they have created, stymied
by actual events and real people. The young hero suggests to his
brother that perhaps only the poet can capture reality with insight,
and thus show mankind by feats of the imagination what the facts of
his existence tell him to be true. "The soul of the poet, which stands
at the side of the road and seeks paths outside the sphere of time, can
tell us of things more essential, can speak more from the center of
the spirit than those of us who are burdened with the task of concep-
tualizing" (KM, 211). To illustrate this point, the letter makes an
atrocity explicable by means of a fable. In the small village of
Laparouse, wounded German soldiers were buried alive by the populace. How can the sensitive and friendly population of France commit such cruelties? First Zweig rejects once more the notion that any
answer to such a question can originate in social theorizing: "Basic
doubts have arisen in me, as to whether or not such simple labels as
treason, crime, enemy are capable of depicting and grasping life"
(KM, 215). The narrated episode of the wasps offers an explanation

for such brutality that is beyond the scope of politics or philosophy. The hero watches a French workman during a lunchbreak. A swarm of wasps buzz about him, lured by the odor of his pork lunch. He does not chase them away but with infinite care and skill cuts in half with an axe every wasp that lands near him. Why? It is not because the man hates wasps, just as Labrousse in "The Beast" did not despise Germans, but "because they are his enemies who can hurt him" (KM, 218). Men act so wantonly not because they are evil, but because they have been made "too dull to be sensitive to what the objects of their games feel" (KM, 218). International politics, academic philosophy, and social psychology have all conspired to tear one man from another, to separate men by superficial and false distinctions, and to prevent a central identification of one man with another by the most basic and natural qualities and needs. Zweig's answer, which he bases heavily on the writings of Martin Buber,[12] is that "the stranger's self must become embedded in the circumference of one's own" (KM, 218).

So ends the letter to the young man in the hospital. The story could end here too. But in a final, bitingly sarcastic comment, he remarks that so distinguished an interpreter of Kant's *Critique of Pure Reason*[13] surely cannot miss the tale's implications: the cause for man's inhumanity to man "is not to be found within the human substance or the fury of war" (KM, 220), but in the failure to distinguish one man from his "type" or his "Volk." Zweig's words now come with a cold fury: "The French, the Germans, the Jews — this is how the poor animal thinks, because one wolf and one cat represent in principle the conduct of life of all wolfs and cats, so that the poor sheep are, after all, quite justified in basing their view of the whole on the individual — and running away" (KM, 221). By the end of this story, the tortuous sentences have been replaced by aphoristic fluency. Zweig's language and thought have attained such maturity that reason and feeling are united in what is for him a new vision of man. The letter to the professor is mailed after the projected end of the war, when its author is working "in the war against misery" (KM, 208) in a slum in London. The final passage is a hymn of joy to his work, which he does freely and happily, and toward which he implores the professor to educate his current students. Such a visionary conclusion — written only six months after Zweig's induction — already offers strong support for his later declaration that "the war gave me the first direct view of the nature of human society" (BJ, 139). Zweig's human response to that direct view in "The Wasps"

shows a new maturity; his orderly expression of it in fiction was still
to come of age.

Two short stories published in 1916 — also in the *Simplicissimus*
— reveal Zweig's attempt at fictional mastery over his revulsion from
war. In both, the human situation can only be grasped through a cor-
responding parallel in the world of "dumb" animals. Zweig was, at
this point, politically uneducated; he was not able to relate the war
to past example or present policy, so he concentrated entirely on the
simplicity of individual experience. Both "Die Tauben" (The
Pigeons) and "Die Laus" (The Louse) seek a common humanity
which shines through the darkness of war, and not surprisingly,
Zweig discovers it in man's animal nature.

He realized in "The Louse" that passive purity, in the face of random violence, may not be enough. A louse jumps from a Bavarian
mountain infantry man on duty in Serbia to a young Serbian woman,
and finally to her lover, who is subsequently imprisoned for attempting to blow up the Berlin-to-Constantinople railway line with two
older partisans. The louse, however, is responsible for the young
man's salvation and its own death. Prior to their capture by German
troops, it jumps from the young man to one of the older ones, since
the youthful fellow could more vigorously combat the itching it
caused. As the Germans approached, young Mita had put away his
weapon in order to scratch himself, and his life is thus spared, while
the louse is killed on the body of its new host. Though lighthearted
and pat, the story nonetheless demonstrates that self-serving adjustment to external conditions, innocent as it may be, is no safeguard
against war's vicissitudes. Animal-like goodness may be touching,
but Zweig was now ready to look for a brave and active stance
against the war. These two stories, almost pastoral in their telling
and tone, are like the calm before the storm. After the publication of
these two stories Zweig was transferred to the Marne and spent thirteen months in the battle of Verdun.

III   *Revolution: Politics and Plays*

Whatever Zweig saw and felt at Verdun, he did not try to write
about it until well after the war. In retrospect, he was eventually to
devote the better part of his life to working out the reaction to his experience on the western front in 1916. But at first he must have
agreed at least in part with the German student who wrote from Verdun that "the best thing of all has been the chance of taking part in
this war. Every day one goes on learning, every day one's horizon

widens."[14] With his customary thoroughness, he learned his daily lessons slowly but well; he reserved judgment until successive layers of truth gained him new perspectives on a conflict which involved the social or political transformation of every belligerent power. From the few statements he published between 1916 and 1918, the process of his education through war can be reconstructed as it must have occurred, before Zweig himself gave it shape in his novels about the war.

The comradeship of trench warfare and the political events of 1917 were the key to an awakening socialism for Zweig, as for many writers. In the work of Ernst Jünger, whose socialism did not take the international and pacifist directions of Zweig's but assumed nationalist and militarist tones, the spark for a socialist future was ignited: "In war's battles one becomes aware, with many other individuals, that a *Volk* is to be created on the basis of the unity of blood. On such moments of awareness, and not on a structure of concepts limited by time and purpose, the socialism of a nation must be built."[15] Zweig's own version of Jünger's vision is remarkably similar, although he adds one very important dimension. As a member of the middle class he had been educated to fear the proletariat's roughness and gaucherie, and had thus participated in the ever-growing separation between the bourgeoisie and the workers. And this "is the guilt of the German *Bürgertum* — one reason for the radical split between the two active parts of one *Volk* united by blood. Such insights are not demonstrable but only accessible to those who have experienced them. And these insights would have been closed to me had not the force and chance of war thrown me as a worker among workers, a coolie among coolies, had I not also been pressed into hard and manual labor, until I left the front as a changed person" (C, 364).[16] This enlightening experience as an ordinary worker was promptly reinforced, when Zweig was given the bureaucratic job on the eastern front, by his observation of the effects of the Russian Revolution of March, 1917. He was intellectually ill-equipped to cope with the historical and social implications of the Communist Revolution. His dismissal of Marxist ideology — which he did not really begin to study until his period of exile after Hitler's ascension in 1933[17] — had led him to identify himself with the "pure" or utopian socialism of eastern European Jewry, as expounded by his friend Gustav Landauer, "the disciple of Proudhon, who placed personal action within social coöperation far above Marxist doctrine" (BJ, 277). Zweig also repeatedly refers to the teachings of Martin Buber as "religious socialism" or "socialist religion" (BJ, 279), and he placed his hope for a future society in Buber's interpretation of the eastern European Hasidism. It is easy to see why Zweig's enthusiasm was inspired by a philosophy based upon a "central doctrine of love: love of God and love of Men. All life was holy. The Evangil of Hasidism was therefore as much of a social-ethical nature as it was of a religious one. It gave the people an affirmative philosophy of life that was warmly emotional, highly ethical, [and] rich in earthiness, though very mystical."[18] But until some time after his arrival on the eastern front he had not made any attempt to convert his bitter disillusionment into a political or social philosophy within a doctrine or party grounded in the reality of actual political life.

But the year was 1917, a year in which turmoil in Russia reached a fever pitch. After the czar's abdication in March, Zweig was a close witness to the July mutinies by sailors and strikes by factory workers, during whch hundreds of fleeing Russians were shot down by government troops. The workers' demands for peace in August, 1917, were suppressed by military force. Simultaneously, there was growing social unrest in Germany, of which Zweig surely was aware. The Allied blockade forced the German government to introduce severe food rationing, and only the rich could still obtain contraband food. Strikes against the reduction of the bread rations took place in Leipzig and Berlin. And after November, when the Bolsheviks first seized power in Russia, then kept their promise to stop all fighting, war-weariness among the German population mounted and led to the spread of Communist ideas and propaganda inside Germany and her armies. During such turbulent times, even the visionary Zweig could no longer expect to create a better world through the spiritual socialism of Landauer or the all-embracing love of Buber. Zweig describes his transformation in strong and clear terms: "It is not enough to have the best intentions and love one's neighbor, we've tried all that before. And don't feel smug and satisfied in a time in which you don't notice the tension between intellectual and cultural life and the boundless misery of proletarian existence. We, too, were well-meaning children — and what has become of us? We are accomplices in the period of terror. Our hands are, at least literally, clean of blood, we never hated along the official lines, and we tried to treat prisoners in a comradely fashion. And yet, and yet! We did not sniff evil, we fell victim to its lie, we did not combat evil" (OA, 166).

Zweig's merely passive disillusionment with war, his revulsion after thirteen months at Verdun, and his search for a utopian and gentle answer had been shaken by events. He had seen not only the brutality of official might, but also the oppressive poverty and hopelessness of eastern Europe's peasants, workers, and Jews. For the first time in his career his writing now constitutes both vigorous protest against social conditions and a firm call for action to change them. In a series of poems written in 1917 - 18 as texts for twelve lithographs by Magnus Zeller,[19] Zweig treats the themes of peace, poverty, brotherhood, and socialism in the high-pitched and exclamatory voice of expressionism. Until the war his poetry had been either occasional or derivative. In the first collection he published in 1909, the poem "Ahnung" (Presentiment) reads like an obvious and pale imitation of Hugo von Hofmannsthal's "Ballade des äusseren Lebens" (Ballad of the Outer Life):

> Wir tun so viel, und reden mehr, und stürmen —
> Und täglich neu erwachen alle Winde, . . .
> Was soll uns dann, zu drängen und zu stoßen,
> Mit andern gierig um den Platz zu ringen?

> We do so much, and talk still more, and strive —
> And daily each wind awakens anew,
> — Why should we do it, why push and shove,
> Why wrestle others greedily for a place?

> (J, 13)

But by 1918 Zweig could supply some rather startling answers to the questions of his early poem:

> Auf Trommel, hinaus und zurück von der Wand
> Der Arbeitergasse[20] geworfen den Ton!
> Wir heben die Fahne, rot flattert sie schon:
> Wirf, Trommel, das Echo des Aufruhrs ins Land!

> Onward, drum, send your sound out,
> And let it resound from the workers' streets' walls.
> We raise the flag, it flutters red in the wind:
> Send, drum, the echo of revolt through the land!

> (J, 119)

His call for revolt was sounded, in similar words and in similar tones, by many other German poets: Hasenclever, Werfel, Toller, and Becher, to name only a few. Zweig's other poems are powerful outbursts about beggars, prostitutes, and consumptives, about all those with no material possessions and no social rights. Zweig was not content merely to point out their shameful neglect but called for active resistance against an order which permits such human indifference. His call to revolution, however, avoids the specific details for such an uprising. Zweig clearly felt its need, but could not yet discover — in politics or in poetry — the springs for action.

On November 9, 1918, red flags flew over Kovno; the war on the eastern front was over. As the formative experience of his life, however, Zweig would make the war a major theme of his works, spanning four decades. He began in 1917 by planning two dramas, *Die Lucilla* and *Das Spiel vom Sergeanten Grischa*. Both plays reflect his immediate experience in the headquarters of the German army on the eastern front. The former turns to the vast administrative bureaucracy of large occupied territories for comic inspiration and fails badly, whereas the latter focuses on one instance of injustice within this machinery of occupation and lays the groundwork for Zweig's lasting analysis of war as a product of Germany's social order.

Die Lucilla employs all the devices of low comedy to make a noble point. Using Roman-occupied Valencia in 55 B.C. as the historical model for Germany's *Drang nach Osten* in 1917, the play is neither earthy enough to be a successful comedy in the *miles gloriosus* tradition nor witty enough for effective political satire. Comparison of this play with other German dramas of the time would be unfair; it is more like the first nervous little joke before serious conversation. *Das Spiel von Sergeanten Grischa* commences that lifelong dialogue.

In the fall of 1917 at a café in Kovno, a noncommissioned officer named Hirschfeld told Zweig the story of a Russian prisoner of war who had escaped but was recaptured "and . . . shot, although the commanding general of an army corps tried to see to it that right and justice in the German army should not be subordinated either to political considerations or to the rising fear of Bolshevism and the troops' rebellion against the continuation of the war.[21] Zweig was deeply moved by this tale, but more important, it robbed him of his conviction that "for the administration of law in the German army the concepts of justice and humanity had to be decisive, just as they were, according to my opinion at that time, decisive in state and society beyond the military."[22] Zweig is reported to have taken notes while listening to the story, and he worked on the bare outline of the incident for four years. The final version of the play was not written until 1921. The period between Zweig's first acquaintance with the case and the completion of the drama was one of the most troubled in German history. The proclamation of the Weimar Republic on November 9, 1918, was followed by four years of violent clashes, revolts, and political assassinations. In addition, the Treaty of Versailles had imposed a heavy burden on an already delicate economy. It is no wonder that by 1921 "the politics of militarism, revolutionary and counterrevolutionary slogans, and direct action was on the ascendant."[23] Although thematically Zweig's play looks backward in time, its tone bears distinctive imprints of this new era.

Zweig could no longer place any faith in the political potential of idealistic socialism in the style of Gustav Landauer, but he was still unable to choose between social democrats and Marxist revolutionaries. With his usual philosophically critical stance, he pinpointed the flaws of both sides: "Both parties no longer are in touch with each other, no longer are aware of the pains jointly suffered and of their joint homeland. The desperate proponents of revolution, of the idea of a new and more humane way of life, appear as brutal enemies and threats to the republic and to national existence, while the defenders of order seem like bloody murderers of the people and cursed defamers of all ideals."[24] To be sure, in 1918 - 19 revolutionary socialism offered no steady social vision to a man of Zweig's reflective cast of mind; Karl Liebknecht assessed the Marxist position as "revolutionary against militarism and the open representation of imperialism: in relation to socialism still divided, hesitant and immature."[25] On the other hand, when Zweig was completing the play Liebknecht and Rosa Luxemburg — the leaders of the Spartacists, a revolutionary political group — had been murdered by fanatical right-wingers aiding a Social Democrat in restoring order, and Landauer had been beaten to death in prison. The treatment of the Grischa material reflects, therefore, not only Zweig's judgment of the past failure of justice within the German army, but the author's growing awareness of the current role of justice as a harbinger of the reactionary counterrevolution within German society itself. Forced to choose between the possibility of future violence and the reality of legalized murder, he espouses the Left.

As early as 1919, Zweig had conceived of the theater as the best vehicle for reaching the largest audience representing all classes,[26] but Zweig's own plays failed to meet the new standards of postwar expressionist drama, and the Grischa play was not performed until 1930, well after the epic treatment of the same material had made Zweig famous. Although the play has been described as "constructed on markedly Expressionist lines,"[27] it is the very model of an old-fashioned, unashamedly well-made play. It is not a loud play; its language and appeal are not strident but cool and controlled. None of the characters declaim or scream as universalized "Man," "Woman," or "Soldier," but they speak as ordinary and highly individualized persons. In short, none of the devices and eccentricities of expressionist drama, from its thematic extremism to its wildly shifting style and tone of dialogue or deliberately disjointed and confusing plots, can be found in *Grischa*.

Most expressionist plays pit the hero's and the author's stark subjectivity against external reality. In such a struggle, either victory or defeat for the protagonist must be hollow, because reality, viewed as senseless and degrading, has not been explored — only condemned. Torn from any social determinants, revolt becomes an empty exercise, at least in sociopolitical terms. In artistic and human terms the fierce subjectivism of expressionist characters may well be considered a "legitimate defense against a social system."[28] Zweig's reaction to expressionist theater and his own failure in that genre is amusingly terse: "In an hysterical era, hysterical plays were performed."[29] He was far too reflective and realistic to accept so sudden and sweeping an enshrinement of man-in-the-abstract as a preventive to war or a solution to social ills. In choosing the specific fate of one individual but simultaneously placing the treatment of his case within the framework of the German army's hierarchy, Zweig attempted to avoid both expressionism's pure subjectivity and Marxism's rigid ideology. It was a noble effort, which pleased neither the theatrical producers of the 1920s nor the Marxist critics in the 1960s. But it offers a more dramatic situation and saner vision of history than its detractors have been willing to grant it, in large part through a candid portrait of the German army viewed from an internal perspective rather than dissected by an external ideology.

The plot, which begins and concludes with the fatal trap sprung on the Russian prisoner Grischa Paprotkin, includes his escape from a German prison camp and continued flight under the assumed identity of a Russian deserter, his capture behind German lines, and his execution under an order given by General Schieffenzahn (a thinly disguised version of the actual quartermaster general of the German army, Erich Ludendorff) to combat the Bolshevist propaganda which, together with news of unrest at home, had "broken the fighting spirit"[30] of the German troops. Schieffenzahn's directive in the play corresponds very closely to Ludendorff's decree: "On June 23, 1918, he published a strict order that promised death and the seizure of property to all deserters and made it clear that these penalties would never be lightened by any subsequent amnesty."[31] Although Grischa's true identity is established after his capture, General Schieffenzahn insists that the innocent Grischa must be executed for the sake of the army's morale and Germany's final victory. The struggle for Grischa's life between Schieffenzahn and a group headed by General Lychow forms the center of the play.

Critics have aptly remarked that Grischa's fate is overshadowed by the tensions and fluctuations of the fight to save his life.[32] But it can not escape the audience or reader that Grischa's escape and execution form the framework within which the entire action takes place and that his desire for escape and his reaction to his sentence diminish the grand as well as petty motivations of the warring factions. Zweig tells us much about the effects of war on men and their society by placing the individual precisely where the machinery of state and its army had put him — on the useful but insignificant flanks of the political, economic, and military strategy of total warfare. Zweig never allows Grischa to hold center stage, either thematically or theatrically; he is excluded from the key scenes in the conflict over his own life, and he is granted neither sentimental nor stirring speeches about the outrageous injustice of his fate. Grischa's escape from the prison camp has little to do with military or political considerations. He tells the band of refugees, led by the earthy peasant girl Babka, who shield him and equip him with false papers and uniform, that he has simply "had it up to here. I just want to get home to the little woman and child" (D, 337). Although Grischa is referred to as "the Russian soul" (D, 337), he never becomes the merely typical, idealized Everyman or Poor Soul caught in the currents of history. He makes love to Babka, and she carries his child when she visits him prior to his execution. He gets roaringly drunk with his German captors, and he glows with the warmth and security in which his protectors envelop him. In short, he is an ordinary man. The helplessness of Grischa's situation is expressed better by his final gesture than it could have been protested by any expressionist scream: he requests that the shiny buttons of his uniform be sent to his little daughter — whom he has never seen.

Grischa's capture, the result of his inability to read the posters

containing Schieffenzahn's order, becomes a catalyst for the airing of
a cross section of German views on war, politics, society, and justice.
The clash of these opinions, rather than unwittingly overshadowing
Grischa's injustice, deliberately intends to illuminate and expand it.
The battle of words and politics, framed as it is by Grischa's passion
for life and fatalism in the face of death, serves to expose the total
discord between what is said at home and headquarters and what is
known and done at the front, between the artifice of politics and the
reality of death. Since the highest-ranking officer at headquarters
and the most potent character in Zweig's play, General Schieffenzahn, seeks Grischa's death, it is inevitable that counterforces, ranging from the firm arguments of General Lychow — upholder of
aristocratic standards of honor and justice — through the ineffective
sympathies of the cautious Private Sacht and the casual cynicism of
the Socialist Engels, to the belated resolve for social change of
Zweig's spokesman Werner Bertin, must all fail. Men of good will
from almost exclusively upper- and middle-class backgrounds,
educated in that Teutonic idealism which blinds them to the
politicoeconomic aspects of the war, they are incapable of seeing the
imperialist, annexationist, graspingly materialist power which will
kill Grischa and strangle Germany. They argue the case in abstract
terms which have no application to the human reality before them,
tossing about *Recht* ("justice" or "right") and *Mensch* ("man") until repetition has made them empty, echoing sounds. Their words,
the fruit of German idealism, cloak and sanctify Schieffenzahn,
clever enough to use war as an extension of political ambitions. The
failure of all the "decent" Germans to act is a moral disaster and a
political failure precisely because morality and politics had never
been joined in public life or private reflection. Too late does Werner
Bertin cry out that the case of Grischa "is the case of all his Germany" (D, 380), or does General Lychow exclaim rather pathetically
"I smell politics" (D, 374). Engels's gentle but perceptive mocking
of Löwengard, the pipe-smoking intellectual who tries to reflect on
the outcome of the struggle and its import, might well serve to chide
the outpouring of words on the war by the entire generation of German intellectuals:

Are they still talking? Still talking? I'm cutting out. (Lights a cigarette) Sure,
Lychow won't go for it, or so he thinks. But I wouldn't give a cent for the
Russki's life.
Löwengard: Man, but that would be murder, after all, he's innocent.

Engels: Call yourself a college man and yet you talk of guilt and innocence in a war! (D, 379 - 80)

With so casual an interest in individual fate, so small a grasp of social reality, all attempts to right the wrong done Grischa fall short. Common humanity fails; Babka's pathetic last-minute attempt to effect a rescue wins Sacht's sympathy but not his consent to an escape, and he understands the significance of his refusal. "The Russian stays here, and he'll be executed tomorrow at noon. Everybody has got to be his own best friend. Everybody has to do his part. (Runs over to Grischa and grasps his hand) Forgive me, friend. With a wife and a kid you just haven't got any other choice. God forgive those who ground us decent fellows down, until out of fear we're only capable of atrocities ourselves" (D, 403). And honorable authority fails; like Engels and Sacht, but more viciously. Schieffenzahn dismisses Lychow's plea, based on the code of justice and honor in the German army, for the life of Grischa. The conversation between the two, as well as earlier remarks made by Schieffenzahn, reveal that power is now in the hands of the Schieffenzahns, and that such men no longer even pretend to cling to the army's code or their society's professed morality. Lychow defends his position with every weapon from the arsenal of German idealism, from "our Lutheran conscience" (D, 376) to "Prussia's moral heritage" (D, 389). But Schieffenzahn brushes aside the evocation of God and Kant. He never bothers to hide Germany's aggression or imperialism, and he openly delineates the recently explored military-industrial complex Germany had created on the eastern front: "What is our future based on? On the preponderance of people dependent on agriculture over the crumbling masses in the cities, the industrial proletariat. We have absolutely no choice. After peace is made we'll be able to keep the empire along the Strip[33] if we will have populated eight or nine provinces with farmers who think along good old Prussian lines. Hell, then the gentlemen in the big cities can vote for the Social Democrats as much as they want. We'll have to exist independently of world trade if necessary, and live on Rumanian oil, our own potatoes and rye" (D, 366).[34]

Zweig's portrait of the shift of power within the ranks of the German army unmistakably reflects the triumph of a bourgeois mentality over aristocratic honor, the victory of crass capitalism over Spartan militarism, and the end of the myth that war, in the minds of the men in battle, is fought for noble causes rather than the national

self-interest. Since armies, at least by World War I, were no longer
bodies distinct from their parent societies, the implications of
Schieffenzahn's victory are clear. Lychow's whimpering protest —
"I am, O Lord, a Prussian General" (D, 392) — in the face of
Schieffenzahn's confident challenge laments the capitulation of the
German Officers Corps. Schieffenzahn represents a new world in
which men distinguish not so much between right and wrong but, at
best, between what is legal and what is not. Such a world is not concerned with justice but with efficiency, not with satisfactory employ-
ment of human beings but with profitable deployment of resources.
Schieffenzahn is Zweig's first industrial technocrat. Given Zweig's
political education in 1917 - 19, the bourgeois opposition to
aggressive, imperialist nationalism of whatever stripe is naturally ineffective.

His view of working-class conscripts surrounding the case of
Grischa is equally varied and equally clear-sighted. If they are not
individualized or articulate, neither is their position simplistically
monolithic. The common soldiers in the play are not deceived by
their country's professed aims in the war, and they perceive the real
case quite clearly. In a very Brechtian song they reveal their disillusionment and resignation:

> Und krepierte Landser, die tun ihre Pflicht, pick pack,
> Und morgen stehn wir im Tagesbericht, schnick, schnack,
> Und der Kriegsgewinnler wird madenfett,
> Und im Drahtverhau klappert das Landserskelett:
> Na, da stürm wir mal, stürm wir mal, jufifallera-ssassassa."
>
> (D, 411 - 12)

> And we doughboys'll die, we do our duty, pick pack,
> And tomorrow we'll be in the morning report, snick snack,
> And the war profiteers'll get feisty and fat,
> and the trooper's bones'll rattle in the barbed wire,
> Okay, let's attack, attack, hip hip horray.
>
> (D, 411 - 12)

And yet this song is followed by a fiercely patriotic cheer for
Schieffenzahn and the munition makers. The almost boyish cheering
betrays both the political naiveté and the complicity Zweig could not
fail to notice. In an essay published in 1923 he spells out what the
play barely hints at: "The Wilhelminian German, who screamed for
annexation during the times of military victories, who approved

every assault, exploitation and diplomatic lie, may not excuse himself today by claiming that he was deceived. He was deceived, but by his own choice."[35] The cynicism of the soldiers' song complements rather than contradicts the innate nationalism of the citizens' cheer. It was Germany's tragedy that the transformation from Wilhelminian nationalism to antimilitarist republicanism was both short-lived and shallow.

As Zweig clearly stated in essays of that time, his dramas were intended to be "pedagogical and character-building."[36] The failure of the Grischa play to be performed, however, cannot be blamed only on the temper and taste of the times. To be sure, passionate or political engagement between the theater and its actual or potential public, necessary to Zweig's ethical mission, had been made difficult by the profusion of shocks and sensations offered by so many expressionist plays. Their portrayals of the war as coldly dehumanized or searingly stylized were in marked contrast to Zweig's solid realism, which offered merely experience without novelty. His admirable understatement of Grischa's case and his refusal to deal in types reveal no universal truths about the condition of man. When other dramatists demanded "the most fantastic truth [*unwirklichste Wahrheit*], the Superdrama,"[37] Zweig was content to show a truth far more terrifying precisely because it resided within the external forms and formalities of everyday life, not beyond reality. It is not sobriety based on historical authenticity alone, however, which prevented its dramatic success. The play's flaws in structure and characterization are obvious. Schieffenzahn is the only strong character, and his opposition is either weak or indecisive, so that the protagonist is really only his victim. Grischa becomes too much like the corpse in a murder mystery — central to the unfolding of the plot but not illuminating to its resolution. Grischa's personal tragedy and Germany's political one are, in short, intellectually related but not dramatically integrated. When Zweig returned to the same material in 1926, political and legal developments in the Weimar Republic had made the historical and social implications of a case such as Grischa's both clearer and more ominous, and he was able to place the death of one individual at the center of the social world and merge symbol and setting into his most successful novel.

Zweig made one additional attempt to reach a mass audience through the drama. In 1922 he composed *Laubheu und keine Bleibe* (Dry Leaves and No Abode), a postwar comedy which Freud "did not find funny."[38] Freud's judgment is accurate and kind. In trying to capture the economic catastrophe and moral confusion of postwar Germany, Zweig only reflects the confusion without grasping the catastrophe. The comic situation in which a group of soldiers, returning from the war, become involved is aimed at contrasting the greed of already wealthy farmers with the professed nobility of already impoverished soldier-workers in order to unmask the power of money over the lives of men. The soldiers are on their way to Persia to start a new and communal life. When they reach the little town of Niedersdorf, in the fall of 1920, they are asked by the mayor to guard a wagon of foliage, in which the major and the farmers have hidden their money from an expected commission of the Ministry for Finances and Taxes. The soldiers soon discover that the wagon is not loaded with army materiel, as the mayor has told them, but with the concealed money. Before they can abscond with the money themselves, however, an old servant of the mayor, following the voice of a religious dream, sets the wagon ablaze. It turns out, moreover, that the commission was never meant to check Niedersdorf after all.

Much is said in the play to point out the power of chance and irrationality over the postwar mind of Germany. One veteran officer summarizes the situation: "The Unexpected became our daily bread, and the completely Wild was accepted as natural" (D, 423). Zweig wished to show that many Germans, in attempting to cope with military defeat, personal deprivation, economic uncertainty, and moral anarchy, had no choice but to dispense with causality to maintain a hold on reality, to give some meaning to their existence. But in the play the comic elements disarm the social criticism and moral barbs. In the early 1920s Germany was, after all, fiercely eager to recapture her pre - World War I position and prestige, and the revelation that "money is the power whom all serve" (D, 440) is an unduly mild rebuke, a mere slap on the wrist for a capitalist crime. Compared to the devastating experiences with money so powerfully depicted in Kaiser's *From Morn till Midnight* ("money veils what is genuine, money is the saddest fraud of them all"[39]) or Toller's *Hinkemann* ("Nowadays Progress is the World. Hundred percent profit in it. Full steam ahead"[40]), Zweig's somewhat tardy and comic comment seems ineffective and out of place. Zweig was keenly aware of the weakness of his approach and method. In his reply to Freud's friendly criticism, he notes that "the piece is neither completely comic nor totally tragic, and its styles really do work at cross purposes."[41] More significantly, he questioned whether "unmasking, without also positing a productive, positive counterpart is really the task of the poet" (E,I, 257).

IV *Deepening Vision, Clarified Form*

In 1922 Zweig began to strive for such a positive solution. To achieve his task, he removed himself from the pressures and demands of theatrical fashions and returned to the freedom of form and theme offered by the short story. Moreover, the tone and temper of his approach had been changed by personal failure and political uncertainty. Since Zweig lived in Starnberg, Bavaria, during the succession of coups and regimes in Munich, he observed at close hand the failure of political ideology and social revolt to merge successfully. Whether one places the bulk of the blame on the pettiness of factional infighting among the Social Democrats, the oscillation between cabaretlike ridicule or visionary utopianism among the intellectuals, or the explosively unpredictable allegiance of the proletariat, it is certain that most literary men had little contact or communication with the workers, because "their formulations of social problems were always on the level of subjective idealism or a mystical objective idealism that showed no understanding of the actual social forces."[42] Much of the political attitude of the *Neue Sachlichkeit* ("New Objectivity" or "Matter-of-Factness") which succeeded expressionism was irritably negative and critical. The feelings of the novelist Alfred Döblin toward the working class are probably quite representative: "Countless times at gatherings of Social Democrats; read Marx, Lassalle. But when I sat next to the workers it was clear to me that my love must remain platonic. I wanted no economic advantages, was no factory worker; at elections I rejoiced over the increasing vote of the reds. But it was clear to me that I was swimming in the air, a hopeless stickler for principles."[43]

"Kleiner Held" (Little Hero, 1922) is Zweig's descent from such intellectual abstraction to the social reality of Germany's worker. It depicts the brutal and brief life of a miner in prewar Germany. It seeks not to explain the workers' political shifts of allegiance, which are more important to polticians and intellectuals than to the workers themselves, but to achieve a middle-class *Einfühlung* ("emphathy") with the daily existence of a miner. Zweig has chosen a young doctor of a miners' infirmary as the narrator, apparently to permit a clinical objectivity that would authenticate any personal response. The physician is learning his trade on the bodies of the miners, "who are delivered [to the infirmary] like the goods death has picked from the warehouse of life" (KM, 62). The doctor, in order to "check the vital signs of my spirit" (KM, 62), writes down the cases which "excite me, which allow disgust or admiration to swell up within me until, once again, my nerve ends tell me that I am still a human being, vibrating with the passions, joys, and despairs of shared experiences and shared responses" (KM, 62).

The doctor's chroniclelike retelling of Michael Mrozik's tragic nineteen years represents a breakthrough for Zweig in the choice of new material, treated in the most traditional form. Not only does the doctor link the miners' sacrifice and death to the conduct of nations, but he raises the level of meaning from its topical limitations by prefacing his account with these reflections: "This story begins with the father — all human destinies begin with fathers" (KM, 63). The physician's platitudinous ruminations, appropriate enough for a young man overwhelmed by social conditions he was never prepared to understand or deal with, signal the author's intentions and perhaps his view of the short story in general. Zweig is suggesting, without ever saying as much, that "no story has really been understood until it has been read as a character study, as an emotional revelation, as a logically related series of incidents, and as a work of art which has something to say about human life in general."[44]

The doctor's summary of Mrozik's life restricts itself precisely to those areas which were open to the working class — the concrete and immediate, the intimate, the sensory, and the detailed. He never even hints at the existence of an inner life, of introspection or self-awareness. Mrozik leaves school at the age of fourteen to work in the mines so that he can support his mother and himself. Outside of the lung-destroying work there exist only the dank and dreary tenements in which miners and their families live and the patriotically named bars in which they gather on the weekend evenings. For Michael and his mother life has circled around a "dull, grieving satisfaction" (KM, 65), a satisfaction derived from the victories over economic necessity which have to be repeated daily, with no hope for anything better. Pleasures of the mind have been denied to workers by laughably inadequate schooling, and the pleasures of a family life, in the manner in which the word is understood among the bourgeoisie, have been put out of the workers' reach by their grim socioeconomic position. Drink and sex are the two means for forgetting or escaping drudgery or emptiness.

At a Sunday dance for the workers at the pub, Michael meets and falls in love with Berta, a salesgirl, and soon they became lovers. For

Michael the aspirations of a young working man should now have been met, for with the others at the bar he can boast of the fulfillment in the four worlds granted him: "work, strength, being one of the boys, and time off" (KM, 67). The German — "*Arbeit, Kraft, Kerl sein, Feierabend*" — emphasizes the comradely manliness and fellowship with its stress on the crisp *f* and *k* sounds. But precisely at this moment of manly achievement, the possibility of anything beyond it is cruelly denied. Steadily Michael's health begins to deteriorate, his strength to decline, and the threshold to adult maturity is never crossed. With ashen skin, dark circles under his eyes, and the arms of a boy, Michael is delivered to the infirmary. Not overindulgence in drink or love, as his mother suspects, but the desperate attempt to break out of the cycle designated as the worker's world has brought about his deterioration and will cause his death. Because Berta bore him a son, Michael has been working twelve to sixteen hours a day to support them and his mother as well.

Just as the physician-narrator uses Michael's father as the starting point of the story's circle, so he returns at its close to Michael's own son. He comments, almost casually sympathetic, that the mother's forgiveness, like all human emotions in an inhuman system, comes too late and means too little. The mother, he tells us, adopts the baby because Berta is too young to be burdened with him. And just as casually, as if to diagnose an illness the symptoms of which we have seen but perhaps not fully understood, he adds that the grandmother has named the baby after Michael's father and put it into Michael's old bed — to illustrate, as she sighs, "how life follows in its rounds" (KM, 71).

It would be enlightening if the second point at which Michael's life intersects with the physician's voice signaled a change in the doctor's tone or attitude. Indeed, he has grasped the human tragedy inherent in economic exploitation and seen the emotional barriers built by social rigidity, but he accepts both as the terrible price to be paid for individual heroism. As the title of the story implies, to him Michael's death can be both terrible and beautiful — terrible for its uselessness, beautiful for its legacy. He, too, just like Michael and the proletariat, lives in a closed system. He cannot speak of Michael as anything but a type or representative of his class. His sympathy with Michael's destruction is overshadowed by his admiration for humanity's indestructability. In a final burst of unintentionally ironic intoxication, he even congratulates himself for belonging to the same race as Michael Mrozik. And yet the doctor is the ideal

narrator for Zweig. Through his very isolation he has permitted
Zweig to concentrate on the externals that form the center of a
worker's life. Our gaze is never averted from them, and we are
allowed neither romanticizing nor condescending interpretations.
The doctor's noble-sounding clichés are exposed as self-serving and
self-justifying, his sympathy as sincere but insignificant. Like
Döblin, the doctor meant well, but . . . Zweig has built, in "Little
Hero", a social reality which stands mute with aspirations never
spoken, hopes never expressed, injustices never shouted, and the
seeds of an inner life never given voice. It is a portrayal that is
historically accurate, but its very silence — there is no spoken
dialogue in the entire story — is forbidding to further fictional
growth. In the next few stories written in the early 1920s Zweig
turned inward and outward to find the voices, to make the circles
meet, to see society as a whole.

In 1923 - 24, Zweig turned to Freud for aid in integrating his psychology; when a few of his stories also turned backward in time, he
began to deepen his knowledge of society. When he saw how the
past shaped the present, or malformed it, he found the freedom to
impose his own artistic forms on his newly discovered vision. The
first step on the road to this kind of communal self-knowledge,
naturally enough, turned out to be a reexamination of Germany's
emotion-filled idealism which had greeted and glorified the outbreak of the war. In 1915 Zweig had published a story, "Der Mann
des Friedens" (Man of Peace), in which the hero's inability to share
in the populace's embrace of war, rooted in an intellectual coldness
and rationality, led to a self-destructive madness. Such estrangement
from the popular spirit was portrayed by Zweig in 1915 in a harshly
negative light as a sense of righteousness twisted into egomania, as
rationalism soured by selfishness, as the defeat of soul by mind.
When he rewrote the story in 1923 as "Helbret Friedebringer,"
Zweig had cast aside the emotional assumptions and intellectual
prejudices of prewar Germany, and in the light of political upheavals
and Freudian revelations the slant of the story and the defects of its
main character become highly ambiguous and complex.

Helbret Friedebringer, a respected Thuringian judge in his fifties,
is the personification of German idealism. His mode of life and
thought is based on his love of the law, belief in justice, and affirmation of reason as the means to govern the conduct of men and
nations. He is a cold but honest and fair man, very serious and
hairsplittingly correct in all his dealings. But Zweig makes it clear

that such rigidity of conduct, even in the case of high-minded
legality, deadens the response to emotional nuances and distorts the
sense of reality. Indeed, the judge stands so far above passions and
politics that he can cope with neither. His trust in the rational conduct of European man is so overwhelming that "he viewed every
political complication with the greatest equanimity. It was with this
sense of calm that he experienced the Austro-Serbian clash" (KM,
362). The ensuing explosion of national pride, ethnic hostilities, and
irrational hunger for battle shatter his world. His personal decline illustrates gloomily that "even before the war, grasp on reality con-
stituted one of the weakest sides of the German national
character."[45] He loses all confidence in reason and justice as the
governing principles of human life. His isolation proceeds from dis-
engagement from his government's policy and alienation from his
people's feelings to separation from the members of his own family.
The volunteer charity work of his wife and daughter and the
patriotic performance of his son at the front become acts of treason
to him. Shut up in his room, he rapidly succumbs to mental derange-
ment and physical collapse. As his final gesture to a world grown
totally incomprehensible and hostile, the judge carefully composes
peace treaties in Latin, complete with instructions for the cessation
of all hostilities, and mails them to all warring heads of government
and their chiefs of staff. In an action that is as ironic as it is mad, a
gesture as logical in its closed system as it is neurotic in relation to
the world, the judge has declared peace. Above the war's carnage
and yet buried by it, his treaties of peace are a farewell in a dead
language to a dead ideal.

With "Helbret Friedebringer" Zweig had traversed the full circle
— from the world of social reality without any ideals in "Little
Hero" to ideals without roots in the conditions of human life, albeit
critically depicted. The disparity between two such stories written
within so short a span of time illuminates the division within
Wilhelminian Germany which Zweig came to understand.
Hypocrisy among the middle class about moral ideals and material
gains in Wilhelminian Germany was exacerbated by the economic
difficulties and political uncertainties of the republic. And in this
hyporcrisy turned vicious, this professed idealism ever more sharply
silhouetted against reality, lay the core to which political extremism
appealed, thus accelerating the psychological collapse of bourgeois
society. Aided by an orientation toward the subconscious drawn
from Freud, Zweig began to probe the moral veneer of the average

German. In "Ein Fleck im Auge" (A Spot in the Eye), written in 1926, he found the perfect fable and character to illustrate the problem of German *Zerrissenheit* ("disunion," literally "torn condition"), and he linked specific psychological characteristics with national modes of thought.

The story signals not only a new awareness and ease of expression, but an autobiographical confession as well. "It does not happen to many people that they experience a basic change between the ages of thirty-eight and forty, especially if they've acquired a bald head, a solidly bourgeois view of the world, and the fleshy red face that goes with it" (SZ, 39). For Zweig, thirty-nine years old in 1926, the change may not have been as shattering as it is for the story's wine-merchant hero Ingbert Maukner, but the wry opening suggests that it cut deep. Maukner strains himself while opening a bottle of wine at a friend's party. The next morning he notes a spot in his left eye, which subtly distorts his vision. His physician diagnoses it as the bursting of a tiny vein on his retina, and suggests that it will gradually disappear. But the little spot remains, and its external permanence represents an inner alteration as well. Maukner cannot but see the world through his left eye, and he sees things he never noticed before. His orderly perception of the world is rearranged, and suddenly he "sees disorder into the world" (SZ, 45), suddenly his smug world has a little hole and can no longer remain as "unambiguous as the Catechism or the Ten Commandments" (SZ, 45). Maukner's altered perspective forces him to question the very validity of his reality, a reality he had accepted as readily as his stomach or walking cane. New possibilities appear in his field of vision, new ideas and doubts invade his mind. The foundations of his old world have been toppled. To the great displeasure of his circle of friends, he now becomes tolerant of political ideas and figures they oppose totally. He begins to question every shibboleth and article of faith that the political Right has adopted: "Why must the *Völkisch* politicians be the sole saviors of the country? Is it not possible that Lenin and Ludendorff can both be great men? Might it not have been better if Erzberger had not been assassinated, or even Liebknecht and Luxemburg had been spared? Can it not be that we were defeated by forces other than the stab in the back?" (SZ, 46 - 48). For such shockingly "left-wing" notions he is cast out by his friends. The squint in his eye and in his mind's eye offends everyone, from slight acquaintances to his own wife. The "maybes" and "not only but alsos" which now stud his speech and thought run counter to the either-or mentality so characteristic of Germany. Maukner does not become bitter. He lives on as a happily squinting friend of his children and employees, the only ones who sense in their father and boss a "warm, good kindness" (SZ, 57), which originates in the "maybe" awakened by the spot in his left eye.

Unlike many stories previously discussed, "A Spot in the Eye" has no extensive authorial frame. The story speaks for itself, and Zweig's voice is sure and strong, the flow of the narrative as rapid as it is clear. Zweig was not one of the intellectuals who saw the dangers to the Weimar Republic early. What he realized in 1926, Carl von Ossietzky had warned against in 1920: "The old Burgher spirit, enriched with a new note, is back again, and dominates the day. Burgherdom not as a social concept, but a mental attitude. Here everything comes together: aversion to the unusual, unwillingness for experience, enthusiasm for authority, servility."[46] Zweig not only understood this danger, but added, through Maukner's tender warmth, the biblical compassion from which the tale's title is taken: "Judge not, that you be not judged. For with the judgment you pronounce you will be judged, and the measure you give will be the measure you get. Why do you see the speck that is in your brother's eye, but do not notice the log that is in your own eye?" (Matthew, 7:1 - 3). Although by 1926 Zweig had moved politically as far to the left as Ossietzky and Tucholsky, his colleagues on the staff of the *Weltbühne*, he restricted his views on class struggle and party politics to his essays and speeches. But, more significantly, he simply lacked the flair for journalistic jousting, the glibness for one-sided condemnation or commendation. He preferred to explore, to diagnose the symptoms and discover the causes of his society's illness. Each of the novellas written in the early twenties exposes one of the flaws or failures of Weimar Germany — the worker's hopeless reality in "Little Hero," the intellectual's baseless idealism in "Helbret Friedebringer," and the bourgeois' rigid *ressentiment* in "A Spot in the Eye." Like pieces of a larger mosaic, each is well executed; yet Zweig had not been able to find a pattern for fitting the pieces together. But when they are read together, a common clue emerges, and that clue points to Germany's prewar period and war experience as the key to an understanding of the postwar period. In Fritz Stern's formulation, "The Germans under Weimar continued to live on the emotional presuppositions and intellectual baggage of Imperial Germany."[47] In 1925 Zweig began to turn back to Weimar Germany's handling of the war and found the issue largely ignored,

at least on a level above prowar pop fiction. When he began to
perceive the significance of such repression, his political vision
cleared and his fictional vision expanded to unite the classes and
types, to take in the full panorama in space and time of his countrymen's psychic situation and political leanings. Until that moment
he, too, "could not develop a politics capable of dealing with the
return of the repressed in the German middle class."[48] "A Spot in the
Eye" acknowledges the ominous foreboding of that return, and
while Zweig wrote it, he was already beginning work on a short novel
in which he could fully confront it.

Zweig's intention in *Pont and Anna* was to expose Germany's
repression of the war. But this repression must be seen as more than
a psychological symptom, although it is that too; its causes and consequences are meant to portray the wider frenzy and malaise of the
Weimar years. Although *Pont and Anna* is Zweig's second major
prose work, critical attention has been scant and the critics have expressed puzzled dissatisfaction with the book's ambivalence. It is not
entirely surprising that recent East German critics voice unease
about Zweig's use of Freudian insight to expose social ills. And yet
precisely the intersection of the "social unconscious" and the "individual unconscious" forms the axis of the novel, shapes its vision,
and dictates its direction. Zweig chose an intellectual as the central
character and involved him in densely emotional and psychological
problems as well as in a politically motivated murder, thereby refus-
ing to permit the separation of spheres or qualities which generate
the delicate tension of *Novellen um Claudia*. The superficial
similarities to that earlier work indicate just how far Zweig had
progressed from pitting unreflective vitality against alienating self-
consciousness, while the significant differences show that the same
problem is now understood in a much broader sense. Pont, to
be sure, is both artistic and intellectual, but also a highly successful
architect, a husband, and the father of two children. Zweig has thus
eliminated the polar opposites within which the battle of
aestheticism versus materialism previously concealed the complexity
and ambiguity of human relationships and social patterns.

Pont's enemy is within himself as much as it is without. As symbolically hinted in "A Spot in the Eye," the Germans of the Weimar
Republic perceived themselves and their history from rigidly drawn
political positions; their angle of vision was narrow and inflexible. In
the case of Pont, the angle has been reduced to its logical extreme:
"What was missing, he discovered, was not the faculty of memory or

cognizance of his own identity, but memories, the remembrance of things past, the origins of his own person in the past. Close to forty years of age, he discovered one day how few memories carried him back to the times before the Great War; a kind of thick fog covered his life with gathering darkness" (PA, 8 - 9). Pont represses not the war itself, but the origins of the war within German society and within the German mind. The question posed by his dilemma reaches beyond personal illness; the wider issue has been summarized as follows: "What of a people that neither celebrates nor distorts its history, but ignores it?"[49] The tragic story of Pont and Anna attempts to sketch the consequences.

Nothing suggests to Pont that his life without consciously known roots is either abnormal or extraordinary. In fact, in 1924 he concludes that "citizens in the hundreds make no use of their memories" (PA, 13), and that they, like him, are "people at the center of things, in every sense" (PA, 9). Pont's temporary amnesia is ignored from the first chapter until the thirteenth, when a combination of shock and associations awakens his childhood recollections. At the center of the novel, constituting the occasion of Pont's repression, is a love story. At forty Pont becomes infatuated with Anna Marechál, a modern dancer and a captivating woman, half vamp and half nymphet. But his "love" is the kind of feverish fantasy that excludes or ignores reality, a tendency Freud termed "idealization." Pont acts out being in love as "fascination" or "bondage," foolishly and fatuously mistaking Anna's invitations and suppressing his own instincts. As he retreats further and further from sexual satisfaction in their relationship, his frenzy and frustration increase. He is the prisoner of the very divisions which characterize his country's thinking and living: "If only the man in me had won out over the human being in me" (PA, 48). The identification of humanity with moral strength and weakness of instinct and of manliness with amoral force and primitive power is one of the causes of Pont's blindness. This psychic blindness, which forces him to ignore Anna's many affairs although he is directly confronted with them, becomes an equivalent of Germany's national blindness to its own history. In this manner Zweig connects individual repression with social character.

When a doctor suggests a journey as a means of recuperation, Pont embarks on the tortured German's obligatory trip to the South. And with his tormented consciousness physically removed from the German scene, repressed urges can come into play. Hans Joachim Sarrow, a young violinist embittered by the war, understands Anna too well where Pont understood her not at all; he knows that "she could love a man tenderly but at the same time could be hopelessly removed from him" (PA, 108). She is about to walk out of his life just when he has been dismissed from the orchestra which accompanies her dance program, and so he shoots her. The murder, like Pont's passivity, has roots in both personal and national maladies. Sarrow kills Anna not only because he has been rejected as a lover, but because she appears to him — in his mind twisted by the war, defeat, and the myths about the defeat — as one who had "committed cultural high treason" (PA, 115). Sarrow acts out the role as "avenger of German music" (PA, 115) by killing one who has besmirched the holy names of Mozart, Gluck, and Händel in using their music to perform lewd "Nigger dances," and who has helped through such decadence to lead German youth astray. Sarrow's suicide, at the end of his trial, only dramatizes the waste of a life that can no longer be salvaged. Sarrow is the all-too-symmetrical alter ego to Pont. While Pont cannot remember, Sarrow is a bundle of burning memories that fuel his behavior. Pont is an apolitical dreamer, Sarrow a political fanatic; Pont turns his experience into daydreams, Sarrow his into nightmares. Pont is a creation of the war, Sarrow its victim. And when Anna is killed, the war's power over these two men dies with her. Anna embodies every evil of warfare: coldness, cruelty, and caprice. Her death — and his own — ends the horrors of war memories for Sarrow, and it lifts their repression for Pont. The news of Anna's death brings about the awakening of the past into the present which permits "consciousness of myself, return to reality" (PA, 195). Pont's memories flood back as he is rolling up his sleeves in anticipation of work long blocked by fantasies. But just as significantly, his return to his craft is accompanied by an awakening to social conditions around him. For the first time he notices the poverty of Italian farmers and laborers, and abhors their dependence on tourists' whims and fashions. Pont is by no means ready for Marxist ideology, but in his own way he has come to accept the Marxist notion that life determines consciousness.

There are many loose ends in *Pont and Anna*. It is true, for example, that we never really know just what Pont repressed, nor do we discover an exact connection between his repression and his creativity. But then Zweig is describing a set of symptoms, not proposing a course of analysis. That he should choose a Freudian approach to shape his fictional depiction is entirely fitting. The random shootings and political assassinations, the madcap quality of life in the 1920s, with its frantic dancing and exotic experiments in art and manners, are well documented. On a deeper level another set of circumstances dictated Zweig's choice of material and its treatment. "In the literature of the twenties there are many sick people, schizophrenics and neurotics, who make gruesome contrast to that which should really be considered as normal. The following explanation offers itself: First, one can say that these writers regarded the period as so apocalyptic that it becomes obvious, through the existence of such sick and abnormal people, just how bad conditions have really become. Second, isn't it possible that many writers had a foreboding that after the twenties a madman would seize power — a madman who styled himself a genius?"[50] Such ominous forebodings few would doubt today. What is extraordinary is that Sarrow's defense attorney and Pont's acquaintance Dr. Preuβ anticipates both points with uncanny accuracy: "This is a time in which the most horrendous deeds are committed by the most mediocre men — time of the wolf, of the apocalypse, time for turning back" (PA, 120). For Germany there was no turning back, and Dr. Preuβ's words ominously ring in the reign of horror that was to come.

For Pont and his creator, turning back meant, in a historical as well as psychological sense, probing the origins of repression; and those origins lay in the war and in prewar Germany. The structure of *Pont and Anna,* with its amnesia and recovery of memory framing the passions, perversions, and politics of the Weimar Republic, is meant to show that Weimar should not be viewed as a separate or disconnected period in German history. Similarly, Zweig realized by 1925 that a return to reality did not mean refuge in easy political answers. Reexamination of his own career, reaching back to the fanatic endorsement of the war and subsequent disillusion in his fiction of a decade earlier, indicated that much in Wilhelminian Germany, whether repressed or revered, had not ceased to exist simply because a republic had been declared or because reflective men now saw the past differently. *Pont and Anna* is an attempt to fictionalize the continuity of German life; in its actual manifestations it is a depiction of the dreary results that occur when continuity is ignored as by Pont, or falsified as by Sarrow. The book allowed Zweig not only to find his enduring theme, but also to settle on the genre to which his style and outlook were most attuned. Though his novellas had fully realized their aims with increasing frequency, neither in them nor in *Das Spiel um den Sergeanten Grischa* — the only one of his dramas even to approach success after the war — was he able to depict the wide panorama of subjects, times, and places which by the mid-1920s he realized were necessary to reflect the social as well as psychological realities of prewar German life. His deepening insights, his moral-ethical purposes, and his scholarly inclinations, frustrated by the prescribed forms of the drama though less so by the short story, required the scope of a novelistic exploration. His second "Glance at Germany" was to be a long, searching study, recorded in six novels which reach back to the turn of the century, that occupied, fascinated, and challenged its author for the rest of his life.

CHAPTER 3

Mars and Mammon

NOVELS about war, particularly World Wars I and II, have been relegated to a separate and, more often than not, minor category. Because the form of the war novel is so completely determined by a subject with limited boundaries, many critics have assumed that little about the structure or texture of these novels is noteworthy. In the most general way, war novels are judged by their endorsement or rejection of the war, while some attention is paid to verisimilitude, verbal vehemence, and the ideological basis of their stance. Few modern books about war have achieved enduring fame. To strain the quality of modern battle into any permanent artistic mold has seemed almost impossible; this difficulty appears, in the case of World War I fiction, to have been a direct consequence of trench warfare — so static, tedious, and fatal to the individual, about whose adventures most great war stories have been written.

A study of German novels dealing with World War I reveals the same range of outlooks, from the picturesque and romantic to the realistic and naturalistic, and the same range of responses, from war as a normal state of human affairs to war as insanity, which the Napoleonic campaigns and the Crimean War evoked in English, French, and Russian novels of the nineteenth century. But such novels, including works by Stendhal, Zola, Tolstoy, and Andreyev, had the advantage of two conditions of warfare from which a fictional quality of heightened life can be achieved, namely, the adventurous and the social — the battlefront and civilian response to it.

For the novelist of the First World War the choice had become limited: the adventurous side of warfare had generally been outpaced by firepower and artillery, and the scene behind the front was accessible to few of those buried in the trenches, nor was it thought by many to be representative of the war. Thus the attrition and stalemate of trench warfare, the characteristic battleline of World

War I, allowed no mobility and therefore no change in perspective or mood. The novelist was restricted to portraying, on the one hand, weeks or months of absolute boredom in the trenches, interrupted occasionally by murderous but tactically futile engagements with the enemy, and on the other hand daily awareness of extremely high casualty rates incurred through steady shellings. Most men were not killed like warriors in battle but slaughtered like cattle in a pen. They did not die while facing a visible enemy in combat but were torn to pieces while brushing their teeth or playing cards, from explosives fired by unseen hands. It is not surprising, then, that most antiwar fiction directed its anger not against a worthy or insidious foe but against war itself. The attitude is summarized in Siegfried Sassoon's statement in *Sherston's Progress:* "I had no conviction about anything except that the war was a dirty trick which had been played on my generation."[1] The consequences of this "trick" are usually seen and cursed from the perspective of a small group of individuals, a few friends or perhaps a squadron or platoon, who come to see the war as an eccentric and destructive shift in the normal course of human events. As a result, the great majority of war novels adhere rather closely to one pattern: "In its driest outline the shape of the experience of the Great War is defined by all or most of these events in roughly this order: the outbreak of the war, enlistment, training, embarkation, the base, marching to the line, the sound of bombardment, the first shell, the line, digging in, under fire, the first death, relief, leave, return, on patrol, in combat, the suffering of hardships or wounds or sickness, the end."[2]

Admirers of war fiction, of course, reject such an attitude. A war novel modeled on the described pattern does not touch the totality of human existence; few of the virtues extolled in the great classics — selflessness, courage, faith — are at the center of such war experiences, nor is the mystery of human existence or its universal affirmation at the core of the response to this war. Even today the normality of war, indeed the necessity of war for the spiritual health of the nation, for the transformation of self-indulgent boys into self-reliant men, and for the development of comradeship that has a high moral value, is compelling to many.[3]

But even friendly critics frequently find fiction about the war preoccupied with human values and ethical problems which can interfere with its art as prose narrative. One study notes that

a cross-section of eleven widely read German war novels reveals a remarkable similarity in several basic ethical and social ideas. Closely related and often even identical is the attitude of the authors as well as that of the characters toward great problems which are cast up by the war. The basis for this similarity is grounded quite plainly in the fact that the inexpressible horror of the battlefield has been personally experienced by these writers and, furthermore, that their reactions to these experiences are subject to universal laws of human nature. The horrors of the war, therefore, shape a common experience which determines the author's attitudes toward specific problems.[4]

And indeed we do find, in the novels about the war written and published in Germany from 1915 to 1928, whether pacifist or nationalist, a consensus of attitudes — toward the encounter with the reality of war, toward the enemy, toward officers, toward the state — which can be categorized or classified according to the political and ideological leanings of the student. The sympathetic critic just cited discovers in the fiction little of artistic merit and treats each novel as a sociopolitical case study. This typical approach divides its discussion of the novels into the following topics: (1) War Horrors and Condemnation of War; (2) God, Religion, Church, and Priesthood; (3) Fatherland and Heroism; (4) Man as Beast, Friend, Enemy, and Master; (5) Revolution, Change for the Better, and Hope.[5]

As Conrad wrote in his preface to *The Nigger of the Narcissus:* "Fiction — if it at all aspires to be art — appeals to temperament. And in truth it must be, like painting, like music, like all art, the appeal of one temperament to all the other innumerable temperaments whose subtle and resistless power endows passing events with their true meaning, and creates the moral, the emotional atmosphere of the place and time."[6] It is precisely the unique moral and emotional attitude of the individual novel which critics of war fiction as a genre have ignored. They have assumed that the "world" created in nonwar novels, that total and final impression great pieces of fiction leave with readers, is given to the author of a war novel in the war itself, rather than imagined by him. To friendly interpreters the author may "achieve some sort of a social and personal attitude,"[7] to hostile critics his work will merely be the result of a single, usually isolated consciousness.[8] The war novel, thus trivialized, becomes a category like the mountain-climbing novella or the avalanche drama.

The history of World War I fiction in Germany tends, at first sight, to bear out many negative evaluations. The early books, written

between 1915 and 1919, were either overwhelmingly popular
because they transformed the dull reality of trench warfare into the
romantic excitement of a crusade, or they were completely neglected
because they instinctively grasped the madness of the slaughter of
World War I in particular and the irrationality of war in general. To
the first group belongs Walter Flex's *Der Wanderer zwischen beiden
Welten* (Wanderer between Two Worlds, 1918). Flex's hero, Ernst
Wurche, is a cheerful warrior, a *Wandervogel* in uniform, the ideal
of the new German spirit motivated by a patriotism that is moral
rather than national or political. Nevertheless, despite the
Nietzschean and ideological overtones, the book is permeated by an
innocence that raises war to the level of an adventure both necessary
and elevating. Wurche saves a ladybug from drowning with the
same bubbly self-assurance and self-righteousness with which he
shoots Russian soldiers. He is following ideals rather than just orders
and fighting not so much to protect his nation as to cleanse it of the
materialism and decadence of modern civilization. Nowhere do pain
or disfigurement intrude into either battle or sylvan scenes, and
death is a glorious ascent to heaven, accompanied by martial music
and angelic strumming. The book is a hymn to the sweetness that is
dying for one's fatherland.

On the other end of the scale are Andreas Latzko's
Friedensgericht (Judgment of Peace, 1918) or Fritz von Unruh's *Der
Opfergang* (The Way of Sacrifice, 1919). Latzko's novel and his
collection of short stories, *Menschen im Krieg* (Men in War, 1918),
polarize all men as either for war or against it. The author scatters his
hatred, which gives tremendous power to his work, on all those who
are responsible for war or profit by it. Such an outlook — as much a
simplification as Flex's of a world where evil is inextricably blended
with good — makes Latzko's vision great in its narrow, passionate
way. While Flex has cast the dreamlike, golden hue of a medieval
contest over the war, Latzko has wrenched from it the ultimate man-
made nightmare in black and white. Because Latzko, like Joseph
Heller in his highly successful World War II novel *Catch-22*, con-
jures up images of lost comrades disfigured beyond imagination and
swathed in white and of generals who seek perennial missions, he
"was regarded as something between a freak and an instrusion."[9]
Indeed both books lack the specificity and verisimilitude to give
their passionate viewpoints the necessary realistic underpinning. Today Flex's book reads like a parody, while Latzko's retains the appeal
of its prophetic insights. Neither author tells much about the First

World War, neither creates an effective sense impression of the particular world that existed in the trenches from 1914 to 1918. Flex yearns for moral ideals in the figures he portrays; Latzko traces the psychic scars on the minds of men.

After the early outpouring of war books, there followed "a strange hiatus, until in 1927 Arnold Zweig broke the silence with *The Case of Sergeant Grischa*. In 1928, ten years after the signing of the armistice, the dam was broken, and war literature flooded over, reaching its crest of popularity in Erich Maria Remarque's *Im Westen nichts Neues* (All Quiet on the Western Front)."[10] Although many popular novels of the war were in fact printed and read during this "hiatus" (which may seem less strange to readers of *Pont and Anna* and to current historians), the flood did bring the most widely respected novels, those which aim to present an accurate picture of the reality of war. The novel by Remarque, Ludwig Renn's *Krieg* (War, 1928), and many others from Germany, France, and England are nonetheless just those books whose form and technique seems interchangeable to careful readers. They have been called fictionalized autobiography or sensational journalism, decried for their attempt to present the collapse of civilized values through an account of the violent events within one man's immediate horizon.

That most of them are intensely personal, occasionally unbalanced in attitude, and sometimes deliberately slanted in the selection of incidents or characters does not detract from the validity and vitality of the composite picture they paint. Missing, however, is an informed and discerning intelligence which weighs and orders the multitude of personalities and forces involved in the war, imbues the picture with a unified, directed vision, and shapes its presentation accordingly. Arnold Zweig's personality, more philosophical than passionate, more scholarly than journalistic, more historically minded than revolutionary or tendentious, was well suited for the task. He saw that most novels of the war, pacifist though they may be, still contained too little philosophical inquiry or scholarly reflection to depict the war as something beyond an elemental force unloosed by human agents. In the succinct words of Byron's Don Juan, "war cuts up not only branch, but root." Zweig chose to make both branch and root his subject.

I *Return to Grischa:* The Case of Sergeant Grischa

Why did Zweig return to the same subject which had failed as drama, which in fact no theater cared to stage in 1921? Since his war experience — ranging over a broad and varied field, from supply duty in Serbia to the hell of Verdun and paperwork on the eastern front — offered a plethora of subjects, why did he choose the very case which had brought him neither public recognition nor personal satisfaction to turn into a major novel? In an interview he remarked that "the material was just too important. I had to get it to the public at any cost. In 1924 I wanted to change my drama into a novel, and even had gone so far as to sign a contract with a publisher."[11] Between 1924 and 1926, financial problems forced Zweig to abandon all literary projects and earn some money through essays and articles for newspapers and journals; but in 1926, when the S. Fischer publishing house specifically barred war stories from its annual best-short-story contest, the drive to combat repression of the war experience stirred in him once again. He composed the Grischa novel on sixty-five mornings late in 1926 and early in 1927; and it was published in twenty-eight installments under the title *Alle gegen einen* (All Against One) from June 12 to September 16, 1927, in the *Frankfurter Zeitung*. It appeared in book form as *Der Streit um den Sergeanten Grischa* (The Case of Sergeant Grischa, literally, "The Quarrel over Sergeant Grischa") in October of that year. His instinctive persistence proved correct, for the book was an almost immediate popular success; by 1929, 120,000 copies had been sold in Germany, while by 1930 an additional 300,000 volumes in translation had been purchased outside of Germany.[12] The novel attained a genuine artistic success as well, for it has been widely praised as fiction from 1927 to the present.

The execution of an innocent man through judicial error offends the principle of due measure as a basis of justice; when his execution is part of planned political policy, as Grischa's came to be, irrationality has turned to horror. Zweig had first heard the story with shock, indignation, and a tingling sense of discovery, but only subsequent political events and judicial proceedings in postwar Germany proved to him how widely the symptoms of the Grischa case had spread in the body of German society. The death of the young sergeant (Zweig could no longer recall his actual name for interviewers), as it had occurred and as Zweig had portrayed it in the play, assumed a significance in the mid-1920s which he had only begun to grasp in 1921. By 1926, however, he understood that each man's "relationship or stance to the world war became a function of politics."[13] In dealing with Renn and Remarque in 1929, one astute observer noted what was missing from their vision of war: "There are only hints at the cause of the collapse. It is impossible to depict with documentary verity how doubt gnaws at silent duty. Where the feelings divide, that is the place where fiction begins."[14]

A stance and a subject remained. The causes for collapse, the division of feelings among the soldiers of the German army as well as within many of them, is exactly the point where the quarrel over Sergeant Grischa is located.[15] Comradeship, boredom, and death are obvious qualities of war; Zweig allows Grischa's life to represent the further insight that war has no category or ideal of its own. Rather, its causes and conduct, its logic and nexus lie elsewhere. The relationship of justice to politics, as exposed by the case of Grischa, originated in the condition of prewar Germany and dominated life in postwar Germany. Zweig had come to see that a case which appeared to be an interesting oddity was in fact uncannily prophetic. Its potential truth had become uncomfortably timely in 1926; its peculiarity expressed the real fact of the tensions in Germany's social and political behavior. He had more than enough evidence to convert his findings into fiction. Between the end of the war and 1922 alone, right-wing extremists committed 354 murders, while left-wingers were responsible for twenty-two. The average sentence handed out to these political murderers, however, revealed that the administration of justice had become a political weapon: fifteen years for the left-wingers, four months for the right-wingers.[16]

The success of the novel cannot, however, be explained by its truthful portrayal of political developments alone. The conflict over Grischa's fate, placed in the spatial confinements of a stage and the limitations of spoken dialogue, emerged as overly intellectual and brittle. The wider scope of the novel permitted Zweig to fill in the historical and psychological details that charged the clash with authenticity and personal motivation. The entrapment and destruction of a human being in the complex bureaucratic machinery of a modern state is better captured by the novel's arrangement of incidents based on causal connections than by the drama's convention of forward movement in time. Given Zweig's leisurely pace of narration, all personal fortunes can be connected with national or political movements without violating the dimensions of character or the cohesion of the plot. Zweig maintains the novel's unity in one perceptual category, causality, focused on the destiny of one central figure, Grischa. Space and time, expressed in a variety of places and actions, are arranged around the figure not by abstraction from experience, but by reproducing the experience itself. Zweig thus tried to avoid two flaws which had characterized the German novel: an absence of passion and a paucity of action.[17]

His choice of subject matter lifted his work above the provincialism and inwardness of much of German fiction, while the breadth of his treatment and the scope of his vision insured his success. He was well aware of the plight of the German novel. "It was but after the War that the universally human and European element was introduced into German fiction, the War itself, the greatest of all European events, and the national and European problems arising therefrom, serving as literary subjects that interested the world also beyond the boundaries of Germany."[18] Unlike his first novel, *Claudia*, *Grischa* confronts the real world without a painful and lengthy struggle against romantic inwardness. In order to attain the cosmopolitan tone and the realism of French or Russian fiction, Zweig also abandoned what he perceived as the predominantly autobiographical mode of German fiction.[19] To be sure, his own war experience serves as the authenticating canvas for the entire cycle, but Werner Bertin, the thinly disguised representation of the author, does not stand at the center of the narrative situation except in one novel. Elizabeth Bowen has written of modern fiction, "We want the naturalistic surface, but with a kind of internal burning."[20] Through the fictionalized figure of Grischa and the addition of much surface detail, Zweig met both requirements to create a compelling social document and a moving personal story.

II *Grischa Iljitsch Paprotkin*

In the novel of Grischa Paprotkin, Zweig broke with a number of traditions. He placed a Russian worker and POW at the center of a German war novel. The execution of Grischa is the only death shown. Finally, Zweig demonstrates that actual combat, the core and substance of the great majority of war novels, is the logical extension of the social tensions, political policy, and economic ambitions of peacetime. The first break is the most unexpected, but probably the most inspired one. Grischa is not, as might be anticipated, the folksy, long-suffering, eternally patient Russian soul. He is an energetic man, full of love of life, moody, lusty, and eager to enjoy the fruits of his work and play. When he is first seen in the lumber camp where he is held prisoner, his impatience to escape has an almost boyishly impetuous air about it. "With the beginning of the new year and the confirmation of all sorts of rumors, his heart had become restless. Slow, heavy-footed thoughts had fixed themselves more firmly in his head, with each passing day: he must go home" (15).[21] Zweig's method, congenial to the subject he is treating, rapidly emerges as Grischa's restlessness, obviously exploding after sixteen months of captivity, is linked to the explosive situation in Russia's political life: "Strange changes were taking place in St. Petersburg. The great czar, The Little Father Nicholas II, had abdicated to save the ancient imperial crown for his son, soldiers were firing on the imperial police, the red flag waving in starving St. Petersburgh, in Moscow . . . criminals let loose, generals imprisoned, ministers driven into exile, admirals drowned, shot, hounded out of the country. And in their place, what a strange bunch was running Russia! Russia was reshaping herself, Russia was awaiting peace with her rifle at her feet" (15). The rumors which had floated across the country to Grischa's ears not only accurately reflect the state of Russia in mid-March of 1917 but correspond to Grischa's inner state of mind as well. Zweig uses this method again and again. The fusion and combination of historic events and private emotions, infinite in their possibilities, are always natural, never forced. In the opening chapter of the first book of *Grischa*, they serve their dual but linked functions by setting in motion Grischa's escape as well as the Russian Revolution.

Most of Grischa's characteristics, however, straightforwardly affirm his independence, love of freedom, and thirst for living. His life, like that of the agricultural worker, is more adjusted to an organic cycle of growth and decay than to the mechanical structure of machine-controlled society. After his escape he survives in the wintry forest because he can carve his own bows and arrows as well as hunt and cook. And yet Grischa is never presented as a peasant, rooted in the soil and limited by the cycle of the seasons. He is a carpenter and construction worker, grave-digger and handyman, and he carries out his tasks, whether for his own survival or for his German captors, with skill and pride. While imprisoned at Mervinsk he cleans the rifles of German soldiers. "Grischa dedicated himself to his work with enthusiasm. He loved rifles. Since his arrest he had returned to the soldier's way of thinking and was now cleaning the lock of a German weapon the way he used to clean his own Russian rifle" (138). As a foreman in a soap factory before the war, Grischa learned to value orderliness and cleanliness as well as efficiency, and he found these qualities stressed once again by the army. That they should offer him comfort yet sap his nervous energy, in the midst of the uncertainty and the vicissitudes of the struggle to establish his identity and save his life, is convincing.

But Grischa is no revolutionary. His escape, in the play as well as the novel, is triggered by rumors of political upheaval but actually motivated by his overwhelming desire to go home. He never shows sympathy for the revolutionaries, although the reader senses an unexplored awe for them in his speech, nor does he react against the German invaders for national or political reasons. In the central episode of the book, the *"Herrenfest"* ("Staff Celebrations") chapter, however, he rebels against his treatment on an entirely different level. " 'Now then, Russki, you can eat till your belly bursts,' said the gray-haired Wedrig cheerfully to Grischa. He was suddenly aware, sharply and clearly, that he was eating leftovers, just like his poor German comrades, that it was shameful to accept such crumbs, and that the shame was not his or theirs. There they sat on their chairs, those men who were privileged to bestow upon him their leftovers, and he and only he felt that it was shameful to toss scraps to a man as to a dog" (249 - 50). Grischa's awareness of the snubs and slights inherent in the hierarchy of classes or ranks never expresses itself as ideological protest or theory. Indeed, all of his comments are shrewd observations or violent outbursts, the former made by the sharpened senses of an illiterate factory foreman, the latter as the painful cries of a battered human being, buffeted about by forces he cannot comprehend. All of his insights still do not coalesce into a world view beyond his justly earned feeling that "somebody's after me" (282).

The very ordinariness of Grischa in Zweig's unadorned portrait may be one key to the book's success and popularity; Grischa appears neither as glorified worker nor as faceless victim. He is representative of the Russian man-in-the-street, as the immediate identification of his restless urgings with the rumblings of the Russian Revolution indicate; but he is also a man of many moods and wishes. His treatment of his mistress and protector Babka fluctuates between tender affection and gruff impatience. Her interpretation of the world as caught in the clutches of the devil does not touch or satisfy Grischa, nor does that of Täwje, a Talmudic Jewish carpenter and his fellow coffin-maker in prison camp, who sees no contradiction in a world governed by a kind and omnipotent God. He accepts Täwje's answer to his agonizing "Why?" — "Whoso sheddeth man's blood, by man shall his blood be shed" (321) — as ultimate justice for his participation in the war's killing, but more for the sake of comfort than with conviction. Täwje's other biblical tales, from Abraham to Sodom and Gomorrah, strike Grischa less as explanations of his situation than as an indictment of those who have placed him in it. And

Grischa is right. He has sensed the profound contrast between the heaven (or hell) of doctrines, be they theological or political, and the earthly reality of the society in which men live and act as private individuals. His earthiness, his noninvolvement in the profits or passions of the war, heighten his insight and innocence. War is not fathomable to him, not as class struggle, not as national defense, and not as heavenly revenge. Freed from any doctrine or dogma, he finally faces death with a natural fear that seems far more liberating than false dignity. The execution scene returns once again to the wintry forest, and here it is Grischa's human vitality which robs the deadly procession of its mechanical advance. "This marching body made its own particular noises and had its own heart that was full of fear, and Grischa was that heart" (527). Again, "One of the Jägers untied Grischa's hands. Grischa smiled gratefully at him" (530). At the moment of death, Grischa conquers the fearsome bonds imposed on him; his death, neither elevating nor debasing, labels the execution as the murder that it is. "Then, at that moment when the sharp voice of Sergeant-Major Berglechner rapped out the command 'Fire!' the certainty of death and the extremity of his terror conquered; his soul burst its bonds, and in the same instant his bowels were loosened" (532). His death is not permitted to attain any tragic transcendence; only in his children may we sense the potential survival of the spirit that inhabited Grischa. "But his sense of life, which had long been broken and effaced by his experiences, was suddenly, in the very instant of death, lit by a flame of certainty that parts of his being would be rescued from destruction" (532 - 33).

Zweig's empathy with Grischa, and his success in creating a believable Russian worker, is not confined to a purely realistic sphere. The only recurrent symbol, the appearance of a lynx, confronts the power of Grischa's vitality throughout the novel. He first encounters the lynx while competing with her for game during his sojourn in the forest immediately following his escape: "Cowering thus, paralyzed by her rage and terror, the lynx looked no bigger than a well-fed sheepdog and not nearly so dangerous as she was, with her sinews of steel, her hooked talons like a panther's claws, her vicious fangs which she bared with a slight snarl. This gave her a grinning look. And Grischa, as he stared more intently at the beast, was struck by her attitude, and then it occurred to him suddenly that the creature was like him, Grischa! . . . He broke into hearty laughter, laughing like a boy, slapping his thighs. . . . That was too much to bear for the lynx. Snarling and hissing, she took off in terror" (50 - 51). The lynx not only resembles Grischa in appearance, with her bright, piercing eyes, frill of a beard, and snub nose, but Grischa's life now parallels hers. They are both cunning hunters, preying upon other living creatures in the forest. What separates them, of course, is Grischa's laughter, and it is his laughter which repeatedly drives away visions of the lynx. The lynx represents deception, furtiveness, desire to rule with resistance to being governed, and its vices and falsehoods become ludicrous when seen from a sufficiently distant perspective. In the end, however, the man-made lynx destroys him: "There was the black beast creeping toward him, the lynx with her brushlike ears and devilish face, tensing to leap upon him and tear him down, but fleeing in terror at his laughter, at his exulting freedom. . . . Once more, now weak and forlorn, he smiled at the beast as she leapt at him out of the five muzzles of the rifle barrels — and this time he knew that she would tear him down" (532). Thus Grischa is ground down by a process of justice manipulated and perverted at the hands of a corrupt elite.

The passage describing Grischa's death leaves no doubt that his case, while firmly rooted in the historical circumstances of the German army and society in the war, has a significance beyond its actual origins, and an emotional as well as philosophical impact which only its fictionalization could have achieved. Grischa's laughter, too, is a lament and a prayer — pain mixed with relief — for one man and for all humanity. It has no power to transcend reality, but it celebrates possibility as the core of man's existence. Writing of another war, Sartre has asserted that "the secret of man is not his Oedipus complex or his inferiority complex: it is the limit of his own liberty, his capacity for resisting torture and death."[22] Grischa has retained his laughter and therefore his liberty in the face of psychological torture and death. His capacity supplies "the internal burning" around which the debate over his case assumes a brighter and more intense light than it ever could in the theater.

III   *The Case*

In the 1921 play, the battle over Grischa's life provides exciting if somewhat puzzling reading. We can sympathize with Lychow's stiff-necked Prussian correctness and faith in justice as the cornerstone of government, and we may relish the pleading and plotting of the lawyers, intellectuals, and workers around him, but their struggle occurs in a vacuum. Their attitudes and actions, as well as those of their adversary and Grischa's, General Schieffenzahn, seem to be unrelated to a set of visible circumstances. The case of a Russian POW topples into a world apparently untouched by the sweat, confusion, paperwork, strife, and mountains of materiel that make up the day-to-day existence of an occupying army. To be sure, references are made to political aims and administrative problems, to the tactical situation of the war and the socioeconomic crisis at home. Nonetheless, such spoken comments tell the truth without capturing the reality underneath it. Their intrusion detracts from concern over, and involvement in, the legal case. The dominant effect is that of a stark outline, with the necessarily feverish atmosphere caused by the taut dramatic development of a life-or-death situation. Each decision or action, whether for or against Grischa, is infused with a grand and lofty air.

In the 1927 novel, Zweig's deepened insights and his greater mastery over the narrative process shape for the reader an experience extended in every dimension. He meticulously shows every detail of the vast network in the organization of the German army in the East. The momentum of the legal battle, racing toward its theatrical climax, is slowed and the final decision no longer represents the whim and ambition of one man. The addition of many episodes and descriptions eliminates the slightly heroic character of the struggle in the play — two parties locked in grim combat — and places the case in the mire of bureaucratic bungling and petty squabbles which represent any large organization. Both sides, caught in an empire that controls them even while they build it, and dwarfed by the character of Grischa, lose much of their stature. Schieffenzahn is less the ambitious bourgeois as black villain and Lychow less the antiquated white knight that they are represented as being in the play, for the whole enterprise of war is seen in shades of gray, which is just as deadly but more accurate than the chiaroscuro of earlier books. Not only do we gain a sense of place, but the life of Grischa is now inextricably tied to all that the German army in 1917 has come to stand for. Thus the reader agonizingly awaits each new turn and twist as the case winds its way through query, reply, and counterorder, and we feel with Grischa and his friends the numbing, ghastly slowness of life and death on the Russian front. Zweig had realized that his scope, the total reality of war, and his method, the enumeration of all material necessary to create a picture that best conforms to truth, could demythologize war through the power of its objectivity.

Zweig's depictions move from the leisurely catalog of army

organization and structures to incisive portraits of greed and crime sanctioned by the power elite of this corporate giant. "Every town swarmed with offices filled with clerks where officers, and officials impersonating officers, strode continually through slamming doors and down flights of stairs with their noses in the air, shouldering out of the way a populace whom they heartily despised as barbarians and by whom they were secretly loathed in turn: town-commandants, inspector-generals, staffs, hospitals, depots, civil administrations, censorship bureaus, and military courts. Every good-sized village contained a lieutenant as town-commandant, or a sergeant-major of the mounted police with his staff, or at least a squadron of *Landjäger*, or military police, for whom comfortable quarters had to be provided" (81 - 82). It becomes clear that so large an apparatus, stretched over such vast territories full of natural riches, cannot remain purely military. "The Higher Powers looked on the whole land (Courland, Lithuania, and Northern Poland) as ultimately under requisition. The only disturbing element was the population, and that obstacle had to be removed as expeditiously as possible. It did not occur to anyone that the land would ever be evacuated. Some influential officers already had their eyes on large estates which they hoped to receive later as gifts from a grateful emperor. They thought as little of the population as a patriarchial squire across the Elbe thought of his Polish stable boys and maids" (82). It is a short step from such disdain for an entire population to the denial of their humanity. German nobility, from the army and the home front, devised a new sport on the eastern front: "Shooting Russians seems to be a field sport with the princes of the empire, since a certain grand duke started the sport. Up north in the Tirul marshes, if I'm not mistaken. Drove up to the front line, where you're as safe as a virgin in the Vatican, and whenever an unsuspecting Russki came along, his highness bowled him over with a head shot. It was a new game for him and, unfortunately, for the Russian, too" (110). Within this context of territorial ambition and murder as entertainment, the roots and the implications of Grischa's execution reach deep and stretch wide into the mentality of Germany's military and political elite. It is not possible to view Lychow and Schieffenzahn simply as polar adversaries, for they inhabit and thus condone the same social order. Their motives strike us as less pure and more complex; their positions in the struggle are still determined by ethical conviction and political expediency respectively, but they are equally influenced by the role which confusion and conservatism play in the administration of a bureaucratic colossus and, ultimately, in the shaping of historical events.

Schieffenzahn undergoes no major change from the play. As a dramatic figure he radiated a total malevolence for which, like Iago's, no explanation or interpretation was available. A repulsive kind of glamour, a raw energy dressed in sparkling uniform and shiny boots, overwhelmed the practical aims and bourgeois sources of the general's drive to power. He seemed less a man than the embodiment of Prussianism, the essence of all those strutting, monocled officers stereotypically portrayed by Erich von Stroheim. His material ambitions and his love of power shone through, but underneath no personality emerged. Neither his arrogance nor his ambition is decreased by Zweig's novelistic opportunity to reveal the general's private reflections and personal habits. And Zweig goes well beyond caricature in a chapter devoted entirely to Schieffenzahn, *"Bildnis eines Selbstherrschers"* ("Portrait of an Autocrat") and in the confrontation scene with Lychow. Schieffenzahn is convinced of Germany's mission in the world: "To his mind, they were the nation chosen to rule, create, and elevate the breed of men" (222). He is equally certain of how this destiny needs to be fulfilled and of his role in its attainment. "In his work nothing bothered him as little as the wishes, views, and traditions of the populace. He, Schieffenzahn, understood what was good for those folk much better than they did themselves. It was for him to command, and his was the responsibility. It was for them to obey, to follow and bow down. . . . He said he had no need for honor, fame, or recognition; power alone sufficed him" (223). Free to supply background in the novel, Zweig sketches in the origins of this lust for power and the reasons for its success. Schieffenzahn obviously is the workhorse of the General Staff. "In the first nine months of the war he had been in charge of the transport of troops, the planning of all offensive campaigns, a great retreat across a network of rivers, and finally the conquest of the country. Then came the gradual organization of a complete system of civil government; . . . not a single soldier's club or cinema was started, not a plank laid for a munitions depot without his consent." We understand his policy of retaining the lands which German forces occupied in 1917, for more than any other German officer or politician his "creative will was embodied and manifest in that land" (220). In Schieffenzahn's world view we find no idealism but a belief in Germany's holy mission, and no ethics but the narrowest version of the work ethic. "He hated opposition, independence of mind, laziness, the vast incompetence of human beings, and remorselessly he hated disorder, sedition, the Western chatter about democracy, and the loathsome nihilistic revolution in the East. He enjoyed his measureless capacity for work" (223 - 24).

Germany could and did produce this combination of tycoon and tyrant in General Ludendorff, whom Zweig is lightly disguising as Schieffenzahn.

The question Zweig did not ask in the play but answers in the novel is, how did such a man become the most powerful political figure in Germany? How does his rise, and his defeat of all opposition over Grischa's case as well as many other affairs of state and the army, reflect on the men who admired or detested him and on the nature of German society in general? Zweig first squelches the notion that every important action or decision came about through careful planning. Much of what happens on the eastern front occurs through oversight or omission, and much of what does not take place was originally intended to take place. Faulty telephone communications prevent Schieffenzahn from calling off Grischa's execution, just as mere chance in the figure of a pouting secretary, choosing the most perplexing case to annoy the Judge Advocate on Schieffenzahn's staff, places the file on Grischa in his hands in the first place. Many other connections are made in similar ways, and some of the central events in the book have insignificant and accidental causes. Schieffenzahn's triumph, however, is not a matter of chance, nor was it forged by his iron will and prodigious work alone. The play suggests, in the nature of dramatic conflict, that Schieffenzahn rose to power and took Grischa's life either against the wishes of Lychow and his supporters or in circumvention of their thought and tradition. In the novel, compilation of historic evidence and exploration of psychological states suggest, rather, that many aims and ideas united the two camps despite the principle that separated them over Grischa. Neither Lychow nor his aristocratic fellow generals have objected to Schieffenzahn's drive for leadership as long as his success brought professional glory and the possibility of profit through conquered territories.

The similarity of phrases repeated by both parties, as well as the description of alliances formed, reveals that each group has hoped to use the other for its own benefit. Lychow echoes Schieffenzahn when he exclaims, "We have more important matters to think of: discipline, Prussia, the empire. Compared to them, what does one Russki more or less matter?" or, "Revolution — I hate that word, it leaves a foul taste in my mouth" (129). He takes up the case for Grischa not so much because he understands the judicial issues of the case, or because Grischa's life or death touch him deeply, but rather to defend his conception of the German state, the army, and justice from the politicization and industrialization that has already taken place. Lychow's most revealing remark, and the one which betrays the frailty of his faith, occurs in a conversation with Posnanski, the Judge Advocate of Lychow's division, who proposes that "we must start our revolution from above [or else] scrap the whole system" if it falls prey to Schieffenzahn's morality (129). Lychow's response reveals the chasm between his professed belief in the teachings of Luther and Kant and his inability to apply their moral philosophy to himself or his times. His view of Posnanski and all those other Jewish lawyers is that "I could swear they love law for its own sake as we love our lands and fields" (130). The tragedy is that he cannot love the law except as it undergirds the hegemony of his class; when he confronts Schieffenzahn with idealistic arguments based on faith and justice, they wither in the face of Schieffenzahn's shrewd intuition that such invocations are mere verbiage. Lychow is deflated by the very mention of the franchise and land reform. He and other Prussian nobles have obeyed the demands of political necessity and the dreams of personal wealth, and now they have lost the reins of power as well as the refuge of ideals. Lychow's expression of horror at Schieffenzahn's dictum that "the State creates justice, the individual is a louse" (357) reveals as much regret at his own share in making the dictum come true as it conceals awe for Schieffenzahn's candid espousal of it.

The potential saviors of Grischa are thus not arrayed against Schieffenzahn alone but against the entire class he represents, which is rising to power in anger and defensive contempt, and against a ruling class, which, in its decline, has grown too weak to outface the forceful general. The Junkers, who abhor his coarseness, ambition, and efficiency, have not only used him but helped to create him. As the son of a middle-class family, Schieffenzahn was subjected to cruel snubs and humiliating tortures while attending an aristocratic military school, and he emerged from his experiences with a deep hatred for "the fools with a *von*. He wanted to become the greatest man in Germany, but that ambition was un-Prussian. He would have to train himself to put all his achievements, all his ideas, and all his work ungrudgingly into the service of a *von*. He would always have to be in the second position, working behind the back of a larger, more substantial *von*, who would grow mustaches and bask in the glory of Schieffenzahn's achievements" (368).[23] This smoldering bourgeois *ressentiment* is not Schieffenzahn's alone. Captain Brettschneider, commandant of the garrison at Mervinsk, harbors similar feelings toward Lychow and the landed gentry. When Posnanski tries to persuade him to postpone the execution, warning that "you don't want to antagonize His Excellency, von Lychow" (430), his anger bursts forth. "Right now he's dressed up as a general and I as a captain, but when we take our uniforms off, as we shall someday, he'll be a little country squire on his Brandenburg estate, and I shall be the junior partner of Brettschneider & Sons, a concern you may have heard of, employing a few thousand workers, and turning out iron tubes and girders" (431 - 32). Brettschneider and Schieffenzahn despise the Prussian nobility not only because they smart under past offenses but also because they sense the future importance of industry. Schieffenzahn's negotiations with Schilles, whose name and appearance resemble the industrial baron Hugo Stinnes, foreshadow the coming social revolution of national socialism, the alliance of a petite bourgeois governmental clique with big industry. This premonitory insight is just one measure of Zweig's laborious development of the role each class or group played in the war in general and the Grischa case in particular. In the tapestry of the novel he could dwell on the weakness of one party as well as on the strength of another, then show the relationship between the two in its psychological and material roots and its consequent fluctuations. In such a careful presentation Schieffenzahn is not facilely allowed to be a scapegoat. The responsibility for Grischa's death ultimately rests in the creation of forces which all classes condoned, or at least did not oppose.

Such a complex interplay of social groups, psychological drives, and random occurrence is the stuff of which *The Case of Sergeant Grischa* is made. It would, indeed did, supply several novels; the selection and the control of all the material posed no easy task for Zweig. Individual vignettes in the novel might well have become separate works, whereas others could have been omitted altogether without serious loss. Zweig welds his episodes together by assigning complementary functions to the central story line of the legal case and to the descriptive or analytic elements in almost every chapter. As a result, the vast amount of background on the machinery of war is split into small fragments, each attached to a similarly short section of the main plot. The narrative flow is consequently slow but steady, and each new development in the case carries with it just enough weight of historical or intellectual substance for successful advancement to the next event. As Eva Kaufmann points out, only rarely do chapters concern themselves solely with Grischa or purely with aspects of the war not connected to his case.[24] And in the "*Herrenfest*" ("Staff Celebration") chapter, placed at the center of the novel and set on the anniversary of the declaration of war, all elements flow together to create a microcosm of the entire book. Every rank, class, and ideology is represented in characteristic behavior and language, and the news that Grischa's death sentence has been upheld, despite all the evidence, crashes into the party like lightning.

Zweig also has built some striking parallel scenes into his structure. The electric clash between Schieffenzahn and Lychow is repeated, with similar results, in the conversation between Brettschneider and Posnanski. Both scenes reveal the impotence of idealism in the face of materialism, and the second version places the intellectual argument of the first into social reality, the world of persons and especially of things. Portentous similarities occur on a political level as well. Schieffenzahn's ultimate gesture, his decision to stay Grischa's execution in order to avoid further clashes with Lychow, is based on the sound tactic of always maintaining one avenue of escape. Lychow's exploratory letter to a courtier, asking if he would be well advised to bring the matter before the emperor is dictated by the same tactical maneuvering. Since all interest groups and power cliques have chosen their courses of action and manipulated each other in order to obtain influence, they in fact use Grischa more to fight each other than to enforce political discipline or to defend a principle of higher justice. Only the common troops, the workers and farmers, have no stake in the games played in the higher echelons. Like a chorus, they occasionally step forward and speak the truth, but they have no power to change the events in which they themselves must participate. German and Russian soldiers express their weariness with the war, their inability to perceive any sense in it, and a comprehension of the Grischa affair that cuts through expedient defense or high-toned condemnation. "It means that there's no more justice in this world. What's going to happen to him might very well happen to you or to me" (307). And so it did.

Yet the book closes not with Grischa's death or with a seminarlike discussion of the significance of his case. The novel's conclusion addresses itself to its much criticized opening message. In the manner of Tolstoy or Dickens, Zweig's first paragraph precedes the setting of the scene with a fatalistic image of the world on its usual course: "This earth of ours, this little planet Tellus, went whirling eagerly

through pitch-black, airless, icy space, forever swept along by waves
of uncharted ether. In darkness made electric by her passing contact,
she moved among mysterious influences, destructive or blessed" (9).
Such cosmic objectivity does not place the fate of one decent man far
from the reader, but permits the indignation we must feel about
Grischa's fate to strike at the proper targets. It encourages the
speculation that the case was not, after all, so individual or unique
that there could not have been thousands of Grischas. It ac-
complishes in a traditional manner what Brecht was to achieve with
revolutionary means — showing us that the extraordinary, or what
we conceive as the extraordinary, is the usual. At the conclusion,
however, another apparently unusual event takes place. Private
Sacht is about to go on leave in late November, 1917. He arrives at
the railroad station seconds too late to catch his train. But then
something occurs that never could have taken place a year earlier:
"In a fraction of a second he realized that the train had slowed down
nearly to a stop on his account. He was hauled into a compartment. . . . The incident cost the state seventy marks in wasted
coalpower and two minutes' delay. And so with rhythmic groans,
shaken by its own strength like a gyrating dragon, along the surface
of the earth's crust where the air is dense and dark, the inexorable
train chugged westward into the brightening moon" (552). Man may
not be able to affect the "mysterious influences" of the cosmos, but
the gesture toward Sacht voices Zweig's confidence that the train
will carry Grischa's laughter and love of freedom onward to Germany. When Zweig completed the novel, he knew that such feelings
had indeed resided in many returning soldiers and that their expectations had been crushed or deadened by postwar events. It required
gritty adherence to the truth to conclude the book on that fragile and
short-lived mood of 1917. But it is a fitting tribute to the memory of
Grischa Iljitsch Paprotkin.

IV   Young Woman of 1914

After the success of *Grischa* there existed no compelling reason for
Zweig not to choose new themes and backgrounds for his next novel.
The hectic politics of Weimar Germany might have provided a
logical and fruitful sequel to a study of the complex relationships
among the administration of justice, the niceties of class structure,
and morality both public and private, all symbolized by the conclusion of one wartime occurrence. But that complexity, together with

Zweig's historical and philosophical inquisitiveness, prompted him to seek not just the immediate causes but the deeper roots of the phenomena with which he had dealt. He later elaborated on the reason that led to his writing a cycle of novels: "At first I did not plan to continue after *Grischa*. The continuation arose only when I realized that my novel provokes questions in the reader which had not arisen before reading the book. And the most basic of these questions is, how could we take part in a war in which a man like Grischa is killed by the apparatus of military power, although many people around him did everything in their power to save him? Right there I began to dig deeper and deeper, and from 1929 on I stuck right to this problem."[25] Acute as the problem is, both for the historian and for the novelist, it does not fully express the scope of the inquiry which Zweig embarked upon. As Kaufmann points out,[26] nothing in the development of the plot or the depiction of the characters points to a continuation of this particular book. The hero is dead, and the other figures have shown no impressive growth or change throughout the progress of the case. Political and social conditions after the war might, therefore, have impelled Zweig to look elsewhere for the answers he sought.

The *Grischa* novel, however, in a stunning but brief flash of insight had concentrated on a single aspect of the case and its participants — the human one. Grischa, as the novel's hero, represents man in general rather than a historical being, that is, a product of the forces of one historical period. His symbolic universality rather than his explicit typicality make his fate so moving. But the case is significant for the Germans around him in a narrower, more localized and particularized sense as well. For these Germans represent political forces and social types which Zweig could analyze and reconstruct; if they do not significantly change in *Grischa*, such static portraits originate in the limitations imposed by the duration of the case itself and the intellectual preoccupation with it. Their ideological positions, their moral judgments, and their social prejudices must nevertheless be the result of prior development. It was to these forces and currents that Zweig turned in 1928.

1. *Young Bertin and the Ideas of 1914*

Junge Frau von 1914 (Young Woman of 1914), written between 1928 and 1930, turns to the world which Zweig knew best, the disintegration of which he mourned deeply — the prewar atmosphere of the educated *Bürger*. The male protagonist, Werner Bertin, who

receives his orders to report for military duty in the spring of 1915, as
did Zweig himself, embodies the essence of the German-Jewish and
middle-class desire for security and intellectual certainty in the first
decade of the century. A moderately successful writer at twenty-six
(Zweig was twenty-eight in 1915) as well as a trained lawyer, Bertin
is no better, and no worse, than thousands of young Germans at the
outbreak of the war. In *Grischa* Zweig had briefly portrayed his fictional double as politically naive and emotionally impetuous. He
reacted to Grischa's execution with an indignation that was all furor
and no analysis, more petulance than reasoned protest; he never
related the judicial murder to social or political circumstances. And
throughout the early chapters of *Young Woman*, emotional intensity
and political naiveté are once again the striking characteristics which
Bertin displays. Such qualities, Zweig implies, are typical of Germany's youth of Bertin's class and education, and of the country's
emotional atmosphere in general; they are the strands with which
Zweig weaves a psychological portrait of Bertin and his generation.

Bertin greets his induction notice with patriotic buoyancy:

To the authorities now calling him up he was just a relatively healthy man.
The fact that he also did some writing just made him look a little odd. Still,
his heart had good reason for thumping slower and louder. After all, the
local authorities were not important in themselves. But behind them stood
the homeland, morality, and all the spiritual and intellectual power of the
fatherland. It no longer mattered how grim and bloody the coming struggles
might turn out to be. War had come into the world, and the world was now
in its grip. What mattered now was to be equal to all demands, with a clear
head, calm nerves, and heightened feelings. Germany was calling him, and
he would heed her call without delay.(11)[27]

Zweig evokes in the reader a rueful but detached sympathy for
Bertin, who exhibits every symptom that historically accompanied
this widespread enthusiasm. The prospect of war, with its reality of
communal life at the front, may also break through the petrifaction
of German social structure and thus weld together a society whose
members have become alienated by the barriers of class. "People in
Germany suddenly felt themselves elevated and united through the
common experience of great events. Messages of joy and grief
charged electrically through the walls which habit, class, and that
nordic fear of baring one's soul had erected between men. Suddenly
people felt that they mattered to each other, that they were a people,
and that they were created to make life easier for each other through

empathy and understanding" (67). Bertin's error — for it is one — has all the charm and restless energy of dissatisfied youth. The previous failure of industrial and bourgeois civilization to provide the younger generation with "the moral equivalent of war" seems to have transfigured the experience of national ´solidarity into a metaphysical liberation. In Bertin's formulation, strikingly similar to the outbursts of real and fictional figures on all levels of German life,[28] the vaguely revolutionary temper and the spontaneous unity merge to form an uneasy alliance of individual release from constraint with the organic idea of national freedom so predominant in German thought.

At first this mixture is deliciously, although ominously, intoxicating. After a few days of Prussian drill and discipline in basic training, Bertin "obeyed impulses which had lain dormant for years. Yes, he heard around him˙ and inside him new languages, a stupefyingly joyous roll of orders from without and within" (49 - 50). But these nonintellectual aspects of his being, liberated from bourgeois fetters, are not allowed to shape a new self or a new society. Instead, they are caged in the pigeonholes of a collective idealism just as oppressive as the selfishness of bourgeois materialism. "He relished the delight of belonging to a giant body, of being responsible for one fixed group into which one blended; the company of soldiers. The intellectual felt lonely no longer, and this was the primary source of happiness. As soon as one had learned to know intuitively what one's superior officer expected, and how he wanted things to get done, one experienced a feeling of freedom, a new kind of collective freedom which previously could not even have been imagined" (51).

Why should Werner Bertin, a highly educated writer and lawyer, embrace the loss of self and its absorption into a communal whole? Bertin is a member of the lower stratum of the middle class; although his intellectual and creative achievements have lifted him above his class financially and in the eyes of the public, his psychological responses are still rooted in middle-class feelings of inferiority. Erich Fromm's analysis of the social character of the middle class in the period before the war explains much of Bertin's eager surrender: "His submission and loyalty to existing authorities were a satisfactory solution of his masochistic strivings. What he was lacking in security and aggressiveness as an individual, he was compensated for by the strength of the authorities to whom he submitted himself."[29] His delight stems from his acceptance as a Jew into the

German national fabric, from his unification as an intellectual with the common people, from his identification of his youthful dreams with the aims of his nation's esteemed elders, and finally from the merger of his ideas with those of the aristocracy. The idealistic glow of Germany's war aims, usually proclaimed in the terms and tones associated with the role of fate in ancient legends, illuminated for each element in society one very clear aspiration which the spirit of 1914 promised to meet. To young men the chance to make a sacrifice for the fatherland stirred their imaginations. Older men regretted their lack of opportunity.[30] Jews proclaimed the greatness of the German mission with a ferocity that matched or tried to overwhelm their countrymen's dedication. Nahum Goldmann, a law student at the outbreak of the war and later the president of the Jewish World Congress, asserted that "the Prussian Sergeant is the personification of Kant's categorical imperative. The military spirit — that is the spirit of our times, and military spirit is German spirit. German spirit controls the world. The spirit of West European civilization stands on the side of military spirit, of the German spirit."[31] In such company, Werner Bertin's exuberance simply must be accepted.

In the heady excitement of the period, belief in such absurdities can be understood, but many young Germans were willing to translate their faith into action, as Zweig easily perceived. During a discussion of the shelling of Rheims cathedral by German guns, Bertin defends the action by summoning a tragic Weltanschauung and generalizing daily phenomena into cosmic impersonality: "Necessity had ensnarled both sides in a tragic knot, and only fate could decide which side would fall to glorious defeat, which achieve inner justification" (43). For the same reasons he is willing, albeit with "bleeding heart," to bombard the cathedral at Strassburg (44). He is so happy to bridge the prewar chasm between the idealism of his education and calling and the materialism of his society and state that he can say, without a trace of irony, "Now spirit and force were one, the war had merged them. Now the power of the German army stood in the service of the German soul" (52). Such an identification of violence with virtue, however, cannot exist in the lofty realms of the Zeitgeist alone. Bertin's behavior soon begins to reflect his faith in the cult of force.

2. Lenore, Learning, and the Generation Gap

Bertin's response to the war both affects and is thrown into relief by that of Lenore Wahl, who is the "young woman of 1914."

Daughter of a wealthy Potsdam banker, she has loved Bertin, son of a provincial craftsman, since their student days in Munich. But their relationship must remain secret, for Lenore's parents will not let her link her life with that of a struggling writer of lower-middle-class origins. At first she, too, like Bertin, is blind to the political and economic reality of the war, but in her case, it is the tenderness of love rather than ideological zeal that blinds her. "So childish. I sometimes think men wage war just to impress us, while pretending that it is a matter of the world spirit *[Weltgeist]* and intending to lead us toward glorious days (22)."[32] Her gentle chiding is soon challenged. When Lenore visits Bertin at his army camp in Küstrin on Ascension Sunday, the two take a stroll in the country. Now the new alliance of "spirit" and "force" *(Geist und Gewalt)* makes its appearance, breaking out in Bertin's character to determine their relation. "Suddenly, without any kind of transition, Bertin wanted to make love to her. But here, out in the open, her modesty refused his advances. She turned him down. And then, for the first time since they had known each other, he grabbed her angrily by the shoulders, hissed commands at her, and raped her" (79). To be sure, Zweig does not intend to show that Bertin's new devotion to force is the only inducement to his brutal treatment of Lenore. His political ideas and his psychological motives are somewhat independent — yet both forces operate interdependently in the total social process.

Since Zweig was deeply influenced by Freudian theories of group behavior and its effects on the individual psyche, Bertin's unexpected assault can well be interpreted through Freud's own words: "When a nation is summoned to engage in war, a whole gamut of human motives may respond to this appeal, high and low motives, some openly avowed, others slurred over. The lust for aggression and destruction is certainly included; the innumerable cruelties of history and man's daily life confirm its prevalence and strength. The stimulation of these destructive impulses by appeals to idealism and to the erotic instinct naturally facilitates their release."[33] Freud thus suggests that ill-assorted appeals to grand idealism and basic instinct can easily paper over the real issues of the war, those rooted in economics, power politics, and social greed and ambition. The complexities of human relationships are lost to Bertin's brutalized psyche, and he mindlessly brutalizes the dignity and individuality of Lenore, whose tolerant, unselfish affection matches his best instincts. Then he escapes to the war.

Lenore, however, is forced to remain at the home front and to confront the social reality she has heretofore been able to avoid. Learning that she is pregnant, she faces the prospect of terminating the pregnancy secretly at a fashionable clinic, but during this period she retains a calm that prevents her from understanding what has happened or will happen to her. Physically and emotionally unaffected, she can still muse, "The most important things in the world are intellectual. They take place independently of all material conditions" (135). But the intrusion of physical reality, when antithetical to the spirit that supposedly controls it, cannot merely be willed away. The shock of her experience at the clinic brings her face to face with material conditions which destroy her belief in the harmony and stability of her vision of the world and her society. The nurse there goes about her business with a commercial casualness: "Everything is sanitary, little miss, I know what we owe our customers. After all, we cater to the finest ladies, the cream of the aristocracy" (139 - 40). Bertin is callously indifferent to her suffering, and her mother urges on her an arranged marriage with a socially prominent lawyer. Above all, the pain, secrecy, and antiseptic horror of her abortion finally compel her not only to see through Bertin's idealism and the hypocrisy of her family's social values, but to perceive the underlying reality that both were disguising or embellishing. Her bitterness slices through false values and their inflated justifications. Now she thinks: "I'd love to jump out of bed and smash everything around me to smithereens: this rotting social order, which inflicts war upon us, brutalizes men, increases suffering in the world. Sitting in seminars at the university she had heard wise sayings about the value of suffering. Well, it is easy to philosophize when all is well and you're doing fine. God, all the verbiage about it is trash: excuses not to come up with something better than abortions, wars, maimings, and murders" (149 - 50). Lenore's epiphany, and with it the content and scope of the novel, proceeds from the personal to the social level, from the disappointment of private insight to the growth of social awareness.

For Bertin the process is less direct and far more extended. His failure to understand his actions and accept responsibility for them and for Lenore reveals his idealism as romanticizing and his forcefulness as immaturity. Since he expects the army and the war to "make a man of him," he seeks to escape from his guilt for Lenore's situation by linking her suffering with his theoretical disquisitions on suffering and destiny. "What you have gone through is terrible, but the earth, trembling from far more terrible pains, is bringing forth a new creed, new and striving creative powers, and we must not dwell on ourselves" (179 - 80). Lenore somberly recognizes that such slogans merely idealize selfish motives; Bertin is still lacking breadth and sympathy, so that his aims and sentiments are indeed narrow, hard, and complacent. But he retains his personal attraction for her, or rather she continues to love him, despite events.

When given the opportunity to serve in Poland, Bertin chooses to volunteer for duty in Lille, although Warsaw is much nearer to the clinic in which Lenore waits for his visit. When he finally does receive leave to see her before entraining to the western front, he cannot bring himself to do what he should have done, and what Lenore hopes he will do. She could be placated for the asking. But Bertin's selfishness compels him to speak of little but himself. Lenore is generous enough to perceive that his self-centeredness is due to insecurity and dissatisfaction with himself, so she hopes that an assertion of his own self will release as well his ability to love others. And Zweig, in one of the many authorial intrusions in the book, notes that "Bertin presumed to know himself well, to see himself clearly with his trained reasoning, but actually he grasped only scanty fragments" (10). Bertin's fragmentation manifests itself doubly in his reaction to the sadness he belatedly comes to feel over having to leave Lenore. He "felt sincerely unhappy about it. She now needed him as much as human beings require water, and he was being torn away from her. He was moved to write verses about it, but only six lines managed to reach paper, nothing complete" (176). Bertin talks of himself and his actions in the passive voice (*es trieb ihn*, "it came to him") as if no center of gravity within him controlled or guided his behavior, as if he were in the hands of forces beyond his own being. Still lost in a haze of intellectualization, he marches off to his unit and "lets himself be loaded onto the train like a sheep" (181).

So much more enlightened is Lenore that, even though the two agree to marry, their relationship must worsen before it can improve. Even at the front, Bertin continues his quest for some external idea to serve nobly, while Lenore grows increasingly bitter. In a letter, Bertin lacerates her affection for him by "just ignoring what didn't suit him. Had he become so dull or insensitive? In no way. His letters proved how vividly he perceived the occurrences of everyday life. Only on one matter did he remain silent, did his heart harden toward the feeling of guilt" (206). Instead of coming to terms with his relationship to the person closest to him and touching her

humanity through his concern, he soars to new abstractions. Lenore
dissects his letter with a cynicism that signals her recovery as well as
the creation of a larger and sharper insight into the nature of human
relations:

Always and only him, the events that touched him, the things that occurred
to him, the ideas that struck him, the matters that made him sad or happy.
And what was it that he discovered out there in France? Get this —
humanity! Face to face with British POWs, Belgian workers, and French
citizens he had learned that, underneath, human beings are all one, that
differences exist only on the surface. Humanity, which had been an artificial
concept in his university days, was a genuine experience now. Now,
suddenly, he felt the unity of the human race in his own body. Terrific, my
dear Bertin, you can have a ball with your discovery! Do tell more of it to a
woman you have nothing more important to tell than that. (207 - 8)

Her biting sarcasm exposes his humanitarianism as an inauthentic
ideal, one grafted on his mind rather than grown from it. In
Fromm's formulation, "a genuine ideal is not some veiled force
superior to the individual, but the articulate expression of utmost affirmation of the self."[34] Bertin is running away from himself, escaping into a false consciousness; still subject to an ideal that is veiled
and far above any single person, he cannot affirm responsibility for
misused force and the abused person in his own life, to say nothing
of misspent power in the public world.

For Lenore, however, the veil has been torn away, and through
her bitter discovery she can cast her glance over the social landscape
and discern the patterns and processes which shaped the Bertins of
1914. If her frustration with Werner's cloud-hopping callousness
reveals the destructive hold of ideologies on men, the treatment she
receives at the hands of her family opens up a gap between her and
her parents which labels the social values and customs of the older
generation as rigid, shabby, and hypocritical. Although her father, a
banker and *Kommerzienrat*,[35] has always loathed Bertin as a fortune
hunter, patriotic prestige — since it is easily transmutable into cash
or connections — easily transforms Bertin from heel to hero for him,
thanks to his service at the front. " 'Fortunately, Mr. Wahl, your
family doesn't yet have anyone at the front?' And Hugo Wahl
needed great self-control to reply imperturbably, 'Not yet, Mr.
Secretary' " (271). With Werner in the family, so embarrassing an
omission could easily be corrected. A son-in-law-to-be in the field,
even if unsympathetic, is better than none at all or even a desirable

one at home. And after all, "many an engagement has been broken before." Zweig draws a memorable portrait of the Wahls as a typical upper-middle-class family climbing its way to prominence and social status, one in which there is little space for values between the façade of culture on the surface and the drive for money and power beneath.

Thus it is Lenore, and not Bertin, who uncovers the reality of the war even before Bertin experiences it. It is Lenore's discovery that her family's priggishness is a mask that first equates personal morality with class standing. These insights confirm her sense of self to such a degree that she can, at the end, dismiss with a shrug of her shoulders the unspoken agreement between herself and her parents to have the wedding in Berlin and not in Potsdam, since Bertin is just a common private with no social standing. Her gesture exhibits the forthright combination of strength and charm with which she can ignore her parents' pretensions to morality and deliberately choose the humanly imperfect. One day, before the wedding, Lenore starts to accompany Werner to his room so that he can enjoy a brief nap. "Mrs. Wahl stared disapprovingly at them. Was it proper for a young girl to accompany a man to whom she was not yet married to his room?" (424 - 25). After an abortion such a prudish concern is laughable to Lenore. The concluding words of the novel, as Werner leaves for his assignment at Verdun after their wedding and honeymoon, represent the triumph of her integrity over Bertin's jingoism and her family's Babbitry. "In the end what really matters to her is love, love which sacrifices, acts, and creates — but above all, simply love" (462). And despite her travail, she loves Werner Bertin. Lenore's victory, like that of Kleist's *Marquise von O . . .* whose story Lenore read and admired in the clinic, is the first step toward liberation from the tyranny of illusion and convention. She is the hero of the novel.

3. *Society and Structure*

The happy ending of the book does not, however, extend beyond the private sphere of the young lovers' lives. The crippling consequences of Germany's class system and the cooperation of industry with the military are not exposed for what they are and for the way in which they intrude on private lives. At least half of the seventh book of the novel is devoted to the extension of personal and social tensions into the spheres of politics and economics, statecraft and warfare. This unfolding must necessarily be channeled through the experiences of Hugo Wahl, the only character whose life touches on affairs of state. At the outbreak of the war, Wahl was delighted with the financial opportunities the war had offered him and equally pleased with the coalition of industrialists and militarists. "Economics runs into politics and thereby into the authority of the army. Wahl felt from his conversations with Colonel Schieffenzahn that the leadership of the army was in the right hands. Big business was ready to back the military all the way and expected to have their trust fully repaid. And that was to mean, at the end of hostilities, more land, more money, and higher profits" (267). Only when Wahl is invited to meet with Schieffenzahn in Kovno and there pressed to support the colonel's scheme for the deportation of Lithuania's Jews to America does he begin to question the motives and the power of Prussian militarism and thus the fragility of his own position. "For fifty years I have admired the Prussian and looked upon the uniform as the finest costume on earth. I never listened to any talk of super-militarism. But it is never too late to reconsider. Reason is the highest form of patriotism, and militarism is a rotten creed. It will one day destroy Germany if someone doesn't force it to curb its appetite" (372). Wahl's estimate of Prussian militarism, when measured by Schieffenzahn's ambitions, is certainly accurate, but his outburst is self-serving. He never acknowledges the involvement of his own industrial group and its common aspirations with the military. Werner Bertin and Hugo Wahl are much alike in this respect: the former refuses to accept the consequences of his personal actions, and the latter ignores the implications of his financial transactions. Ultimately, the sentimentality of the wedding ceremony and the nagging doubts voiced by his daughter force Wahl fully to identify and admit the damage militarism has brought upon German society, as a social and economic phenomenon. For the first time he questions the desirability of war, despite its usefulness to business, and he concedes that "the manners of bourgeois life will collapse if treated so ruthlessly" (428). He envisions quite sharply the breakdown of prewar morality and shivers at prospective changes in private and public life if the war should stretch over a long period. Obviously still not disinterested, still a man of his class and protective of its interests, he knows at least that the war will continue to undermine the foundations of bourgeois existence, which affords him luxury at home and a position in society.

Young Woman of 1914 wraps no cosmic framework around its story but, rather, remains highly personal in its tensions. Zweig opens the book, characteristically, with a deftly realistic description of the mailman who delivers the induction notice to Werner. Occasionally authorial intrusions predict historical effects beyond the perspective of the characters or connect the events in Germany with parallel developments throughout Europe. But among the characters, only Werner Bertin delivers pronouncements about national destiny and cosmic necessity, and his pomposities shrivel when set against the pleasures or pains of the social reality they are meant to encompass. To create the private texture of the novel, Zweig shifts regularly from Lenore to Bertin. While the books or chapters concerned with Bertin remain essentially the same, focusing on the unchanging ideology of a young man pitted against a rapidly changing reality, the chapters in which Lenore is the central character vary in tone and grow in scope. Her tone shifts slowly from smug satisfaction through dark despair to mature criticism. It is as if Lenore's intelligence gathered experience and knowledge to confirm some truths her intuition had always asserted about subjects to conjure with, like war or love. The third book, in which the abortion and Werner's remoteness plunge Lenore to the lowest point of her life, opens with the Tolstoyan observation that "families always remain the same; neither war nor depression changes the course of their actions" (133). But in the first chapter of book IV, entitled "Stocktaking," Lenore's reflections have already lifted her out of such universal sameness. "What made her different from the working women vacationing nearby? Nothing but the cushion of her parents' money!" (202) — her realistic analysis will restore her self-esteem and force her to change her ideas and actions. At the end of the book, her affirmation of love and her opposition to the war spring from the same knowledge. The value system around which she intends to organize her private life can no longer be divorced from the politics and economics which have thus far denied her that opportunity.

But, as has been observed before,[36] Lenore does not directly pass this knowledge on to Werner. Such insights must be gained firsthand. Her attitude does transmit, however, the first hint of doubt to Werner. "He was just a tiny rivet on the German ship of state now struggling in dangerous waters. But that ship was manned by a pilot not truly reliable, a swaggering captain, and high-handed mates. Was it permissible for a rivet, under these circumstances, to spring from the hull of the ship that was protecting the lives of those most dear, like the woman beside him now?" (442). Bertin's doubts about Germany's regime and leadership are still cautious questions more concerned, like Wahl's, with personal security than with the common good. He has much to learn. Werner must experience his conversion under real fire. The road he has to travel is political, whereas Lenore's was personal, and Zweig has only begun — in this depiction of the effect of the early months of the war on a few individuals — to sketch the background that permitted the Grischa case to arise. He has more to say, and Bertin more to learn, about the kind of thinking which engulfed German society in the First World War. The trenches of Verdun were to become their catechism.

V   Education before Verdun

1. *The Case of Sergeant Kroysing*

In the afterword to *Erziehung vor Verdun (Education before Verdun)* Zweig describes its difficult genesis: "It was sketched in 1927, and begun first in 1928, and again in 1930. The confiscation of my manuscripts and my expulsion from Germany delayed its publication, and the steady deterioration of my eyesight made the final revision of my redictated manuscript even more difficult" (628).[37] Despite political upheavals and personal problems — perhaps more because of them — the novel succeeds in capturing the complexity of war as well as revealing its meaninglessness. Without robbing World War I of the spiritual mystique and physical excitement it exercised over its participants, the novel shows that the values or virtues occasionally gained through the soldier's existential confrontation with death — discipline, hardness, clarity of mind — neither repay the cost in physical and mental suffering nor define the core of the war experience. The attempt to remove war from the material universe and from a realistic approach to it has been continuously successful in Germany. In the preface to *Das Wäldchen 125 (Copse 125)*, for instance, Ernst Jünger offers a lofty celebration of war: "No — war is not a material matter. There are higher realities to which it is subject. Values are tested in comparison with which the brutality of the means must appear insignificant. A strength of will concentrated in the highest untamed expression of life [asserts] itself even in its own annihilation."[38] Zweig's novel sets out to refute all such claims. The case of Sergeant Kroysing, around which the book is structured, demonstrates that grubbiness and greed are not extinguished by the initial high-minded enthusiasm for war but, rather, are intensified by its dreary routine and personal deprivations. The education of Werner Bertin demonstrates that the "brutality of the means" inexorably becomes the sole end and value of the war itself. And finally, the case of Kroysing and the education of Bertin merge to deny the validity of Jünger's´final dialectic absurdity and to reveal its horror. Bertin learns that the use of brutality diminishes whatever values may originally have inspired it. The lesson of Verdun for Bertin has been brilliantly described by Simone Weil: "As soon as the practice of war has revealed the fact that each moment holds the possibility of death, the mind becomes incapable of moving from one day to the next without passing through the spectre of death. That soul daily suffers violence which every morning must mutilate its aspirations because the mind cannot move about in a time without passing through death. In this way war wipes out every conception of goal, even all thoughts concerning the goals of war."[39] Probably no single engagement could better establish the truth of this vision than the one which Zweig himself participated in and recreates in *Education* — the ten-months-long struggle for Verdun in 1916.

Sergeant Christoph Kroysing is a young man of a good Nuremberg family with some poetic promise. During a chance meeting in July, 1916, with Bertin, in whom he senses an artistic and intellectual kinship, he explains that

for the last nine weeks he and his men had been living in the cellars of Chambrettes farm, and it looked as if Captain Niggl, a former tax collector, and his orderlies intended to keep him there until he got killed. He had done a pretty stupid thing. In the fall he was supposed to enroll in an officers' training course, and by next spring he would receive his commission. But for now he suffered the misfortune of being unable to close his eyes to the treatment of the rank and file by his fellow NCO's. They had established their own kitchen and confiscated all the best supplies — fresh meat and butter, sugar and potatoes, and above all, beer — while noodles, dried vegetables, and canned meat were considered good enough for the men, although they worked hard and got hardly any leave. And because of his family's traditional passion for justice, he committed the folly of writing a long letter full of complaints to his uncle Franz, who was a big shot at the Military Railway Administration in Metz. Naturally the censor's bureau was mighty interested in what an NCO might have to tell the Chief of the M.R.A., and the letter went back to the battalion with orders to put its author before a court martial. But under no circumstances would the company let the matter get as far as an inquiry. Their fear of that was clearly considerable, and strangely enough the court martial did not take up the matter. (43 - 44)

And so Kroysing is shipped off and kept at Chambrettes — a forward position exposed to close artillery fire — where a French shell kills him only a day after his meeting with Bertin.

Zweig has invented this case not only in order to involve and thereby educate Bertin in aspects of warfare far removed from individual heroism or staff tactics but also to establish that human behavior in warfare is largely governed by the same desires, instincts, ambitions, and patterns as civilian life. The incident Kroysing wished to report, moreover, cannot be considered an isolated phenomenon. A study of the letters and diaries of young Germans at the front uncovers many similar disillusioning experiences. "We hoped that this community of sacrifice, this facing of death common to all, would bring about an end of all class distinctions. This is not the case. You do not believe it? I will give you an example: in the trench three privates are fighting over a loaf of bread; inside the dugout the officers have more wine than they can drink."[40] Zweig has selected the small-scale thievery of a few sergeants not merely to give vent to his antimilitarism but to demonstrate that the ordinary self-serving quality of social and economic life in peacetime inevitably finds new arenas and new forms of expression in war. For entrepreneurs war is business as usual, whether on the corporate level of Hugo Wahl or on the petty one of hoarding NCO's.

At Christoph's funeral Werner meets the boy's older brother, Eberhard Kroysing, a lieutenant in the combat engineers, and gives him Christoph's letter. From this point on, the case's paltry origins and motives are subjected to judicial scrutiny and ethical debate. The survival, if not the triumph, of meanness and deceit soon reduces the ersatz grandeur of war to the ordinary scheming of civilian life. After all, in peacetime a disruptive Christoph might also have been transferred to an isolated provincial post for his egalitarian idealism. When Professor Mertens, a famous jurist and the Judge Advocate at Montmédy, examines the file of Christoph Kroysing, neither he nor his assistant "noticed anything unusual" (97). The cumbersome apparatus of military justice, even if well intentioned, cannot effectively deal with the labyrinthine network of favors, privileges, deals, and delays that exalts private loyalty over concern for the common good or individual rights.

Mertens is horrified at the injustice of Christoph's fate, but he finds that he cannot combat the machinations of Captain Niggl and his NCO's by sheerly legal means; this inability gradually undercuts the tenuous philosophical structure on which his life is built.

Mertens's disintegration, like that of Helbret Friedebringer, proceeds from knowledge of his impotence in one case to condemnation of all human affairs. "That was what had begun it all. This wretched little case of Sergeant Kroysing had given the impulse, faint at first but sufficient to release the doubts dormant within him. By now, however, individual cases had ceased to count. The whole scurvy race of man stood ripe for judgment. Men had ceased to exist; there was only a nation" (358). Mertens, in allowing himself to be overcome by the number and the severity of crimes committed by German soldiers against civilians as well as their fellow soldiers, falls into the same blind absolutism of which he accuses his countrymen. His condemnation of the whole human race and his unwillingness to distinguish among individual cases prevent him from engaging precisely in the one activity the loss of which he laments most: "The spirit of inquiry had vanished from the earth" (369). He allows himself to sink into a void of clear-headed nihilism, for "clarity had always been one of the central concerns of his life" (370) and nihilism takes the place of perfect justice denied. He commits suicide while listening to the music of Brahms, the only remnant of a "nobler world, cleansed of all the impulses and savageries of our bestial nature" (373). Mertens prefers the delusion of dying for a perfect philosophy to the risk of exposing and compromising it in the world of "impulses and savageries." He expresses the polarity of his legal thinking shortly before his death: "From the point of view of legal theory two spheres could be distinguished: the unassailed sanctity of justice, existing objectively, and on the other hand a right of retaliation and revenge, ultimately based on the interest of any given unit or group" (367). When Mertens abdicates the first position, removing himself and his philosophy from the Kroysing case, he leaves the field free for Eberhard Kroysing and the second.

Kroysing approaches his brother's case with an understandable if unholy desire for revenge, although his decision to transform desire into action is prompted by Mertens's capitulation and his own insight that there is a "little catch in it" (98). Stung by the injustice, he sets out to wring a confession of guilt from Captain Niggl. But in his battle for revenge he employs the same tactics used by the men who cast out and killed his brother. He manages to have Niggl and his men transferred to Fort Douaumont, which has come under French counterattack, and thus he exposes them to the same dangers under which his brother suffered. Niggl's company does indeed incur very high losses; when Werner Bertin subsequently accuses Kroysing of

being responsible for their deaths, Kroysing dismisses them collec-
tively as mere *appanages* (195) of Captain Niggl — exactly Niggl's
own attitude to enlisted men. Kroysing's intense and absolute subjectivity has led him to the same lack of discernment to which
Mertens plummets from his total objectivity. Under the pressures of
war, neither man can continue to make intellectual distinctions or
accept moral nuances. Thus Zweig allows Bertin, beginning his own
road to moral discernment, to reject decisively Kroysing's
rationalizations for his campaign of revenge, whether based on
analogy to the biblical tales of David and Uriah or on the acquiescence of Niggl's men in the persecution of Christoph. He sum-
mons the courage to tell Eberhard, "the world is out of joint, all
right, but it seems crazy that you should put it still further out of
joint" (198).

What are the qualities of the Kroysing case itself, of Mertens's inability to place it in his legal framework, and of Eberhard's private
vendetta to conclude it, which make it particularly apposite as the
core of a war novel? Like battle, this conflict moves to a violent and
brutally senseless solution, which, on one level, is the only possible
resolution to a struggle between two sides equally touched by evil.
After Mertens's suicide, which destroys Eberhard's best hope for the
restoration of Christoph's good name, the French save Niggl by
retaking Fort Douaumont in such a way that Niggl not only escapes
the eagle eye of Kroysing but receives the Iron Cross and promotion
to Major as well. And finally Kroysing, who has so relentlessly
hounded Niggl, strikes a ludicrous bargain with Niggl's confessor
whereby Kroysing will abandon his campaign if the priest will help a
nurse obtain a divorce so that she can marry him. At this juncture,
the hospital in which Kroysing is recovering from a wound, under
the care of the nurse he is to marry, is bombed, and he is killed. The
hospital is hit only because the nurse left a light burning while, at
Kroysing's own thoughtful request, she telephoned her old acquaintance, the Crown Prince, to ask for Bertin's transfer to the east, far
from the anti-Semitic captain who is persecuting him for such un-
patriotic behavior as his association with the troublemaker Kroysing.
Ironically, the superbly named Niggl has become the sole living
"hero" in the case.

So bizarre, convoluted, even absurd an ending to a tightly conceived and executed novel seems, at first glance, to leave all motifs
and developments fragmented or suspended. Such may have been
Zweig's aim. The Kroysing case contains, in its conception and un-

folding, almost every socially accepted rationalization or myth about war. The chaotically thorough ending literally and symbolically explodes them all and cuts off every possible line of defense for war as the continuation of politics, economics, social life, or any other form of human aspiration. If we examine the origin and growth of Christoph Kroysing's complaint and its consequences, we see that it moves through and rejects war as a socially unifying force, as a biologically valuable or politically motivated competition, as a legally justifiable or manageable duty, or as a Christian and thereby holy venture. The "catch" at the center of the case cannot be fitted into any of these categories; all of the rationalizations crumble in the face of either external reality or an inner search for the meaning of war. No ideal, neither the destiny of the fatherland nor the sanctity of one human life, is attached to the struggle. The notion that so inspired young men to march off to war, that warfare could ennoble their characters or purify their souls, is first belittled and then quashed. Glory or greatness, selflessness or decency, if not present in the factory or at home, will not suddenly emerge with the donning of a uniform or the possession of a rifle. Zweig observed in an essay that "war is nothing but a form of human life in its most naked expression,"[41] and therefore subject to the same standards of conduct as every other human activity. The utter physical destruction and spiritual barrenness at the conclusion of the novel testify to the meaninglessness of war as such a form of life. The Kroysing case has served the novel as the *Fabel*, or plot, as a vehicle for suspense and cohesion, but also a means to divest war of any superhuman attributes. It proves the conviction of Zweig and Freud that "our mortification and our grievous disillusionment regarding the uncivilized behavior of our world-compatriots in this war are . . . unjustified. They were based on an illusion to which we had abandoned ourselves. In reality our fellow-citizens have not sunk so low as we feared, because they had never risen so high as we believed."[42]

2. *The Education of Werner Bertin*

As usual, Zweig was not satisfied with a merely negative exposure. As Werner departs for a leave prior to his transfer to the eastern front at the end of the novel, he reflects that "there was something like a lump in his throat. It had been a lousy company, it had tortured him with drill and treated him with growing cruelty and injustice as time went on, but no matter; it was his company, it had taken the place of father and mother, wife and profession, home and university" (619).

The army and the war had to exercise a formative influence on Bertin, thanks to their all-embracing structure and total power, the duration of the war, and the absence of other, inimical forces. The Kroysing case makes it relatively easy for Bertin, as it was for all young soldiers, to discover what war is not. But as a reflective man, he is still tempted to inquire like St. James in his epistle, "Whence come wars and whence come fightings?" (James 4:1). The Freudian reply, that man's irrational and aggressive nature is to blame, strikes both Bertin and his creator as a symptom rather than a cause, and one true not only of men in war, but of society during peace. Bertin's education proceeds beyond the intellectual boundaries of the Kroysing case when Zweig seeks to place the case's conclusion in a larger framework rather than tendering its cataclysm as a final answer.

Bertin's personal development parallels the Kroysing affair, but it arises from totally opposite problems and expands in scope, whereas the Kroysing case steadily constricts in scope. Bertin's conflict with army discipline, and ultimately with war, is rooted in his basically decent, guileless nature. His difficulties begin with his kindness to a French POW, whom he offers a drink of water against officers' orders, and they increase as his innocence continues to irritate his superiors. If Kroysing was murdered because he betrayed the unwritten code of noncommissioned officers, then Bertin is persecuted because he really tries to follow the written code for lowly privates. He attempts to remove every sign that brands him an outsider, as either artist or Jew. Shortly after the water episode, he shaves off his beard because "he wanted to look inconspicuous" (23). But his desire to merge with the crowd of recruits subverts his own identity and thwarts his idealism. His two worldly-wise teachers, the typesetter Wilhelm Pahl and the innkeeper Karl Lebehde, realize that "idealism was one of the best baits with which society prevented smart people from following their own interests, and lured them into serving the ruling classes, without any reward but honor" (30). Very slowly Bertin grasps the relationship between enlightened self-interest and self-abnegating idealism, and the need to distinguish the real from the illusory, if he is to develop and maintain his identity. Werner, however, does not learn easily by counsel from others. The two proletarians and socialists can be his guides, but "their friend Bertin was the kind of man who learned only from experience" (315).

Bertin's experiences constitute a frame around the novel's matrix and, as the novel's most insistent pattern of narrative organization, coincide and yet always contrast with the episodes of the central plot. Just when Christoph's case is diagnosed as hopeless by Mertens and its "catch" grasped by Eberhard, Bertin's illusion of war has reached its highest pitch: "For him it was a primeval force that roared above his head, like an avalanche, for which natural laws were responsible, not men. The war, planned and carried out by human beings, appeared to him more and more in the guise of a storm decreed by fate, a release of malignant elements, not subject to criticism or accountable to anyone" (138). While Eberhard's vengefulness swells to bursting and he longs to be an airman in order to "hurl bombs that would scatter gas and bullets among the crawling multitudes below" (297), Bertin's laborious analysis is gathering momentum. "He had greatly changed in everyone's opinion, since he had been up front" (256).

From this moment, the Kroysing affair rotates on a very personal axis while Bertin's outlook revolves around larger, suprapersonal issues. Although Pahl and Lebehde have tried to convert his revulsion against man's inhumanity to man from intellectual opposition to active, class-conscious involvement, Bertin's educational background and reflective nature resist at least their verbal assaults. But certain examples begin to impress him. When Crown Prince Friedrich Wilhelm, the commander of Germany's Fifth Army, visits the front, his car tears along the road while "the men stood in the mud, with their hands against their trouser seams, awaiting the inevitable splash of mud into their faces" (258). The Crown Prince, who "took time out from playing with his greyhounds, pretty Frenchwomen, nurses, or tennis partners," has scattered three packs of cigarettes along the road for his troops. As one man bends to pick them out of the slime, "someone grabbed him by the wrist. 'Let them lie,' said Lebehde the innkeeper, in a harsh undertone. 'They're not for us. Anyone who wants to give us a present will give it to us properly.' And stepping forward Lebehde stamped the nearest pack into a pulp" (258 - 59). The effect of Lebehde's action on Bertin is striking: "God damn, thought Bertin, that really was something. That Lebehde has guts. Bertin caught himself wondering what he would have done but for Karl Lebehde. He had laughed in philosophic superiority when the cigarettes flew out of the car . . ." (259). With that "philosophic superiority" wiped from his face and mind, Bertin begins to look at the world around him with clearer eyes and to probe the relationships underneath intellectual generalizations and nationalist slogans.

He begins with small things and hesitant questions. "Next morning he reported for sick call. He was certainly feverish; the examination showed his temperature to be a hundred. That wasn't anything serious, as the doctor observed, but since Bertin was an educated man he had better spend the day in the infirmary. 'Ah,' thought Bertin, as he stood at attention, 'if I had been a waiter or typesetter, and were running a temperature because I experienced a shock, I would have to go out into the wet and do my job and catch my death of cold before I was sent to bed.' Health and sickness seemed to depend on the class to which a man belonged" (311). Lebehde's forceful gesture in defense of the dignity of man "had set something in motion within him," and he discovers "an idea the like of which had never come into his mind before" (311). Awareness that the existence of classes also means inequities between them awakens deeper and more critical faculties of thought in Bertin. The inequalities he now begins to notice are not superficial observations, nor are they restricted to his immediate surroundings or firsthand experience. "All that these men suffered, all that the world suffered in the war, slipped through the films of consciousness into the deeper chambers of the soul. Then, in time, it would reemerge to disturb and to demand a hearing" (352). Bertin has progressed so far that at Christmas, 1916, just as Mertens acknowledges his inability to cope with reality and departs from it to eternal peace, Bertin has acquired enough hardheaded cynicism to mock the chasm Mertens could not face: "From the darkness outside came the roaring of guns. It was Christmas night, a holiday of great emotional importance to the Germans, but they felt they must discipline the luxury of such feelings by a display of rugged manliness. Their guns were scattering Christmas gifts made of lead and steel, and the French followed their example. Peace on Earth, sang the Gospel, war on earth thundered reality" (353).

Gradually Bertin perceives the full range of ramifications to the Kroysing affair, ramifications which place the case outside the physical and spiritual hell of Verdun, outside even of war itself. Not all, in fact by no means most, of these connections are made by Bertin, but he is always present at their airing and participates in the discussions concerning them. In his hearing, Dr. Posnanski, the successor to Professor Mertens, dares to suggest that the Kroysing case is not a product of the special conditions of war. "Was such a case possible in peace? Of course it was! Instead of the supply battalion, just picture a large industrial concern which clothed and fed its workers through its own canteens and shops, provided them with housing and medical treatment. The opportunity for corruption and intrigue at the expense of the majority would be no less than in the Prussian army" (476). Bertin is not yet equipped, however, to examine the nexus of relationships that shape German society and discover there the evils that war has so starkly brought to his attention. Indeed, he tries to escape from the painful conclusions which the evidence of his experience and his reason force upon him: "He wanted peace. He wanted to turn his back on the horrors that tried again and again to engulf him; he wanted to escape this persecution of intellect and its possessors. . . . He no longer cared for the praise of lieutenants and men of his own class. He was just plain sick of everything connected with the army and with soldiers, he wanted to take refuge in books and indulge in the play of fantasy" (491). Bertin listens to debates about the relative merits and attitudes of German and Russian workers, and to evaluations of Liebknecht's theories about infantilism and war, but any application to the hustle and bustle of daily life in peace or war still remains beyond his grasp.

Finally, when the bomb bursts on the hospital killing Kroysing and the Socialist Pahl, Bertin begins to question his own intellectual heritage against the background of social and physical reality. Now he leaves behind the depersonalized view that "death was not the evil thing" and concentrates on the personal action of killing: "But devilish indeed was the process of murder, the thousands of methods humanity had devised for the extinction of human life" (557). His vision of the world has shed the hazy glow of his idealism and glitters with cold clarity. "He was faced with a black and derisive world, a world in which force ruled, blank violence, open and unadorned. It was not the justice of a cause that determined its outcome, but the jackboot that decided the issue" (564). With his newly gained sobriety he reviews the past and stands naked before the delusions which, like the emperor's new clothes, he was trained to see and wished to see. His past motives and actions, personal, social, and intellectual, are now linked and illuminated in the harsh light of reality — human mistreatment and inhuman death. He recalls his wish not to serve on the eastern front, and now he can see that his aversion to the "unsavory" manners and appearance of eastern European Jewry was not a purely aesthetic reaction. Of course he is still no saint, and he resents the very process of his disillusionment. "He admitted it now, but he found the punishment a bit stern for so minor a transgression. After all, didn't a Jew have the right not to like some

Jews but to like the Prussian military system, its discipline and
organization, its neatness and drill, its jazzy uniforms and its fighting
spirit, its proud traditions and its unconquerable power? Hadn't he
been educated to feel just that way about it? And now, after two
years' service, here he stood, a truly pitiable figure. Many illusions
had been unmasked in these two years, and one of them was the old
saw that it was sweet and glorious to die for one's country" (580 -
81). For the first time Bertin relates national policy to personal
behavior and responsibility, and he understands the psychological
consequences of accepting lifeless principles or ideals.

At this point, Bertin's state of mind may be described as
restlessness, flux, a deep-seated unease, a sense of frustration — but
by no means as political commitment. He has come to terms with his
past illusions, but he has not yet asked about the causes of his self-
deception and patriotic aggressiveness. None of Zweig's characters
ever mentions German bellicosity as a national characteristic, nor do
they or their author speak of any other qualities as peculiar to one
race or culture. Only Lebehde suggests at the end that certain conditions in prewar Germany must have produced the attitudes that
embraced the war and welcomed force as the solution to social
problems. In his view "capitalist society and its wars — those are our
enemies" (610). Werner is willing to accept the Marxist dream, but
not its theory. He is not yet ready to endorse or even consider practical politics. Very faintly, however, the direction of his future
political thinking is hinted at. He recalls the dying words of a fellow
soldier: " 'Tell my parents it was worth it? Tell Lieutenant Kroysing
it wasn't?' The truth lay somewhere between these two extremes but
not, as a wise man had noted, in the center" (619). The center from
which the unpolitical Bertin is about to move had held most
educated Germans tied to a high-minded passivity, to noncommit-
ment for fear of imperfection, and finally to meeting untidy social
problems with tidy but insufficient national solutions. Without
much preparation, with too many hopes and too few experiences, the
generation of Werner and Lenore was about to turn from ethics to
politics. What Bertin cautiously anticipates, Walter Gropius expressed bluntly: "This is more than just a lost war. A world has come
to an end. We must seek a radical solution to our problems."[43]

Education before Verdun may justly be called a social war novel.
Every aspect of the journalistic war novel, from boredom to
brutality, is covered. Yet, while his characters are always on the front
except for a few leaves, Zweig shows the reader the progressive

demystification of the war through the growing awareness of those fighting it — that is the novel's central theme, in reflection of the character of the entire German society. The fusion of the archaic social forms revealed in the Kroysing case with the modern technology employed in the war emphasizes, in its unraveling, the dangerously split nature of that society. But more important is the indication that Bertin may finally cast off his very German fatalism about social position and all the areas of life it determines. Such fatalism hovered over the Grischa book, in its structure, in the choice of its central character, and in the philosophizing of its secondary figures. The opening vision of a timeless earth was never altered. In *Education* the earth changes from a "blood-drenched planet" in book I to a "rusty" one in book V, and it finally becomes this "stony" earth in book VII. Responsibility gradually shifts from the planet to man; as the earth's stony neutrality is established, men must answer for the bloodletting. The war is no longer allowed to be abstractly horrible, with the individuals who wanted or caused it left blameless. In the face of the vicissitudes of war and the impositions of society, Zweig is asserting the self as the source responsible for all actions. Bertin's education affirms the significance of personal value and evaluation which a character in Sartre's *The Victors* calls for: "A cause never gives orders; it never says anything. It is we who have to determine what it needs."[44] *Education* is just as stunning and original a novel as *Grischa*, but it offers a more mature and provocative critique of the totality of war. War neither begins nor ends with the horrors it creates.

VI   The Crowning of a King

1. *Fiction as History*

Einsetzung eines Königs (The Crowning of a King) extends the analysis of war from the social and psychological atmosphere of *Young Woman* and the military and moral limbo of *Education* to the economic and political sphere. *Sergeant Grischa* — chronologically the apex of Zweig's vision of the folly and outrage of World War I — intervenes by implication to complete Werner Bertin's realization, then gives way to the bleak panorama of this final volume of the tetralogy. Writing between 1936 and 1937, Zweig noted the aim of *The Crowning* in the afterword: "This was the first of my works to be deeply changed by the events of 1933; influence on a work of art

expresses itself in its form. . . . The novel is intended to demonstrate
why the German ruling class had to abdicate and hand over the
direction of, and responsibility for, German affairs to the middle
class and the workers, and the tasks of these two new classes were
made difficult and burdensome" (573).[45] There is little doubt that
the book means to deliver a powerful indictment of the Junker-
industrialist alliance, which determined German military and
foreign policy in the waning years of the war. The complex subject,
however, had an unfortunate influence on the form of the book;
Zweig lost the force of his indictment in the labyrinth of
machinations and plots which he intended to expose. He chose as his
specific vehicle the intricate maneuvers of Ludendorff, the kaiser,
and the *Reichstag* to annex Lithuania and transform it into a fiefdom
of the crown. Buried in the mass of historical facts and political
chronicles are the clear outlines of a story, the characters to give it
personal appeal, and ultimately the motives and morals of the clique
whose demise it celebrates. One reviewer pithily observed that "the
plot is not firm enough to retain the author's interest, to say nothing
of the reader's."[46]

The framework of the story is shaped by the political rivalry over
the newly-to-be-created throne of occupied Lithuania, a kingdom to
be united by dynastic ties with the fatherland. The Prussians want to
install one of the kaiser's sons; the Saxon party favors a duke of the
House of Wettin. Only the Lithuanian *Taryba*, the National Council
elected in September, 1917, and the German *Reichstag* support the
more liberal duke of Teck, a Swabian. The historical complexities of
the situation, however, emerge in the novel only gradually, and
Zweig's backward glances serve largely to cloud the scene he means
to present.

Into this cauldron Zweig sends Captain Paul Winfried, nephew of
General Otto von Lychow (the righteous Prussian of *Grischa*), who
has the youth transferred to the political section of *Ober-Ost* just as
the struggle is getting under way. Winfried appeared in *Grischa* as
an unassuming young officer whose quixotic attempt to rescue
Grischa and whose general behavior were indicative of a natural
goodness and a sense of politeness and honor. Serving now under
Captain Ellendt, Paul's impulsive humanity soon gives way to hero
worship of Ellendt and General Clauss, chief of staff of *Ober-Ost*; he
soon sees himself as "an officer in body and soul" (130). But upon his
arrival at the political section, he finds his quest for acceptance into
the ideological and aristocratic elite of the Officer Corps blocked by

two ready-made enemies. One is Colonel Mutius, head of the political news section, whose business it is to ferret out sedition and Bolshevism in the army. He warns General Clauss, who is strongly modeled after the historical General Max Hoffmann, that young Winfried may have "Red" leanings, since he has tried to arrange the escape of a Russian "spy" sentenced to death. There is also Major Buchenegger, who has heard of the Grischa affair and who knows, moreover, that Winfried's beloved, Bärbe Orsann, is the daughter of the Tübingen professor Orsann, who supports the candidacy of the duke of Teck. Winfried thus finds himself between two camps, for it is his duty as a member of the staff of *Ober-Ost* to work against Teck, the *Taryba*, and the Liberal faction of the *Reichstag*, yet he is suspected of sympathizing with the Teck faction and un-German causes in general. While on an official visit to Germany, he does indeed call on his prospective father-in-law and on Teck.

His associations are reported to Clauss by Mutius, and Clauss grants Mutius and Buchenegger permission to play a practical joke on Winfried as an object lesson — a "joke" which turns into a horror. The opportunity arises one evening when Bärbe, having contracted influenza, fails to keep a rendezvous with Paul. Disgruntled at her unexplained absence, he puts on civilian clothes and visits an after-hours café. The café is raided by military police, and Winfried, caught without any official identification, is arrested as a spy and sent to one of the labor camps in whose existence he has refused to believe. During the week he spends in the camp, his uncle Lychow is assassinated by one of the forest-bandits who had sheltered Grischa, and Bärbe fights a losing battle with illness. Winfried is released only in time for her to die in his arms. By this time, the German armies have lost the war in the west, in part because of the reckless offensive launched by Schieffenzahn,[47] and the whole fabric of Winfried's officer-world falls apart. He disengages himself from Clauss: "Now the spell is broken. I have been bitterly deluded, and so has Germany. All that remains of the dreams of my youth is the conviction that you are a dangerous and disruptive luxury we can't afford any longer, and that you have no notion of the destruction your antics cause" (556). In the novel, as in history, the *Taryba* hesitates as long as possible in its choice of king and then checkmates the German political machinations by offering the crown to the liberal candidate — historically, Duke William of Urach. But in reality, on November 2, 1918, the Lithuanian Council revoked its tender of the crown to Urach and declared that the country's form of government would be decided by a constituent assembly to be elected by a universal secret ballot. Winfried's wish and prophecy to Clauss was realized; "The days of the masses are at hand" (558).

Around Winfried's personal journey, Zweig has attempted to portray the complex background of politics without which the disintegration of the German armies and social order cannot be understood. Partially from personal experience, his knowledge of the intrigues on the eastern front was immense and accurate.[48] No reader of the novel can fail to be convinced that "Germany's war aims were an unattainable conglomeration of the aspirations of industrialist and agrarian interest groups, bureaucratic *Machtpolitiker*, militarists, and Pan-German dreamers."[49] Unfortunately, however, the story of Winfried's reversion to the ideals of his youth is tied too closely to the political forces and issues to establish an ambience of its own. Unlike *Grischa* or *Education, The Crowning* provides no central plot as an analogue of the world. Winfried's disregard for the truth, his acceptance of suffering as an inevitable and necessary price for the aesthetically pleasing formality and order of war, last too long and are described in too much detail to permit his change of heart to ring true. His political wisdom, gained through brief confinement in the labor camp, emerges too suddenly and unexpectedly. His fierce militarism, his devotion to duty, his absolute trust in the fatherland and its leaders — all these qualities are described with great authenticity. Even his language becomes coarser and more violent as his nationalism grows bolder and more wild-eyed. In this frame of mind, he dismisses a letter from his father, who deplores the hunger and deprivation of the population at home, as garbage *(Mist)*, and he spits out *(er spuckt aus)* his indignation in the terminology used by a Goebbels: *heimtückisch dem Volk, das sich wehrte, die Kniekehlen eindrückend.*[50] Yet after his return to human values from military priorities, he never expresses his rediscovered convictions in anything but vague, hollow clichés: "Are there still races, parties, and nations? No, just humanity, and the common task for it to find a way out of this slaughterhouse" (410). Events in Lithuania receive no specific definition in the thought of Winfried, and they are overshadowed by his personal disillusion with Clauss.

The choice of Winfried as the hero of the fourth volume of the original tetralogy may, in the light of political developments in Germany in 1936 - 37, imply that at that time Zweig still hoped for a change of heart among the German Officer Corps. Perhaps he expected, from the German officers who respected the old Prussian code of honor, a reaction to the camps Hitler was building similar to the response Winfried exhibits to the Lithuanian camps. Zweig notes in the afterword that the name of Major General Clauss was picked to remind the reader of "Rudolf Clauss, disabled in World War I, whom the current regime and its supporters executed by the axe in 1936 for his political views" (574). A check of recent major studies of the German army and the resistance to Hitler shows no reference to a Rudolph Clauss.[51] The obscurity of his case reveals how timidly the flame of decency and democracy flickered among the German officers, and how frail was Zweig's hope for a turn for the better in Germany. All the innumerable details Zweig presents in *The Crowning* cannot strengthen the weakness of Winfried's conversion; the ray of light at the end only serves to reveal the vastness of the darkness all around it.

2. *History as Fiction: the Tetralogy*

The reader who opens any of Arnold Zweig's novels about World War I finds a meticulously textured, total kind of realism already old-fashioned in the 1920s and 1930s. His vast novels, divided into books and chapters in a Dickensian way that enforces leisurely, thoughtful reading, employ no expressionism, no surrealism, no reductiveness or stylization of any sort. The vision is long; the author's controlling mind and hand are readily apparent. Zweig's point of view is usually omniscient, with a heavy use of indirect discourse and a manipulation of character signalized by casual movement into minds and from first-personal narration to third. We read Zweig for the power of his moral imagination, for his generous yet incisive vision of the political folly and moral absurdity that developed from German social life in the period surrounding World War I, a vision fully epitomized in *The Case of Sergeant Grischa* and continually extended thereafter. His leisurely pace and omniscient view afford ample space for that fullness of things necessary to political and social realism.

Moreover, a broad philosophy of life is adumbrated by his habits of style and his typical structure. The animal imagery natural to a disenchanted vision of the degradations that war imposes on men is offset by the biblical references which, in almost every novel, act as icon to recall the worthiest characters to a higher standard for human endeavor. Man may often be reduced to the bestial, but he can also approach nobility. This judicious balance of mind, a temperament that looks on all with equanimity, is best shown by Zweig's structural use of adversary relationships and legal imagery to depict the case of Wilhelminian Germany. The direction in which the balance tips is revealed by the persistent figure of one just man, who, as an intellectual, is considered an outsider to be sure but also a perennial cause for hope in social affairs. Zweig seems profoundly to believe that men *can* learn from experience, however panful, and so raise the ethical level of their insights and aims.

Compared to the emotional impact of such antiwar writers as Remarque, Renn, or Latzko, Zweig gently moves the psychological response of his characters and of his readers to the side of the stage. He chooses, rather, to dramatize the external events that affect his actors as they affected the course of twentieth-century history. A critic has summarized Zweig's approach thus: "It is rather as if this calm and scholarly Zweig, setting down in all its intricacies the pattern of a nation turned into a unique and gigantic war machine, were sketching for some academic journal of the future the outlines of a world which once existed."[52] The four volumes taken together do indeed provide such a panoramic outline, but the growth of Zweig's vision and technique, as well as the differences among the subjects he chose, necessarily reveal a distinctive tone and temperament in each book. *The Crowning of a King* may be a thinly fictionalized study of Germany's latter-day *Drang nach Osten*, but *The Case of Sergeant Grischa* meets higher novelistic standards, for its "ultimate subject is man in history, or human life conceived as historical life."[53] Beginning the cycle in the relatively calm period of 1926 - 27, he could invest the *Grischa* novel with an optimism that almost belies the novel's outcome but reflects the author's persistent hopes. *Grischa*, more than any other fictional work of Zweig's, corresponds to the aims and historical perspectives of other pacifist authors:

They hoped that realistic descriptions of violence and human sacrifice would convince the public of the need for universal and perpetual peace. Yet they managed to depict war as an inexorable fate that governs the lives of men. Zweig's Grischa as well as Remarque's young men and private Renn were its victims. It appeared as though destruction rained down on man like an act of providence the cause of which was unknown and the repetition of which rational means would be powerless to prevent. The reader could easily be led to conclude that since war was an emanation of an unknowable fate, conscious struggles for peace would be in vain.[54]

But even in the static *tableau* that is *Grischa,* Zweig asks the
questions that, merely by being posed, begin to dispel the interpretation of war as an act of providence. The course of the Grischa
case condemns human inactivity more than it laments cosmic actions.

Zweig's enterprise fluctuated with the deepening crisis of the
Weimar Republic; his search for the roots of Germany's failed
political life in its social divisions and economic inequities grew more
pointed and persistent as, all around him, chaos gave way to a new
surge of nationalistic fervor and class resentment. In the novels subsequent to *Grischa,* as the implications of events symbolized by
Grischa's death became clearer, Zweig constructed a past state of affairs out of imaginative threads, verified by data that uncover the
human and historical forces which operated on the German army. In
Young Woman of 1914, that peculiarly German tradition of unpolitical idealism is tenderly but critically explored, while in *Education before Verdun* its crassly materialistic underside is revealed under the strains of war. Focusing on his theme with increasing purpose, in both novels Zweig fuses individual experience with historic
occurrences, and he does so without sacrificing either adherence to
objective truth or the full vitality of his characters in their mul-
tifaceted motives. Only in *The Crowning* does the tangled legacy of
the campaign in the east overwhelm the human experience meant to
illustrate it. By 1937, Zweig's fiction had developed far beyond the
limitations of the war novel as narrowly defined. The full texture of
German public life had pressed itself on him as a theme, and his own
political wisdom was bitterly extended even as he depicted the social
education of Lenore Wahl, Christoph Kroysing, Werner Bertin, and
Paul Winfried. The pressure of deadly events drove him from Germany, and to different subjects.

All four novels in the cycle which Zweig called *The Great War of
the White Man* occasionally suffer from the problems and dangers of
so gigantic a project. Zweig offers no easy solutions, only thoughtful
analysis of very complex situations. In that sense he attempts to
function as both novelist and historian, and at his best he achieves
the rare and happy synthesis of both:

Each of them makes it his business to construct a picture which is partly a
narrative of events, partly a description of situations, exhibition of motives,
analysis of characters. Each aims at making his picture a coherent whole,

where every character and every situation is so bound up with the rest that this character in this situation cannot but act in this way, and we cannot imagine him as acting otherwise. The novel and the history must both of them make sense; nothing is admissible in either except what is necessary, and the judge of this necessity is in both cases the imagination.[55]

CHAPTER 4

Insulted and Exiled

IN a letter to Sigmund Freud, Zweig described himself as a
"late bloomer. It always takes me six months longer than
others to get to the bottom of anything, but when I do, as you know,
I really get to the very bottom of it."[1] Zweig indulged in poetic
license in claiming that he took a mere six months longer than
others. Just as almost a decade passed before he converted his experiences at Verdun and the eastern front into fiction, so the threat
of fascism and the actual National Socialist seizure of power in Germany did not occupy a central place in his works until considerably
after the fact. While his backward glance from Weimar to Wilhelminian Germany in the Grischa cycle illuminated the course of German history and society, however, his political idealism distorted for
a long time the shape he assigned to events and movements after
1928 in the works he published from Palestine in the 1930s through
the mid-1940s.

Two of the war novels, *Education before Verdun* (1935) and *The
Crowning of a King* (1937), were already products of physical exile,
if not of intellectual realization of its meaning, for Zweig had
traveled to Palestine in 1932 to explore it as a possible new homeland
and, after another year in Germany, returned to stay for fourteen
years. The final volume of the original tetralogy manages only to sus-
tain historical authenticity; both simplicity and empathy are severely
undercut not only by the tangled political web described but also by
the bitterness of Zweig's experience of exile. He was aware of his difficulties, but temporized about their possible origins or consequences. Beginning *The Crowning*, he wrote that the material "cries
out for organization and contraction, and the latter I worry about.
Am I not obliged, for this work, to sacrifice form and become German, that is shapeless, and merely to sketch the breadth of the topic,
even if I cannot control it?"[2] Zweig was not able to perceive at this

125

time that the shaping of the material might have brought him into a confrontation with its ominous significance that he did not want. In the evolution of new material, Zweig was as deliberate as always. Finally, all that had happened in Germany since his departure, and the particularly difficult adjustment to life in Palestine, took their toll. For Zweig, as for all exiles, the words of Lion Feuchtwanger became valid: "Gradually, whether we want it or not, we are changed by our new surroundings, and everything we create changes with us."[3] For Arnold Zweig the change meant the shattering of one more ideal — the dream of a just society under Zionist leadership — and the new creation reflects this loss of every illusion about his successive homelands.

Zweig's road to exile paralleled the grinding paths of flight and hectic searches for refuge encountered by thousands of others. In February and March, 1932, acting out of an awareness of imminent doom and a curiosity about the practice of Zionism, Zweig visited Palestine. Although charmed by the landscape, and disturbed by doubts about his return to Germany, he later reported that he soothed his instinctive fears upon his return by glancing at his writing desk, where he sighted the photograph of Sigmund Freud, which "was so like a greeting from the center of European creativity, of the most sincere goodness and the greatness of European intellect, that, sighing and laughing, I turned around and told myself to attend to my mail and get to work and stay put — Freud did not run away either."[4] The burning of the Reichstag, about a year later, finally awakened in Zweig the recognition that Germany was about to enter an age of illegality,[5] and three weeks later he traveled to Prague, where he made the decision not to return to Germany. Reunited with his wife after some tense and terrifying experiences, he joined a large and distinguished group of German refugee intellectuals in Sanary-sur-Mer on the French Riviera.[6] There he worked on a study of German Jewry, *Bilanz der deutschen Judenheit 1933* (Balance Sheet of German Jewry, 1933), which was published as *Insulted and Exiled; The Truth about German Jews* in London in 1937. Late in 1933 "we had a choice of two countries as homes in our exile, the USSR or Israel. My wife and I chose Israel."[7] The Zweigs arrived in Tel Aviv on December 21, 1933, and for the next fourteen and a half years lived on Mt. Carmel in Haifa, a period interrupted only by trips to Europe and the United States in the summers between 1936 and the outbreak of World War II.

I   *The Shattered Dream: De Vriendt*

For a "conscious Jew and Zionist" (BJ, 140) arrival in Palestine should have signaled a gratifying return to his own people and the opportunity to aid in the exercise of the mission of Zionism in daily life. Until 1932 Zweig enthusiastically endorsed Zionism, including the colonization of Palestine by Jews from eastern Europe, less to give all Jews a homeland than because the particularly Jewish traditions of justice, progressiveness, intellectual drive, and endorsement of civil liberty would here create a more humane state and society. He expected the "civilizing or moralizing influence of Judaism"[8] to be incorporated into the practice of politics and the administration of government, and to merge, somehow, with the other peculiarly Jewish tradition of socialism: "Jews have been driven into the ranks of the proletarian parties less by their intellect than by their socially sensitive blood, blood which was the mainstream of every form of socialism in the world, from Moses to Gustav Landauer."[9] That Zweig should think of the Jews in the terms and categories he had applied to other nationalities and religions, in terms of blood, is more regrettable than it is surprising. Easy generalizations, high-sounding theories, and involved profundities had been among the dangerous tendencies of German academic and serious journalism since the nineteenth century. Zweig's Zionism was indeed originally based on the slogan *"zurück zum Volk"* ("back to the people"), on the notion of spiritual rebirth through return to the "genuine, old foundations of *Volkstum* ("ethnic nationhood"), and not reliance on the false and artificial bases of the Bismarckian conglomeration of principalities."[10] But his vision gradually evolved toward the special synthesis of Jewish nationalism and international socialism for the practice of which he considered the Jews equipped by their origins in the Mediterranean and the history of the Diaspora. What Zweig expected from this amalgam was a kind of high-minded nationalism that would be peaceful, tolerant, democratic, and elevated above an aggressively *völkisch* nationalism through its union with socialism. In Zionism "nationalism and ethnicity [*Volkstum*] would overlap but not exclude each other" (BJ, 304 - 5).

The trip to Palestine in 1932 damaged but did not yet destroy this vision. The results of his confrontation with the reality of Zionism are apparent in the last novel Zweig wrote in Germany, one characteristically based on old news filtered through his current state of mind. He had heard of, and occupied himself with, the case of the Dutch poet and legal scholar Jacob Israël de Haan well before his journey, when the incident had made international headlines in 1924. De Haan — who, in his youth, had flirted with every ism from anarchism to socialism, written mystical poetry, described his battle with homosexual tendencies in novels that are thinly disguised autobiography, studied law, and joined the Dutch Socialist party — finally abandoned his family and emigrated to Palestine in 1918. At first, working as a correspondent for Dutch papers, he was an ardent Zionist. Disillusioned by the growing particularism and combativeness of the movement, he joined the ultraorthodox and rabidly anti-Zionist Agudat Israel group. He became known and despised in Zionist circles for his pro-Arab memoranda, primarily on legal issues dealing with religious practice in holy places, which he wrote to the British Mandatory authorities, and for his alleged involvement in intrigues with Arab nationalist leaders. His lectures at the Jerusalem law school were boycotted by Jewish students, and he was repeatedly warned to cease his pro-Arab activities. On June 20, 1924, he was assassinated in Jerusalem, not — as Zweig learned to his great shock in 1932 — "by Arabs, as I had believed for seven years, but by a Jew, by a political enemy, a radical Zionist, whom many people know and who is still alive. Now I know how terribly that struck me, although at first I scarcely noticed it. I revised the outline of my work; the new information forced me to look at the affair without pro-Jewish prejudice, to illuminate the murder of one Jew by another Jew as if it were a political assassination in Germany, to continue on the road of disillusionment as far as necessary, as far as possible."[11]

To Zweig, the news of de Haan's real murderer served the same function as the first report he heard about the execution of the deserter on whom he modeled Grischa — in that instance a sudden flash of insight laid bare to him the true nature of German militarism, while fifteen years later, piercing knowledge grew of the unsuspected violence of Jewish nationalism. But what was now worse, the central distinction he had made between Jewish Zionism and German nationalism — the renunciation of violence and aggression — suddenly proved to be questionable. In 1932, while Zweig wrote the novel based on the case, he interpreted it as the disconcerting symptom of a single disorder. The character and fate of de Haan, as portrayed in De Vriendt kehrt heim (De Vriendt Comes Home, 1932), mirror the author's private fears, his doubts about the nature of Zionism, and his confusion about the role of the individual in a society which sustained its direction from sources and peoples strikingly varied and often clashing. Subsequently, his personal fears were justified, his doubts confirmed. But for the moment, he was able to view his disquiet with impartiality, molding it into a taut and suspenseful novel. He uses the troubled life and death of a volatile man first as a symbol for the distress of uprooted European Jews, then as a focus from which to examine the nature of justice in an emergent and threatened society, and finally as an occasion to prescribe his own remedy for the question of Palestine.

The character of de Haan, "this orthodox man who cursed the God of Jerusalem in unpublished poems and loved an Arab boy — this significant and complex figure gripped me while he was still in the news."[12] What fascinated Zweig and led him to depict this man as the main character in his only Palestinian novel is the duality in the man's nature between theocentric rigidity and the vital pulses of natural existence — a duality Zweig recognized at the very center of Palestinian life and at the core of any future Jewish state. De Vriendt laments the split in his life and soul:

Such was the terrible caprice of God, who had selected him for his toy. He alone and nobody else had been chosen, and God was having fun with the Black-Whiteness of his two worlds. During the day and on the outside he was a man of will and intellect, a loyal servant of the Torah, but since he had met the boy Saud, when it turned dark the strength of his will and the boldness of his arguments departed, and he was left the prisoner of a cursed passion which he had not picked for himself, but which had been plucked for him by a mocking God. The more he fought against his passion — and he had done so without interruption — the more powerful it seemed to become. (DV, 55)

In De Vriendt's revolt against a playful and incomprehensible God, Zweig sees a struggle against the role of the Jews as a chosen people, a role which has brought little glory and much suffering and one which thwarts the pride achieved through accomplishments of one's own will. De Vriendt's passion represents the price he must pay for the power of his intellect, just as his people must pay for being chosen — or considering themselves chosen. He cries to God that "your ears are stuffed with wool and cotton and wax" (DV, 86), but he is as little able to free himself from the worship and study of God's word as he is to liberate himself from the passion that controls his instincts. Torn between the law of the Torah and the finely chiseled beauty of Saud, De Vriendt's existence is drained of purpose and energy.

In the strongly psychoanalytic ending of book I, Zweig suggests that Jewishness, the "Jewish essence" which he has described, can exist only in the Diaspora, when it is free to soar or sink without attention to, or responsibility for, such mundane matters as government, economics, or transportation. De Vriendt's affliction is analyzed as an attempted return to his innermost nature, for "whenever an adult loves a child with passion, he seeks himself in that child" (DV, 118). His passionate attachment represents a personal search for national origins which the Jews experienced too long ago to hold in memory, a longing for that childlike innocence first denied by the special role chosen for them and then destroyed by the brutal persecution unleashed by it. Jews, Zweig implies, have been unable to integrate the rigid moral demands and strict requirements of the Torah and ritual practices on the one hand and, on the other, suppressed natural instincts — the same conflicting demands of God's law and human nature which cruelly mock De Vriendt. Denied the social roots and national identification which Zweig believes could have led to integration and thereby to a healing of the internal division, the Jews have been forced to nourish the very duality that sets them apart. But De Vriendt's dramatic bifurcation, "the boldness of his arguments" with God against his condition, has had no social equivalent, no maturely developed external counterpart in most periods of recent Jewish history. Thus, like De Vriendt, the Jews have been forced to turn inward, to seek in themselves what was unavailable or forbidden outside. And Zweig compiles a Jewish "Who's Who" of European culture to support the argument that Jewish achievement is intellectual, dominated by the heartfelt desire for social progress, by a tendency to logic to the point of "revolutionary capacity for abstractions" (BJ, 214), primarily in mathematics, and by a skill in verbal expression. But he leads us to conclude that both intellectual achievement and predisposition to socialist utopianism are consequences of the inaccessibility to Jews of expression and activity in the spheres of power and politics. Zweig, in one of his early Marxist insights, remarks that

the Jews, although they don't want to admit it, although their external life style and culture speak against it, are essentially not bourgeois but proletarian — judged by their social situation. They may be proletarians in comfortable ten-room villas, with academic degrees and learned professions, but the distinguishing characteristic of the proletariat's condition is also theirs: they are unable to determine or secure their present or future circumstances through their own power, since they neither possess political guarantees nor own the means of production. Wherever they have been granted equal rights and civil liberties they deceived themselves about their situation. Most of them never realized that once these privileges were revoked, they had no means by which to regain them. (BJ, 280 - 81)

Palestine, to be sure, offered a large number of Jews the first opportunity in modern history to determine all aspects of their destiny. No longer were utopian dreams or mathematical abstractions required as substitutes for social roots or political and economic independence. But Zweig's title for book I of *De Vriendt*, "An Intellectual Alone," and his fascination with de Haan/De Vriendt reflect his doubts about the survival of these very same Jewish qualities.

While book I concentrates on De Vriendt's internal conflict and external isolation, book II shifts its focus to the political circumstances of his murder and its repercussions. After De Vriendt's death, with the exception of Zweig's customary intrusions at the openings and conclusions of many chapters, the novel is reported from the viewpoint of Lolard B. Irmin, chief of the British Secret Service Administration for southern Palestine. Irmin is very much the externally wry and cynical but genuinely sympathetic and humane Englishman described in Graham Greene's fiction, and his dry logic serves as a cool focal point from which to view the hot politics and intrigues of Palestine. Discovery of De Vriendt's relationship to Saud, after the assassination has taken place, elicits from Irmin no raised eyebrows or pained shock. Irmin "thought that love was love, and everything else just humbug and prudery" (DV, 187). It is unduly harsh to identify Irmin with his government's "imperialist and exploitative policy,"[13] for he is shown to be skeptical of England's intentions and understanding about the entire area. De Vriendt wins his friendship for the stubborn integrity of his orthodoxy and the seemingly total dedication of his battle against hedonistic Zionism. Thus Irmin serves Zweig's purpose by drawing out De Vriendt's misgivings about the situation in Palestine. To prevent the victory of "imperialist Zionism" (DV, 60), he is willing to enter into alliances with the Jordanian throne, the notoriously anti-Semitic Grand Mufti of Jerusalem, or the Communist party of the USSR. In Irmin's response and in Zweig's asides, this obstinate dwelling on a Messianic resolution to the Jewish problem and its accompanying contemptuous underestimation of quotidian politics and economics represents nothing short of "the inaccessibility of reality to De Vriendt and his followers, their imprisonment within themselves and their intellectual world" (DV, 98).

Reality, however, eventually intrudes on De Vriendt. Three recent young Zionist immigrants, filled with bitterness against those orthodox Jews who "bring the ghetto along with them wherever they go, even into the heart of Jersualem" (DV, 157), plot the assassination of the treacherous De Vriendt. Much like Sarrow in *Pont and Anna*, who killed Anna in part to avenge her betrayal of German youth and *Volkstum*, these young men speak of De Vriendt and orthodox Jews as *Volksfeinde* ("enemies of the people"), and decide that "it does not matter who among us performs the assassination, it will be an anonymous deed. It shall be carried out by the people" (DV, 158). After De Vriendt is shot on a Jerusalem street one dark night, through a series of circumstantial clues and the agency of Saud, Irmin discovers and confronts his friend's killer. Alone with the assassin in a rowboat on the Dead Sea, he listens to Mendel Glass's justification of his action: "Violence makes right — that is common practice today, in Africa, Asia, Europe, everywhere. And yet it is still considered immoral. Where on earth is there still an uncompromised institution, with the authority to make moral judgments?" (DV, 328). Irmin admits lamely that indeed "absolutes are in a difficult position, these days" (DV, 328), and he decides to let Glass live if he can swim to shore. In an age in which political murders had become the *modus vivendi* not only of political parties of all shades but of governments in power as well, it is fitting that Glass should escape alive. "He was acquitted. The spirit of the times had saved him" (DV, 333).

With the ominous thunder of events in Germany inevitably in his ears, Zweig uses De Vriendt to signify the end of the line for Europe's intellectual Jews, for the fiercely individual and often highly eccentric outsiders whose contribution he had chronicled in *Balance Sheet*. Within a nationalist Jewish society the outsider's role must bring him into deadly conflict with fellow Jews who are insiders. The beleaguered colony of Jews in Palestine, struggling with parched land and coping with an Arab population angered by Jewish expansion, offered neither patience nor understanding to those not willing to submit themselves to communal life and spirit. The morality to govern social and political customs had to be shaped by, and tested against, daily reality — not, as De Vriendt would have had it, determined by categorical imperatives. His capricious idealism, which Zweig has depicted as insidiously admirable, derives from private and cultural traditions of a pre-Fascist Europe. His literary allegiances are Zweig's own. The artistic hero, whose achievement and intellectual strength stand in a subtly proportional relationship to a private weakness or deviation, reminds us of Thomas Mann's Aschenbach in *Death in Venice*. His blasphemous poems recall expressionist man's challenge hurled at the forces which seemed arbitrarily to determine his destiny.

Because Zweig felt both a sympathy for De Vriendt's passionate stance and, at the same time, concern for the integrity of a future Jewish state, he was compelled to inquire, in books II and III, into the broader implications of the political murder of a Jew by a fellow Jew. To do so, he had to sketch an entire spectrum of possible ideologies. With his usual thoroughness, Zweig reached back to stories he had written before World War I for the origins of the Palestinian problem. He reintroduced Heinrich Klopfer (see pp. 19 - 21 above) and Eli Saamen (see pp. 35 - 37 above) as representatives of the diametrically opposed strains among Palestine's settlers. Saamen, whose central experience of life as a Jew in Russia was the pogrom in which he lost his father, argues for bold and ruthless acquisition of land and an equally harsh treatment of Arabs or dissidents within the ranks: "We Russian Jews have used up all the patience we had in us, and now we must act impulsively. That must have been what the fellow felt who gunned down poor De Vriendt. 'Finally I am here to build something useful for us Jews, and now this scorpion De Vriendt crawls around and stings us in the legs. Away with the pest! Bang! There it lies!' " (DV, 204). Klopfer, the introverted and ethereal German intellectual, quickly points out to Eli that he is endorsing the creation of a superrace, and indeed Eli's language, with its reference to "pests" and "vermin," matches the worst outbursts of Goebbels or Streicher against Jews, Slavs, and other undesirables. Klopfer, ever so gently, reminds Eli that "you can't pump a man full of holes and then soothe your conscience with talk of building greater things. A human being simply is not a pest" (DV, 205). Between Eli's brutal combativeness and Heinrich's lofty idealism — he echoes Zweig's belief in the "moralizing mission" (DV, 197) of European Jewry in the Near East — there thrives no down-to-earth decency, no synthesis of healthy self-preservation and generous coöperation.

Only two sources offer hints of an interpretation of events free of passionate prejudice. A few Communist laborers suggest that it will not do to "ignore a tragic situation, only because it creates great difficulties for us. After all, who got the money from our purchase of land? Certainly not the fellahs or the dockworkers in Haifa's harbor.

Instead we enriched our enemies — Arab nationalism, too, is a
product of the big property owners — and made the situation here
more explosive by increasing poverty in the country" (DV, 260).
Clearly Zweig feels very strongly with Klopfer that no ideal can ever
justify inhumanity, but he also begins to imply that even
humanitarian ideals require concrete manifestations in daily life.
Levinson, a Communist foreman, condemns all such acts of individual terror as the murder of De Vriendt as "deplorable, childish
outbursts of madness, not necessary in the struggle of the proletariat
against its exploiters" (DV, 288). These associations between
socioeconomic reality and the struggle for Palestine occur only twice
in the book, and are easily passed over.

Central to Zweig's view of Zionism and Palestine, however, is the
death scene of N. A. Nachman. Nachman is meant to represent
Ahron David Gordon (1856 - 1922), one of the founders of the
Zionist labor movement. Gordon, who emigrated to Palestine in
1904, preached a "religion of labor," a renewal of the spirit through
settlement on the land and communal agricultural labor. Man, not
the regime or society, must be changed. In the novel, Nachman is hit
by a stray bullet, and Irmin is among the many volunteers who
donate blood to the dying man. On his deathbed he speaks once
more of the philosophy he has lived so long and well, offering a
Tolstoyan vision of hard work and harmony as he recalls "the endless
toil and hardship of the first seven years after the war, the gradual
flourishing of the settlement, where there existed no private property or special privileges, and where he had performed his daily tasks
as an equal among equals" (DV, 277). Nachman's theory of self-
realization suggests a policy toward the Arabs directly opposed to Eli
Saamen's militancy. Nachman only hints at what the actual Gordon
expressed so eloquently: "Our attitude toward them must be one of
humanity, of moral courage which remains on the highest plane,
even if the behavior of the other side is not all that is desired.
Indeed, their hostility is all the more reason for our humanity."[14] On
the other hand, settlement life excludes Klopfer's idealism and
Levinson's socialism as well. Zweig, unwilling as yet to commit
himself to Marxism, unable to return to German idealism, embraced
Nachman/Gordon's "organic socialism" for its gentleness and
simplicity. This, the only calm point he could find in a landscape of
inflamed passions and grandiloquent slogans, seems sadly outdated
and impractical for 1932. His actual experience of life in Palestine
within two years after completion of the novel, taken with the course

of world politics, was to propel him toward the programmatic form of Marxism with which he had been flirting since the early 1920s.

De Vriendt is free of the superstructure of cosmic viewpoint and fatalistic comment found in most of Zweig's novels. This does not mean that Zweig's novelistic ambition was content with a simple representation of life. Zweig carefully takes to pieces, reassembles, and elucidates for the reader a particular group of human beings, their social situation, and their private emotions. The novel is constructed in his typically centrifugal fashion, moving outward from De Vriendt's inner torment to the people caught up in his assassination and finally to the broad scope of the politics and ethics of Zionism. While the first book, with its emphasis on De Vriendt's psyche, is a bit overrefined, Irmin's pursuit of Glass and the description of the hostilities attain a direct intensity. How easily minor skirmishes can turn into major tragedies Zweig had learned from his preoccupation with the outbreak of World War I, and in this novel his insight turns to prescience. Over thirty years after its publication *De Vriendt* has not lost any of its timeliness; together with Arthur Koestler's *Thieves in the Night* it is one of the few original and incisive works of fiction about Palestine and Zionism.

II *Disillusionment and Retreat*

Zweig in exile has been described as feeling "misunderstood, unfairly treated; two of the talks he gave in Palestine were entitled 'The Psychological Consequences of Deracination' and 'Emigration and Neurosis.' He could not and he would not renounce the continuity of his creative writing in order to get closer to the new world. He made no effort to learn Hebrew, he did not go out to the people but waited for them to come to him. The landscape profoundly attracted him but his human contacts were confined to people from Central Europe."[15] The picture is accurate enough, but it lacks insight into his special needs. Zweig not only faced the usual difficulties of exile — worries about his livelihood, the effort of acclimatization, and the absence of any response to his work — but he attempted simultaneously to come to terms with his intellectual past and his former homeland. The continuous flow of his writing was one of the few constants left to him and the only road open to reach an understanding of his life. By continuing his World War I cycle in exile, he slowly worked his way toward an approach to the present, while his essays and journalistic pieces reflect his more superficial, day-to-day reaction to events since 1933. When the two lines of thought and work merged in the late 1930s, they determined Zweig's decision to become a "Marxist socialist" and allowed him to write about the present as well as the past within the framework of his new ideological orientation.

His attitude toward Palestine, however, was direct and unsparing. He reacted to most things Palestinian with immediate irritation or hostility. The first letter from Haifa to Freud, written on December 21, 1934, is filled with complaints about Haifa's unpredictable central heating. After repeated references, he becomes aware of the pettiness of his grumbling and concedes: "You will note, dear Father Freud, that I am overflowing with information about central heating. But such questions of practical life, with the barely functioning machinery of civilized life, create the major problem in this country. We are not willing to give up our standards, and this country is not yet ready to meet them."[16] This sweeping judgment sets the tone for Zweig's reactions over the next years. But what is worse, the carping over small matters leads rather directly into renunciations of more important associations. In the same letter, he announces that "I no longer attach any importance to the 'Land of the Fathers.' I have no Zionist illusions left."[17] The correspondence reveals a deepening alienation from the country and its people. In 1936 Zweig breaks any remaining ties with Zionism: "Everything in me opposes life here in Palestine. I feel completely out of place. Provincial conditions are made even more provincial by Hebrew nationalism which permits no other language access to publication. Therefore, I must lead a translated existence. But if I have to be translated into English, why here? I have little connection to Jewish nationality. But Heaven knows, I am a Jew."[18]

In response to Zweig's complaints Freud offered wry puns (turning the preoccupation with central heating into his central problem) and an expression of hope that Zweig will cure himself of his "ill-fated love for his alleged fatherland" and similar "gush" (*Schwärmerei*).[19] Inaccessible to such gentle remonstrance, Zweig remained as naive about Germany as about Judaism. He viewed events in Germany as if unable to distinguish Hitler and his followers from Kaiser Wilhelm and his court. He predicted for the National Socialists only four years in power, and as early as 1935 he already speculated on the post-Nazi period: "How long do you think the brownshirts will last in Germany? Afterwards I don't expect a red or pink regime, although logic demands it. Instead I imagine a liberally tinted monarchy, perhaps Wilhelm's grandsons, as soon as they have removed the Nazis with the help of the Army."[20] That someone who had written so penetratingly about the German army and German aristocracy could expect an alliance of these two forces to possess either the will or the power to oppose Hitler shows how much wishful thinking had replaced clear-headed analysis.

An observer of exile literature, commenting on the revival of historical settings among many emigrant writers, suggests that "it must have fulfilled a need to escape the insoluble problems of their time; but it also led to the creation of several important works which held up the mirror of history to the distorted face of the present."[21] Although Zweig continued work on his World War I cycle through the 1930s, he also turned to historical drama for relief from present tensions and, he hoped, new perspectives on current events. Between 1934 and 1938 he wrote *Bonaparte in Jaffa*, a drama based on an incident in Napoleon's Egyptian campaign of 1798 - 99. In the spring of 1799, Napoleon's army captured three-thousand Turks in Jaffa. Since the French navy had been destroyed by Lord Nelson at Abukir and Napoleon's forces, already reduced to ten-thousand men, were preparing to march on Acre, neither transportation nor provisions were available for the prisoners, and they were executed. Out of this historical episode Zweig fashioned a morality play about the relationship between war, revolution, and human responsibility. It opens with the decision of the generals around Napoleon to shoot the prisoners for strictly tactical and logistic reasons, to which Desgenettes, Surgeon General of the Army and Zweig's familiar "just man," promptly resonds, "we are soldiers, not butchers" (D, 503). But neither he nor anyone else can find an acceptable solution to the dilemma. A proposal to let the common soldiers decide if they wish to share their meager rations with the prisoners is tested, with calamitous consequences. Given the choice between food or "upholding the ideals of the Revolution and human rights" (D, 522), one soldier coins the Brechtian slogan "Human rights are valid only as long as our stomachs are full" (D, 523). As so often in Zweig's depressing chronicle of historical decisions, from Grischa to the Turkish prisoners, power and materialism emerge victorious over morality and humanity.

Focusing on the distant past, Zweig attempted to draw contemporary philosophical implications from his treatment of the material. Grosjean, Desgenettes's chief assistant, tries to justify the massacre by arguing that the ideals of the revolution will survive only as long as they survive in the minds of human beings, in the minds of the

French populace. But after coming face to face with the sight and stench of the dead prisoners, no man can mouth words of higher justification or military necessity. The soldiers curse the campaigns into foreign lands which force them to "attack the defenseless like robbers and murderers" (D, 559). Grosjean understands that in Napoleon he has endorsed a dictator, not a liberator, and therefore has defended not the idea of the revolution, but merely its ruins. His suicide at the end of the play confirms Desgenettes's — and Zweig's — conclusion that any revolution is only as good as the men who make it. When Zweig completed the drama, he was convinced that one should not base one's hope for peace and humanity on the Lychows in Germany or the Grosjeans in France. Their "no" to evil power comes too late and from suspect motives. Desgenettes resists Napoleon from the beginning, and only such consistent opposition to every abuse of power and violation of human rights can truly call itself revolutionary or humane.

In response to the obvious question, Zweig emphatically denied that he ever thought of "comparing the figure of Adolf Hitler with Napoleon Bonaparte in any way whatever" (Fk, 177). To be sure, the resemblance between Zweig's Napoleon and Hitler is not exact. Zweig's character, apart from his military talent, is an indecisive and humorous bourgeois. To his mistress he is "Polly," who cannot make up his mind and worries about Josephine's affairs while he should be paying attention to her. When he paces up and down in their bedroom, mulling over his decision about the Turkish prisoners and engaging in geopolitical fancies, she taunts him with, "Aren't you ever going to knock off work today, shorty?" (D, 544). Even without the inopportune mixture of tones, it is difficult to discern a specifically anti-Fascist intention in the work. Unnecessary military adventuring, grand national ambitions, offenses against the "rules" of warfare — all these Napoleon commits, but they do not comprise an indictment of fascism as such. If, as Eberhard Hilscher argues, "we experience the transition from republic to dictatorship,"[2] we must accept it as having taken place prior to the play's opening scene. Nor does a comparison between the downfall of the French Republic and of Weimar Germany seem to be warranted simply by the fact that both were succeeded by dictatorships. Zweig's intentions for the play's wider resonances strike his usual, very generalized note. He described the play as a "drama of war and peace,"[23] and as such it offers two notable innovations from his prior treatment of the theme. For the first time the portrayal of the common soldiers is not altogether favorable. The French grenadiers exhibit little of the common man's goodness and tolerance granted German, French, and Russian troops in *Grischa* and *Education*, and Napoleon convinces his men of the rightness of his decision with ease. Zweig's new, disillusioned outlook was no doubt shaped both by the events of Hitler's seduction of the German masses and by the theories of group behavior he learned from Freud. In addition, Grosjean's suicide represents Zweig's rejection of revolutionary fervor not supported by constant examination of the revolutionary performance. It indicates that Zweig was ready to replace his admiration of the vague socialist dreams of Landauer or Gordon with the acceptance of a concrete party program and plan.

In 1946 Zweig wrote another historical drama, *Austreibung 1744 oder Das Weihnachtswunder* (Expulsion in 1744, or the Christmas Miracle). Like *Bonaparte* it is a meticulously researched study based on the expulsion of Prague's Jews by Empress Maria Theresia for their alleged cooperation with Prussian troops during the city's occupation. Zweig ascribes the reversal to miraculous means. The unseasonal blossoming of a rare plant at Christmas time, rather than the urgings of the Czech merchants or the British ambassador, persuades Maria Theresia to permit the Jews to return. Only two young people, a Jewish student and the daughter of a Prague aristocrat, foresee the consequences of the expulsion for Europe's Jews and depart for Massachusetts, where the young man plans to study medicine at a new university near Boston. Almost an afterthought on the Jewish theme, *Expulsion* is weak and unconvincing. Perhaps Hitler's death camps had tempered Zweig's disillusionment with Zionism and left him with the desire to write something positive and conciliatory about Jews. The miracle is either the resort of an exhausted imagination, or the *deus ex machina* of a nontheistic man. By 1946 Zweig had been occupied with current politics for almost a decade and was convinced of the right course to world peace and the formula for a just society. Within his newly constructed political framework, Judaism, merely another manifestation of nationalism, no longer had a place.

III *Politics: Past and Present*

As early as 1930, Zweig alluded to the future direction of his political thinking. After Freud had attacked the "Soviet jumble of despotism and communism,"[24] he replied rather coolly that "the capitalist economic chaos is not prettified by the awful consequences of communist terror. We live in a difficult period of transition, and no one knows what it will lead to. The class struggle of our society becomes more open by the day. In the past one could escape through an ideology — into the future via socialism, or out of modern society, the discontent of which you illuminated so brilliantly, into Rousseauian Zionism. Gradually we learn that there is no escape, that the social conflicts must be confronted and, I fear, still in our life-time."[25] In an autobiographical essay, Zweig accounts for the root of his confrontation and its significance:

After 1934, surrounded by emigrant families who were all products of the Jewish bourgeoisie, I realized that it was their social background that had shaped these peoples' consciousness. Until then my educational path had not led me to the works of scientific Socialism by Marx and Engels, since my professors at German universities had assured me that their dialectical method derived from Hegel and had no greater importance for our time than Hegel himself. (Fk, 160).

But even before Zweig received a collection of works by Marx and Engels from German exiles in Moscow in 1940, he had moved to an endorsement of Marxism and exchanged the Schillerian ideal for the Marxian statement that "society determines consciousness."

It may be correct that Zweig's Marxism was initially more ornamental than fundamental,[26] but from the midthirties until his death he adjusted his writing, first his journalistic pieces and during the war his fictional work, to his own interpretation and acceptance of Marxism. His essays begin to express solidarity, no matter how knowledgeable, with the aims and the theory of communism. Thus in an essay of 1936, dedicated to the imprisoned leader of Germany's Communist Party, Ernst Thälmann, he lists himself among the ranks of the "working men and women of Palestine," and refers to "the battles we fought side by side with Thälmann and his party" (E II, 93).[27] The pieces written just before the outbreak of World War II reflect in style and vocabulary his espousal of Communist doctrine. "Congratulations to the USSR" in 1938 concludes with a hymn of praise to the Soviet Union whose efforts "defend peace in Europe today and combat the victory of lynch law and lobotomizing on the European continent. Whoever writes or speaks today must count himself a fellow combatant on the side of the Soviet Union unless he wants to become a liar" (E II, 115). True to his word, Zweig rolled up his sleeves and worked and wrote for Russia when World War II began. He was one of the chief spokesmen of a German-speaking group of Communist intellectuals, and he was chosen as chairman of the V-Liga ("Victory League"), an organization dedicated to raising financial and moral support for the Soviet Union in Palestine. He gave speeches to collect money for ambulances for the Red Army and attempted to persuade his listeners that the USSR was the major protagonist in the fight against fascism. In addition he was cofounder of the journal "Orient," to which he contributed political and literary essays. Because of the socialist and internationalist stance of the magazine, it attracted few advertisers. Even then, it might have survived longer had not rabid Zionists threatened its distributors and sellers. A bomb attack on the printing plant forced Zweig and his coeditors to cease publishing after only one year on April 7, 1943.

While Zweig was thus actively involved in the politics of his time, his creative work caught up only slowly with his journalistic concerns. Before confronting the issues of the period, he cast two long glances backward and examined the end of two eras, each prior to the outbreak of one of the world wars. The short novel *Versunkene Tage* (Days Faded Away, 1938), published as *Verklungene Tage* after 1945, is the rewritten version of a manuscript dating from 1909, saved from the Nazis only because a typed copy existed.[28] Zweig treats once more the sexually and socially inhibited young student hero typical of his earliest stories. But in the afterword to the 1938 edition he recalls that "after 1933 everything changed, including the point of view from which I saw the manuscript of this novel. Suddenly it became a historical document, testimony to the life-style of German youth at that time" (VT, 221). Although the same afterword refers to the novel as "green apples" (VT, 222), it had become a sharp yet humorous and pleasantly sentimental evocation and critique of the last years in Germany before the lights went out for the first time. The novel can be divided into three parts. The first, comprising three of the twenty-two chapters, describes successively "The Hero," "His Milieu," and "His Friends." Carl Steinitz, a twenty-two-year-old student of English and German literature in Munich in June, 1908, is at war with an ego which conceals both the world and his own feelings from him. He "wants to be rid of this self. . . . I don't want to think, he thought, here it is June and spring and I am not getting any pleasure out of it" (VT, 10). His every attempt to break out of the prison of self stumbles over yet another manifestation of his all-encompassing self-consciousness: "I ought to fall head over heels in love. Now *that* would provide interesting stuff to observe and think about. Maybe it could even develop into a grand passion, if I am still capable of anything so marvelous" (VT, 13). No exhortations or commands will liberate his feelings.

Zweig depicts with brittle humor Carl's immediate surroundings, the bourgeois world of Munich, secure and smug in its beery *Gemütlichkeit,* and the proudly Germanic headiness of the university. Carl is aware of the brutal and bigoted core underneath the *Gemütlichkeit.* "I had to move in the middle of the term because I could not stand it anymore that my landlord, the upright Mr. Schmautz, beat his eight-year-old boy. He only did it when drunk, but when I tried to interfere, he verbally and physically attacked foreigners, Prussians, Jews and me" (VT, 8). His seminar on Shakespeare, given by Professor J. J. Calw, "only rarely treated the dramatist William Shakespeare from Stratford-on-Avon, but rather a German of the same name, who exhibited striking kinship to Schiller, Wildenbruch, and Richard Wagner, and whose Hamlet is transformed into the young Siegfried" (VT, 15 - 16). Yet Carl and his fellow-Silesian friend Georg Berndt lead a pleasantly Bohemian existence. In their regular café they mock the petite-bourgeoisie, exchange literary and cultural ideas and gossip, and keep up with the latest contributions to the fashionable journals. They regularly attend performances at the opera and the theater. Life would be altogether normal for Carl, were it not for his inability to enjoy things, his need "to experience something great, something robust" (VT, 13).

The opportunity to fulfill his mini-Faustian drive arises in the second part of the novel. Chapters IV through IX chronicle Carl's infatuation with and rejection by Hermine Altmaier, a pretty and clever music student. Carl's love basks in its own glow. Hermine allows Carl to escort her to operas and picnics but mocks the precious comments meant to impress her. Her probing conversations elicit from Carl an infatuation with Nietzsche and the individuality of the poseur. He insists on the absolute "purity of art" (VT, 52), "believes in nothing but life" (VT, 54), and subordinates all of life, "from daily affairs to intellectual recreation, to the dictates of artistic taste" (VT, 58). Unsurprisingly, Hermine rejects his declaration of love, presented to her in the form of a poem. His reaction, ranging from compulsive chatter about love, God, music, and night to contemplation of suicide, is interrupted and undercut by his awareness "that he was really just performing his unhappiness for her eyes; in reality he only felt pitiful" (VT, 81).

After the episode Carl loses himself gladly in delicious degeneracy at the beginning of part III. Neglecting his work and appearance, he of course is "delighted by his run-down condition" (VT, 85). He shaves off his moustache and, as his friend Berndt observes, "cultivates his precious ego like a vest-pocket deity" (VT, 119). Still harder to bear is his own awareness that even his fantasies of injured pride and *Weltschmerz* are false. Yet they are now all that he is capable of. The search for a great romance and the worship of *l'art pour l'art* have blunted the capacity for all detail, whether in the world around him or the sensations within. Like the new and proud German Empire, Carl has elevated all aims and ideals to a grand scale, and thereby lost any eye for the small things which are at the heart of private life and public affairs. During a vacation in the Bavarian mountains he makes the brief acquaintance of a man who looks like Heinrich Mann, and Carl rather haughtily announces his philosophy: "The most important thing to my generation, to use Schiller's words, is the aesthetic education of man. Politics doesn't interest us, we prefer to leave it to the professional politicians. And the masses, well, if only they weren't so ugly. So unrefined and common. So hostile to things of the mind" (VT, 137f.). The stranger's admonition that "man needs much bread and hope before his sense of beauty can be developed" (VT, 138) is greeted by a Wildean sneer.

Carl's earthy education commences with alacrity shortly thereafter. Seduced by the sensual Nadja, Carl discovers the aesthetics of the body. His conversion to the new pleasure is instant and total. After making love to Nadja for the first time he feels "as if he had discovered the meaning of life only just now" (VT, 161). However, Carl does not merely swing from disembodied aestheticism to revels of the flesh. Involvement with Nadja leads to an awareness that neither books nor bedroom alone shape and determine our lives. Nadja tells him of her recent participation in the 1905 Revolution in Russia and of the efforts of the Czarist police to drive her out of Germany. Gradually, political events, such as the kaiser's scandalous interview in the famous *Daily Telegraph* affair, become an integral part of his life and thought. Urged on by Nadja, he chooses contemporary characters and backgrounds as themes for his creative writing. Zweig has Carl write the story about the pogrom in which Eli Saamen loses his father (see p. 35 above), and slowly the bits and pieces of twentieth-century Germany and Europe become trenchant material for his literary imagination. Since the first meeting with Nadja, the word *Gegenwart* ("present") has become a leitmotiv which occurs with increasing frequency in the last chapters of the book, until the real present overtakes and separates the two at the end. Nadja is hounded out of the country by the kaiser's police at the request of the Russians, while for the young men of Germany "induction was in the air, mobilization, and soon thereafter war. War in Europe, the unimaginable was about to happen" (VT, 198). As Nadja's train is about to depart for Zürich, tears well up in Carl's eyes. "Nadja looked at him incredulously. 'You are crying,' she cried out, 'for Nadja! You are a human being!' " (VT, 204).

Carl's growth to maturity is not restricted to a physical or emotional affirmation of life alone. Intellectual activity, in Zweig's favorite Marxian phrase, can now also be determined by social awareness. In *Days Faded Away*, ideas are adequately symbolized by — and in turn adequately motivate — events in the plot and the psyche. From the outset, Carl had been working on a lecture about the poet Walter Calé (1881 - 1904), a brilliant scholar of Neoplatonism who wrote *Ich-Dichtungen*, highly egocentric poems in the style of Hofmannsthal, based on a distortion of Kant's philosophy. Although Calé destroyed the greater part of his manuscripts, the one extant poem considered characteristic is "Der Denker" (The Thinker):

> Was sich in Zeiten je begeben,
> hab ich vor aller Zeit gewußt:
> es springt der Quell von allem Leben
> geheimnisvoll aus meiner Brust.
> Und als ich in der Schrift gelesen,
> erlas ich nur, was ich schon bin;
> in Finsternis sind alle Wesen,
> doch ich das Licht und ich der Sinn.

> All that has happened in the past
> I have known long ago;
> the source of all life
> mysteriously resides in my soul.
> And when I read the Book
> I merely found, what I already was;
> all beings are in darkness,
> but I am the light and the meaning is me.

No reader will be surprised to discover that the author of these verses killed himself at the age of twenty-three. Prior to his *Bildung* through Nadja, Carl had planned to concentrate his lecture on a justification of Calé's noble suicide. After Carl has become "a human being," Calé's glorification of self as the source of all light and wisdom seems an excessively other-worldly mystique, hardly an attractive philosophy for a young man enjoying his first love affair. Carl's lecture explores Calé's life and closely analyzes a few poems, but then he departs from the prepared text to announce that "life is reborn every day, and its forms cannot be prescribed by poetry. To affirm the nine-hour workday, and the treadmill of school, and after that the treadmill of the office, that is a task we can't expect young people to perform without great effort. But genuine and creative criticism cannot proceed without this affirmation, which should not be interpreted as approval or blessing. However, daily routine must serve as the springboard of art" (VT, 181). In Carl's statement Zweig has described, however glancingly, a quality found previously only in the Grischa cycle and which his early stories lacked, but which now infuses this novel. It may be best explained in Lionel Trilling's term "moral realism," defined and defended thus: "Is it not of the first importance [in a novel] that we be given a direct and immediate report on the reality that is daily being brought to dreadful birth? . . . Any defense of . . . moral realism must be made not in the name of some high-flown fineness of feeling but in the name of simple social practicality."[29] But Zweig suggests that Carl Steinitz was an exception rather than the rule in his generation; in 1938 he endows Carl with a social vision which he surely wished he himself might have possessed in 1908.

Skilled practice, as well as advocacy, of "moral realism" gives *Days Faded Away* its substance and effectiveness. Zweig evokes the student world of Munich in 1908 not in a naturalistic inventory but by an artfully realistic selection of the sights, sounds, and smells of dark student cafés and of the bacchanalian madness of a Munich *Fasching*, when "bourgeois life takes a break and releases its instincts" (VT, 191). Threading through Munich life, the novel's parallel lines of development — Carl's psychic liberation and his social awakening — carry the evocations of time and place along until the themes merge in the end. Carl hears about Hermine once more, and the reader is led to expect that she may now accept the man she rejected as a boy. Moreover, Zweig sprinkles the story with much unexpected humor; even the usual Freudian allusions are lighthearted and often self-mocking. By gently refracting his country's cultural past and his personal life Zweig obviously found surcease. Thomas Mann would have liked *Days Faded Away*.

A second study of Europe at the eve of war places Carl Steinitz, now the father of two children and an art dealer, *Über den Nebeln* (Above the Fog) high in Czechoslovakia's Tatra mountains in the last few days of 1932. Originally written in 1936, but published in revised form in 1949, the lengthy novella sketches the dreamlike lethargy and naiveté with which Europe's Jews drifted into the holocaust. A middle-aged Steinitz is portrayed as the devoted father of two sons whose mother has been absent for some time, because she has resumed her career as a singer. Carl and his twenty-three-year-old secretary-mistress have come to the Tatra so that Lutz, the younger son, can recover in the mountain sun and air from the deprivations of the Weimar Republic's lean years. Little happens in the forty-eight hours during which the daily activities of each member of the family are traced with meticulous care. Meals and walks, a skating accident and afternoon naps, political discussions and the New Year's Eve ball in the hotel are presented like pictures from the family photo album. The note of unreality derives both from the isolated locale and from attitudes just as rarefied as the air in the snow-capped mountains. Steinitz, well aware of the "unfathomable tears in the moral crust of the world beneath them" and of the thin hold which "the deception called European culture" (N, 31) has on reality, offers in response only what is, in retrospect, a self-destructive hope "that everything remain as it is now" (N, 152). Only authorial intrusions, prophetic rather than reflective in nature, predict the bloody fate that awaited millions of Steinitzes and their children: "In the fog down there a world was being created which, without shame and in broad daylight, would assemble, deport, and exterminate thousands, legions of children like Lutz and millions of adults with them — barely noticed and unimpeded by the rest of the world" (N. 31).

Steinitz, still the man of culture and taste, can only explain anti-Semitism to himself in August Bebel's definition as "the socialism of fools"; the deeper causes within Germany's society remain unexplored in his mind and in the novella. In an authorial intrusion Zweig comes to Carl's aid by suggesting that "the Jews, in their stupidity and fear, were politically moving to the right" (N, 113), but this notion — almost certainly added when Zweig revised the manuscript after his return to East Germany — also ignores the truth.[30] More important, Steinitz dismisses the gloomy predictions of a friend by blandly stating that "he takes the moment too seriously. He already sees our doom when everything is just talk of parties and their foolish programs. Life doesn't follow party programs, I assure you. Germany is not going to turn into one of those Balkan powder kegs of our youth or into a South American banana republic" (N, 137). The tragedy of Steinitz lies buried within the period between 1918 and 1932, in the complex social and psychological responses of German citizenry to the trauma of defeat and the chaos of democracy. The young Steinitz of the previous novel understood the situation when he proclaimed, during a sober moment at the carnival, "knowledge, consciousness, self-knowledge, and intellectual discipline have made us great. And now we are paying for it" (VT, 190). The Germans continued to "pay for it" even after the war, since the public virtues and private standards of Wilhelminian Germany remained essentially intact within the educational, judicial, moral, and even political institutions of Weimar Germany. Steinitz grasped one reason for Germany's road to dictatorship in 1938, but he fails to see even its late fruits ripen in 1949. It remains for Zweig to enter and reveal that "someday you [Steinitz and family] will look at 1932 in the same light as 1913" (N, 116).

The striking similarity between the endings of these two works also offers the key to their real difference. The young Steinitz offers melancholy but wise criticism of his whole generation and time, while the older Steinitz's vague simplifications of Freud's analysis of anti-Semitism are only sad. The artful world-weariness of Munich created a useful distance between self and world, while the tired other-worldliness of the high Tatra permits the self to slide into the night and fog below. In place of the earlier judgment there is only a sigh. Perhaps too many things in Weimar Germany had been left undone to produce the vision to understand or the will to oppose the barbarism that was coming. *Days Faded Away* concludes with a discriminating look to the future while in *Fog* the characters are caught up in "the present that had arrived, but a present misunderstood and underestimated" (N, 153). Zweig could only compose a gentle indictment of Steinitz for his lack of foresight and commitment and a Kaddish for the fate of his generation.

With the two "end of an era" works Zweig had prepared his literary imagination to cope with the present. If his historical plays followed one trend common in the literature produced by exiles from the Third Reich, *Das Beil von Wandsbek (The Axe of Wandsbek)* coincides with another: "The emergence of novels concerned with contemporary society as a whole. This was a new development with only very few antecedents in Germany."[31] For Zweig, of course, the development was not new — he had sufficient antecedents in his own work of the 1920s. His investigation of the political role played by the German army in World War I and his portrait of the involvement of all social classes in the war distinguish him from "the emigrants [who] saw Germany with a new detachment and in a radically changed light."[32] Always something of an outsider, he had looked at society as a whole with detachment. The revelation in *The Crowning of a King* that camps for political prisoners existed on the eastern front links the first thrust of German totalitarianism in the past with its official victory in the present as portrayed in *The Axe*. In 1937, the year in which *The Crowning* was published and *The Axe* conceived, the camps of 1918 had been reestablished in greater numbers, and the brutality practiced within had increased. By this time, Zweig's firm political allegiance to Marxism and the reports of increasing National Socialist atrocities propelled him to concentrate on current events above past origins — the new novel, written between 1938 and 1943, forsakes the long historical view of the cycle to telescope a whole social spectrum into just one year.

The immediate impetus to write *The Axe* was similar to the flashes of inspiration, generated by news events, that served for *Grischa* and *De Vriendt*. In the afterword to the English edition of *The Axe*, Zweig relates how the book "was inspired by a report which the author found in 1937 in the *Deutsche Volkszeitung*, at that time published in Prague or Paris, and was worked out and brought to completion during the following years. By spring, 1943, it was finally committed to paper, so that its translation into Hebrew could appear that year."[33] The newspaper account, although full of minor inaccuracies,[34] tells of the suicide of a Hamburg butcher and his wife in 1937. Four years previously, while the official executioner was ill, this butcher beheaded four anti-Fascist victims of National Socialist justice for a fee of two-thousand marks. After the news of his role in the execution had spread through the district, boycott of his business had driven the man and his wife to end their lives. Zweig saw in this story "the seed of decline in the very rise of the Third Reich;"[35] In order to illustrate how nazism's fall was contained in its rise, he condensed the time between execution and suicide into the year between August, 1937, and September, 1938. Within that brief compass, he attempts to present and analyze all possible answers — psychological, cultural, socioeconomic — to the anguished question, "Why?"

The first two books of part I set the scene for Albert Teetjen's encounter with history. For some time his store has been losing business to the meat counters installed in department stores. With the aid of his wife Stine he composes a letter to his old World War I comrade, the rising and ambitious shipowner Hans Peter Footh, and asks for help. Footh's mistress is Annette Koldewey, the daughter of the director of Hamburg's central prison, so he suggests to Koldewey that Teetjen carry out the execution of the four condemned prisoners, thereby doing his mistress's father a favor, helping out an old friend, and hoping to advance his own career in the eyes of Berlin, since Hitler had vowed not to visit the Hanseatic city until the sentences were carried out. Within the initial pages, Zweig's intention to present a kind of passivity of evil as the atmosphere of Germany in the thirties becomes clear: "The events we are to witness here, culminating in four swings of an axe, a pistol shot, and the tightening of a soaped noose, often have their origin in a trivial action. In this case it was the energetic thrust of a pen into an inkwell by the powerful hand of Albert Teetjen" (W, 7). Teetjen's individual course, however, is meant to be exemplary for Germans of all classes and backgrounds. Koldewey, an admirer of Nietzsche and gentleman of taste, expresses to his daughter what Teetjen slowly comes to sense: "You are only an instrument, and so is your friend Footh, and so am I and so are all of us. Something is being performed in the world today, and we have the honor of being allowed to play along" (W, 20). Perhaps, like most Germans, not committed to national socialism, he "learned to look the other way. Races are distinguished by the quantity of things they deign not to notice" (W, 56). Within this vast body of acquired ignorance and self-imposed impotence, Zweig charts the network of human irresponsibility that spanned National Socialist Society. With the exception of the four condemned men and their comrades, even the "rabble" are shown to accept — and in most cases to welcome — the inevitable. The prophecies implicit in the Grischa cycle have been realized in *The Axe of Wandsbek.*

The remainder of part I, following the execution, dissects the intellectual and social attitudes of educated and intelligent Germans. While the Teetjens retreat into lower-middle-class anonymity, Zweig explores the German rejection of western Europe's nineteenth-century achievements of individualism, equality, and freedom. Koldewey's ruminations reflect a particularly German and strikingly egocentric view of life: "The world, he thought, was curiously comparable to his shaving bowl. From the little table on which it stood, it curved invariably outward, and seen thus it was convex. But to him it curved invariably inward, and from his viewpoint it was concave. So it was with human relationships" (W, 16). This statment typifies a widespread attitude. One commentator on the German scene goes so far as to suggest that the German

spends his life (after childhood) creating a network of established relationships centering on himself. Since this is his aim in life, he sees no need to make any effort to see anything from any point of view other than his own. The consequence is a most damaging inability to do this. Each class or group is totally unsympathetic to any point of view except the egocentric one of the viewer himself. Yet at the same time [the German] insists that his vision of the universe must be universalized, because no people are more insistent on the rule of the absolute or the universal as the framework of their own egocentricity.[36]

The human relationships depicted in *The Axe* delineate the stubborn power of such egocentricity as well as individual efforts to break its power. Zweig shows that Koldewey's casual reflections, when applied to social relations and political maturity, lead to deplorable consequences. Thought, action, and inaction in the lives of Koldewey, Footh, and Dr. Käte Neumeier — the former sweetheart of one of the executed men, who exposes Teetjen as the executioner and later marries Koldewey — betray the individual abrogation of judgment and therefore the collective responsibility created by the abandonment of private opinions to external and mass discipline. Koldewey escapes from the discomforts of his own situation behind the protective shield of culture: "It was the duty of an educated man neither to aspire to know everything nor to let anyone else see his cards. If a man was smart he lay down on his bed with a volume of Nietzsche and smoked a good cigar" (W, 16 - 17).

Koldewey's benign retreat into drawing-room privatism contrasts with Footh's opportunistic manipulation of group acquiescence and individual paralysis to advance his career. On a trip to Berlin to gain support for his plan to take over a Jewish shipyard, he observes that "behind desks of various heights and sizes sat German men with nothing particular to distinguish one from another. Their faces were thin or round, their eyes were brown or black or blue . . . but their functions were always partial, they refused any responsibility, they always referred him for decisions to a higher authority, enthroned above the clouds in the realm of the gods, controlling the triumphant renaissance of Germany, according to a definite plan and goal, and with total ruthlessness and guile" (W, 192). Zweig paints a dismal picture of German abnegation of responsibility at every level and in every sphere — social, moral, and legal. Footh attributes his good fortune to "God [who] must surely have a great destiny in view for the Germans or He would certainly not have sent them Adolf Hitler" (W, 192). Thus he echoes the deification of Hitler expressed by Göring's "God sent you to us for Germany" and Goebbels's "Above all was God's hand which has visibly guided the Fuehrer and his Movement."[37]

Only the gradual awakening of Käte Neumeier, a scientist and a woman, focuses attention on the gap between national socialist program and practice, ideology and reality. Her attention is drawn to the very individual helplessness which Koldewey and Footh excuse as culture or glorify as destiny. The execution of her former friend Friedel Timme destroys her faith in the possibility that Germany's new order could combine nonmaterialist aims with material order, classless ideals with a just distribution of wealth and power. Her discoveries of the hypocrisy and inconsistency, however, are restricted to general social comment and based on personal response — she is no flaming rebel. Zweig places her in the same position he assigned to Private Sacht in *Grischa*. She, too, is asked to help in an escape, and she, too, refuses. When Friedel Timme begs her to supply him with a steel file, 500 marks, and a motorcycle, Käte "looked at him with horror in her eyes, and rose slowly from her chair. 'You mustn't ask me to do such a thing,' she whispered. 'I can't do it!' " (W, 106). With Friedel's laughter at her refusal ringing in her ears, Käte begins to observe daily life around her, the viewpoint of other classes and groups, and the ethnocentric vision that permits rigid judgments and condemnations of everything not German. In complete reversal of Koldewey's escapism and Footh's fatalism, Käte accepts her role in the four murders as one she shares with all other Germans, a collective plunge into intoxication or madness, a shared sense of abandon. On the return trip from a visit to the zoo she asks herself if she, too, has become "capricious, and incapable of self-control — indeed should she rank herself with the inmates of the institution whose huge buildings they were just speeding past, the Friedrichsburg lunatic asylum? Friedel Timme and the innocent and decent Mengers beheaded; a butcher, Albert Teetjen, promoted to be executioner; an admirable person like Annette involved as an accessory in the affair; and Käte Neumeier too cowardly to supply the five hundred-mark bills that were needed" (W, 167).

Käte convinces Koldewey and Lieutenant Lintze of the accuracy of her image; soon they, too, come to see Germany as an insane asylum with Hitler as its mad director — a surreal vision captured long before in the brilliant film *The Cabinet of Dr. Caligari*. But their insight, primarily psychological and limited to reflection, frustrates rather than liberates them. Although they talk and scheme, their plots lack sufficient grounding in social reality to convert plans into action. As Zweig grew convinced of the Marxian critique of capitalist society (and national socialism is shown to be a form of state capitalism), he began to question Freudian theories of group behavior as the central explanation for Germany's turn to fascism. Thus Käte and Koldewey discover works by both Marx and Freud in the library of the executed Mengers; while she reads both, Koldewey refuses even to consider Marx. He is already sure that he cannot agree with Marx's idea that "man's consciousness was determined by his economic condition. The phenomenon of fascism, with all it had brought into being, contradicted such a contention — neither the romantic nor the sentimental attitude to life, with all they involved, could be thus explained." He offers instead theories he draws from Freud: "In fact, political mentality and mass consciousness were subject to the law of group interests. It was quite likely that the advent of a savior, a miracle worker, did indeed put man's critical faculty out of commission" (W, 258). Koldewey's shallow objections to Marx testify to the futility of Freudianism in the face of sociopolitical terror. Moreover, purely psychological explanations for mass hypnosis must apply to the analyst himself, must be turned inward on his own psyche and shred the very logic that built them.

The destructive potential of Freudian analysis is fully revealed in a dream of Koldewey's which climaxes and concludes part I. Zweig thus depicts truth in a Freudian way, but he reveals as well the utter powerlessness of merely psychological insight to take any action, effect any change in a complex and terror-laden world. The dream is a phantasmagoria of German culture and German cruelty, of Brahms and blood, but soon the Brahms turns into marching music, and the axe of Wandsbek is laid before Koldewey in the innermost chambers of his dream house — which smells of Brahms and fire and roses — until he awakens to a voice calling from the abyss. "He would gladly have peered into the abyss from which Brahms' grandiose inspirations came, and the great rose, and the cushion with the axe on it, but he could not do so now, not even in remembrance. He had seen men standing there below, with high bald foreheads, mops of wild hair, Brahmsian beards and Nietzschean moustaches, genuine nineteenth century" (W, 306). Even in his subconscious mind, he posits only German high culture as the cause of Nazi butchery. After the cathartic dream comes a return to the "cool air of Hamburg's lucid critical intelligence, the conviction that two and two make four" (W, 307), but also the bitter regret that it is

"too late, too late, because we Koldeweys did not indulge in revolutions when things didn't go our way. We kept quiet and waited, and knew that everything would turn out all right in the end. In such quiet aloofness we survived the Weimar Republic, in which a party governed that preached such doctrines as 'Material existence determines consciousness.' As if the autonomy of the spirit were not one of the most precious discoveries and achievements of European civilization! And as if the higher element in man were not so precariously poised as barely to protect him from the slime in which materialism and Karl Marx were trying to engulf it. Every reasonable man is ready to pay a price for the expulsion of such intellectual poison." (W, 301)

None so blind as those who refuse to look outside their dreams. Koldewey's dream, like Freud's analysis of cultural discontent, can only describe the progress of a disease, while it provides a very limited answer to its origins — and no remedy whatsoever for its prevention or cure. Neither Marx nor materialism engulfed Germany in the "slime" of 1933. The origins of that disaster are rooted, as the dream suggests, in the nineteenth century, including the development which Marx perceived as man's alienation from his own humanity and his fellow human beings. In 1940, when Zweig began to write the novel, he had learned from Marx that man is shaped not by ideas and family alone, but by society as well. Having gently mocked exclusive dependence on psychic and intellectual roots, Zweig turns in part II to an examination of the social and economic forms which made and in turn were made by Hitler's Germany.

A recent study of the book remarks that "reference to economic conditions as determinants of the Fascist state of affairs remain external and are only presented as occasional anecdotes."[38] Close examination of part II reveals, however, that — while a thoroughgoing Marxist critique is missing — socioeconomic conditions of Nazi Germany become the focus of attention for the reader and the decisive force in the shaping of the characters' lives. The opening of the second half returns once again to the Teetjens and their economic

decline. By January, 1938, four months after the execution, Albert's
business has come to a standstill. He is compelled to think about the
inclusion of the two-thousand marks on his tax returns, about the
reasons for the boycott of his store, and eventually about the social
and economic situation which such small matters imply for all of
Germany. Teetjen belongs to that group of small businessmen and
petite bourgeoisie among whom the dual appeal of national
socialism had its widest-based success. The emotional voice of
nationalism and the much-relied-upon promise of socialism, as Karl
Bracher points out, never "aimed at any concrete socialization, but
only toward a change in social consciousness, an unconditional
loyalty to the political regime."[39] Teetjen's reflections represent the
total victory of such Nazi propaganda:

He, Albert Teetjen, an independent butcher and owner of his own store,
stood in an ambiguous relationship to the workers. When their women came
into his store to buy bacon, pork stomachs, and beef stew, he was pleased. A
well-paid working class formed the backbone of trade and commerce. But
when they united to demand higher wages, exercised trade union terror and
waged class war, when they pushed their representatives into the Reichstag
and organized strikes — then Albert Teetjen slammed his fist on the table
and worked himself into a fury. That was insubordination and sedition. They
exhibited neither patriotism nor loyalty to the Reich! Moscow lurked behind
every corner. This part of the thing had to be dealt with — and if necessary
by means of an axe. (W, 70 - 71)

Thus his personal decline, sudden and seemingly unfounded, forces
Teetjen to explore and finally to expose the central role of class interests and private greed in a regime that claimed to represent
national interests and suprapersonal unity.

Teetjen's financial decline parallels Footh's economic rise. The
success of Footh and his assistant Vierkant proves the truth of the
slogan that the rich got richer in Hitler's "social revolution," which
exploited Teetjen's ambivalence to announce a war against
bourgeois civilization, and then turned around to use the middle
class to strengthen the growth and power of capitalist trusts.[40]
Moreover, Footh and Vierkant mock the so-called "socialist" element of the Nazi program, a reality revealed in a chapter appropriately headed "The Law of the Jungle." Vierkant candidly exposes for what they really were the ideals and promises that won the
support of Teetjen and millions of others. He coolly forecasts the
doom of the small businessman, a group from which the Nazi party

drew moral and monetary support essential to its rise: "There no longer is any room for little one-man businesses. The key to the future, gentlemen, is organization, and we all must subordinate ourselves accordingly" (W, 438).

Zweig clearly wants to link the willing hierarchical subordination, practiced in Germany since Bismarck and brought to a climax under Hitler, with its emotional as well as social and economic effects. Teetjen's economic collapse is accompanied by a process of alienation rooted in insight and disillusionment. His SS squad, with whom he had felt united in bonds beyond base materialist designs, decides to accept or reject him strictly on his payment of 10 percent of his executioner's fee to its funds. In the chapter ironically titled "Comradeship," Teetjen realizes that in that realm, too, sanctified by the memory of World War I and supported by the mystique of National Socialist ritual and communion, "The Law of the Jungle" has taken over. His first thought of suicide occurs just when he has seen through Nazi ideology and simultaneously lost his personal, although very subordinate, role in the Nazi hierarchy. As he cleans his pistol he "did not know against whom he would like to use that weapon. Yesterday he still believed in his Führer, but today something seemed to have gone wrong with the party, some impenetrable and impalpable evil presence had descended between him and his people. Had Hitler not proclaimed to the Reichstag just the other day with thundering voice that his will alone prevailed, that nothing could be done except through his knowledge and by his order? But what about the outrageous nonsense of last night, the business with the two-hundred marks! That was blackmail and usury!" (W, 424). With his dim recognition that the inner shrine of national socialism, in which he had worshipped, served Mammon and Mars, the psychic underpinning of his allegiance begins to crumble. His bloody deed no longer stands as an isolated act of opportunism or a dedicated show of loyalty. He asks Stine, " 'Why did I make such use of my axe last year?' 'Because your Führer wanted it,' she replied with conviction. He nodded and lighted his pipe as he glanced at her agonized face with its wide eyes penetrating the darkness. 'But why do people like us need a Führer?' 'Because you all shouted for one,' and Stine touched his right hand, 'and because you learned to follow a Führer.' 'Yes,' he nodded and sighed, 'that's God's truth. There was always someone to follow. First my father, and grandpa was around too, and the teacher and the pastor, and the classmates in my school. Then the sergeant, the company commander, the battalion, and the regiment. And then the speakers at the party meetings. One after another.' 'You were always a good fellow, Albert,' she said to him" (W, 481).

Zweig has used the economic deception practiced by National Socialist leadership to lay bare the history of German middle-class obedience and insecurity, its tragic refusal to identify its aims and share its power with the working class. The maintenance of position and class, with its emphasis on status and culture, obstructed a clear view of reality and a healthy pursuit of economic goals — to say nothing of social justice. Not only Teetjen would pay the price for his ambivalence toward the workers. Intellectuals and idealists, with their aesthetic distaste for politics and proletarians, are shocked by the raw drive for power at the core of National Socialism. Koldewey's daughter Ingebottel tears down the last veil from the mantle of Nazi idealism and reveals underneath what Hans Kohn called Germany's "self-centered power and self-glorification."[41] "I asked daddy what he would do if Nietzsche's doctrines were actually put into practice and the blond beast waged total war against the west or the east. He explained that the realities of thought were purely intellectual. They were valid only within that realm and did not count in the crude world of daily life, and then he blabbered on about a cave and Plato — fortunately I can't remember all the things he said. These old gentlemen are going to be surprised when the younger generation, with the Führer in the lead, puts them all out of business" (W, 538).

Zweig's broad panorama of Nazi Germany cannot be viewed as either exclusively psychological or wholeheartedly socioeconomic, although his interpretation of Germany's acceptance of Hitler corresponds closely to that of Georg Lukács.[42] Zweig treats both the ideological seduction of the upper middle and the intellectual classes and the economic deception of the petite bourgeoisie. Nor does he absolve the working class of its responsibility for the triumph of national socialism. Although a 1968 postscript to *The Axe* depicts the people's role in the course of Germany's tragedy as that of followers of its upper classes, as "guilty and guiltless," the first edition dryly comments that "a people is always responsible for what is done in its name" (W, 388). In Zweig's version, only four dead men escape from complicity in the creation and support of the Third Reich. The fact that the Reich consumed its own children, that the perpetrators of evil could become its victims as well, strengthens rather than weakens Zweig's interpretation of Nazi society. Teetjen is not made more sympathetic by his troubles, or ennobled through his suicide. He never shows regret for his action or sympathy for the four men he has executed. He remains always a small and weak man, not particularly incisive or reflective, easily influenced and swayed. The political and social passions and prejudices which are shared with millions of others he has picked up along the way — in school and in the trenches, in his bar and on the streetcar. He was, after all, not trained to ask the right questions, and many better-educated Germans did not ask them either. Zweig sees the inability or refusal to ask such questions rooted in the structures of Wilhelminian Germany and their continuation in the Weimar Republic. The economic disaster of the republic was merely the final step in the conversion of the German Everyman into the Hangman.

With *The Axe of Wandsbek* Zweig completed the last step in his own intellectual development. The Marxism of the novel is implicit rather than explicit. The emphasis on economic and social affairs in the second half gives meaning to the tortuous intellectual debates and psychological monologues of the first half. The details of daily life and the disappointment of economic reality authenticate the bits and pieces of intellectual history and psychological speculation of the first three-hundred pages. Ingebottel's prophecy for Germany, which was soon fulfilled, returns us to the core around which Zweig's search for the basis of a just society revolved again and again: the cautious, well-judged thinking of wise and humane men absolutely must be brought to bear on public life. Cultural pursuits for their own sake lead to sterile snobbery, while politics without the staying voice of enlightened intellect soon becomes a jungle of greed and opportunism. Zweig's own unwillingness to commit himself to any policy or program, knowing it would be imperfect when realized, was finally crushed by the ultimate vulgarization of German idealism. In the 1940s he granted the stature of public model to Heinrich Mann, whom he had summarily waved away in 1908, then revived in 1938 as a Cassandra. In an essay of 1942, Zweig writes, "We all recall that a few years before World War I, under the leadership of Heinrich Mann, there began an era in European intellectual life, which was called the period of Activism. Activism demands the unification of mind and action in all spheres of public life — social, political, ethical and intellectual" (ÜS, 64). Zweig's cycle of war novels had uncovered repeatedly the gaps that existed between those spheres, in public life and in private thought. Zionism proved no exception in the history of failures to achieve the desired synthesis, for it merely brought European divisions to foreign soil. *De Vriendt* reveals the ruthlessness of idealism unreconciled with humane practices in the conduct of daily affairs. In his glances at Carl Steinitz in 1908 and 1932 German and German-Jewish blindness to Mann's Activism and a churlish refusal to engage in the vulgarity of action show the pleasures and dangers of acquiescence in the status quo. *The Axe of Wandsbek* finally transforms acquiescence into action — destructive and self-destructive. Missing from Zweig's work is what one might have expected as a successor to the Grischa cycle — a novel of Weimar Germany. The fragmented vision of Weimar Germany that emerges from his novellas of the 1920s attests to the difficulty of a question Zweig did not want to answer too easily or simply: was Nazism the inevitable outcome of the course of German history? The Grischa cycle outlines its origins and *The Axe of Wandsbek* its triumph and consequences. Zweig's always thorough and orderly mind found no clear bridge, manageable in fictional form, within Weimar Germany. At the end of World War II, Marxist socialism offered that bridge from the many yesterdays into the tomorrow always dreamed of.

CHAPTER 5

Twice-told Tales

WHEN World War II ended in 1945, Zweig entertained no doubts about who deserved the major share of the credit for the defeat of Nazi Germany: "Long live the democratic front of all free men, groups, and nations! Long live the Red Army which, along with the whole Russian people, like Atlas held aloft a world threatened with extinction by the forces of fascism!" (E II, 229). Although the Royal Air Force and American bomber crews are granted a minor role in the war effort, it was "more than anyone else the fighting Russian people" (E II, 228) whose spirit had withstood and finally destroyed national socialism. Of course, Zweig has the right to place emphasis where he wishes, but unfortunately he was not content with stressing the Soviet Union's role in the war. When he writes that "until 1939 and with the exception of the Soviet Union the democracies refused to realize that only a larger stick in the hand of an adult will prevent the misuse of a stick in the hand of a nasty adolescent" (E II, 254), his image is obliterated by the historical fact that in 1939, while the Western democracies finally declared war on Hitler's further advances, the Soviet Union simultaneously signed a nonaggression pact with him. But by 1945 Zweig was less interested in historical truth than in ideological certainty, and his commitment increased thereafter.

Three years after the conclusion of the fighting in Europe Zweig left Palestine for what was then the Eastern, or Russian, Zone of occupied Germany. After a brief stay in the Czechoslovakian mountains he settled in East Berlin in the fall of 1948. Clearly he was convinced that only socialism could prevent another alliance of militarism, nationalism, and capitalism, in whose combined greed and aggression he saw the seeds of both world wars. And the Eastern Zone, soon to become the German Democratic Republic, was the only country in the socialist camp in which "a large reading public

159

was eagerly awaiting my books" (Fk, 161). The intellectual climate in East Germany must have appeared irresistibly attractive to a writer stranded in a country in which the language was inaccessible, the religion meaningless, and the growing nationalism ominous. What Zweig heard and read about the Russian Zone, moreover, was not simply propaganda. "For many German intellectuals, the spring of 1945 ushered in a period of great expectations. The Soviet army and the German Communist administrators returning from exile did nothing to discourage these hopes; for about four years (1945 - 1949) it appeared that everybody was cooperating in an effort to revive the experimental art that had flourished brilliantly in the Weimar Republic."[1] In so open and fertile a climate Zweig immediately directed his energies into the channeling of artistic efforts for the common good. He played a central role in the creation of the *Deutsche Akademie der Künste* ("German Academy of the Arts"), and when its president-to-be Heinrich Mann, who had planned to move to Berlin from California, died before assuming his post, Zweig was elected to the academy's presidency, in 1950. But by then things had changed. "The transformation of the Soviet zone into a German Democratic Republic on October 7, 1949, put an end to tactical tolerance; as Soviet policy became more hostilely anti-Western, so in the cultural sphere the vestiges of 'decadent bourgeois' culture came under attack. Early in 1950, the topic of socialist realism began to fill the papers and to dominate discussion in the cultural organizations. In the spring of 1951 socialist realism was proclaimed the doctrine binding for all artists and writers, and a State Commission for Affairs of Art was instituted to control intellectual production."[2]

Zweig's tetralogy of novels about World War I is readily classifiable by most standards as "realistic." The four volumes fall well within the tradition described by Harry Levin:

The role of the great realists — as who but Gorky pointed out? — has been to transcend their own class, to criticize the bourgeoisie. It does not necessarily follow that their successors ought to panegyrize the proletariat. Middle-class culture, with all its faults, has had its virtues — the redeeming virtue of self-criticism. "*Kunst wird Kritik*" ["Art becomes criticism"], Thomas Mann has lately remarked, and the bourgeois novel is nothing if not critical. It may have told the whole truth very rarely, and included many other things than the truth, but it has kept open the question, "What is truth?" in the teeth of dogmas and systems that strive to close it.[3]

Simply to criticize Zweig's own, middle-class culture, however, did not suffice, and he turned to the closed system of dogma. He was prepared, after his arrival in Berlin, to abandon the critical realism which had infused his past work for socialist realism, "more precisely, an uncritical idealism"[4] in which living reality is adapted to a prescribed ideal image. He accepted the new dictum that "the old realists, . . . men like Balzac, Tolstoi, and Chekhov, . . . not having been instructed in the genius and teaching of Marx, . . . could not foresee the future victories of socialism, and they certainly did not know the real and concrete roads to these victories."[5] That Zweig should now want to fashion his novels as roadsigns on the way to socialist victory, as guidebooks for proper German behavior, is a dismaying departure from the philosophically searching mind and historically exhaustive method that marked his previous novels. But in the many essays he wrote in the early 1950s he enthusiastically endorsed the concepts of socialist realism. Now, he says, he perceives the need for literature to "lead us from the great ideas of socialism into a more productive form of social life,"[6] and the novel in particular as a form of art "in which the structure is translated into the structure of the plot."[7] Perhaps Zweig already sensed what socialist realism at its most insistent would come to be, for he cautioned readers in the same essay that "nothing is further from my mind than to inject a pedagogical element into literature. Literature's function cannot be realized in a didactic fashion, cannot be achieved with the schoolmasterly forefinger raised high to drive home the point."[8]

Zweig's literary conversion to the official position of his new nation was matched by a turn to political orthodoxy, as well. Just as the young Zweig had prepared the way for his fiercely nationalistic propaganda stories by numerous essays justifying his intellectual position in 1914 - 15, so the last novels of the aging Zweig were preceded by a set of explanatory essays. At the height of the Cold War and the McCarthy era in the United States, his was one of many voices in the socialist camp denouncing and renouncing the ideas of Western Europe, past and present, as remnants of a doomed bourgeois culture. In 1950 he declared that "everything which shaped the pleasure and luster of Europe and America since 1920 has been revealed as a deception" (E II, 346), and "we have now entered the final phase in the struggle between the ascending working masses and the declining clique of profiteers" (E II, 335). As the Cold War heated up, Zweig's tone became more strident and harsher, his condemnations wider and more unequivocal. In the

past, his sharp mind had repeatedly espoused, and his fiction induc-
tively arrived at, a view of life dedicated to intellectual discernment
and the proposition that "the truth usually lay somewhere between
two extremes but not, as a wise man had noted, in the center" (see p.
116 above); now he moved from a humane position left of center to
one of the extremes. Old and weary, having experienced German
nationalism and Zionist utopianism, in search of one final and enduring philosophical doctrine, Zweig succumbed to the
revolutionary romanticism which is at the intellectual core of
socialism. That Zweig could write, in 1954, "what Christianity began
two thousand years ago is being realized by socialism today" (E II,
302), should be observed with more understanding than scorn.
Zweig's attacks on the Western liberal tradition, which rigidly follow
a Communist-party line — like his early diatribes against the same
tradition, based on a fiercely Teutonic mystique — betray the
weaknesses of a particularly German intellectual tendency as much
as a youth's fiery idealism and an old man's last commitment. His
early hope that "philosophy was supposed to provide answers to all
questions of human existence" (see p. 15 - 16 above) had found and
then been disappointed by the answers provided successively by
German philosophical idealism, Jewish utopian socialism, and
Zionist nationalism. Only socialism was left to solve the many
problems to which he had so honestly and thoroughly addressed
himself in his fiction.

Whether or not the practice of socialism in the Soviet bloc cor-
responded to Zweig's acquaintance with its theoretical projections
for a just society was a matter he had neither the energy nor the inclination to investigate objectively after 1948. It was under socialism,
after all, that his works were republished and studied, that disser-
tations were written about him and honors bestowed upon him. His
espousal of Marxian socialism, though arrived at late, was genuine.
Although the critical examination of Germany's intellectual currents
and social reality had been the central motive and unifying force in
his work, he expressed an uncritical Marxism, motivated in his
lifelong desire for social justice and socialist humanism, in the three
novels he produced after 1948. These novels lack not only a critical
stance but also the sense of excitement that comes with the discovery
and organization of suitable material to express it. Reality is determined and described by dogma. To perform this task Zweig no
longer sought in external reality events which could trigger his
historical insight and literary imagination, but turned back to past

inspirations to reshape them in the light of his new ideological framework. This method, so inimical to his usual procedure, produced the dismal results one might expect. Zweig's case is by no means unique in the literature of East Germany; "Anna Seghers, Arnold Zweig, Stefan Heim, to cite the three most prominent examples, have never duplicated their fine pre-war and wartime novels; their work of the 1950's has been depressingly retrospective, schematic, and generally unconvincing."[9]

I *Old Wine in New Bottles:* Ceasefire

No work required or received from its author so elaborate a justification as *Die Feuerpause* (Ceasefire, 1953). In the afterword to the first edition Zweig recalls that the central plot of *Education before Verdun* was originally conceived as a first-person story in 1930, then discarded in that form when he again occupied himself with the manuscript in Palestine in 1934 because "as a German intellectual it was my duty not to construct a first-person narrative out of my experience but rather to paint an authentic and objective portrait of the army and, by implication, of the state and its class struggles, which were reflected in the world of the army."[10] Fifteen years later Zweig wished to revive the original version, so that young writers might benefit from a comparison of the earlier, autobiographical account with *Education before Verdun*. But when he submitted the manuscript to the editors at his East German publisher, it was returned to him with corrections and queries. Zweig notes that "I reexamined my attitude of 1930, tested it against my current view of life, and made the necessary additions and changes dictated by my present state of mind."[11] So embarrassed and convoluted an admission of censorship as well as the long hiatus in its genesis says much about the reasons for the book's dichotomies.

Ceasefire is intended to cover the period in "The Great War of the White Man" between the conclusion of *The Case of Sergeant Grischa* in November, 1917, and the opening of *The Crowning of a King* in February, 1918. Zweig places Werner Bertin on the eastern front in Mervinsk as assistant to Judge Advocate Posnanski. To pass the idle hours in the army bureaucracy while waiting for the peace negotiations at Brest-Litovsk to commence, Bertin retells his most memorable experiences at the battle of Verdun to Pont, Winfried, Posnanski, and other characters from *Grischa*, as well as to a few figures especially created for this book. The paraphrases of Bertin's experiences should, Zweig suggests, be interpreted in the new light which the events at Brest-Litovsk cast on them. Interesting as such a conception may seem at first, Zweig's execution of it reveals a nearly complete incompatibility of new material with old, an apparently schizophrenic contrast between the Bertin of *Education* and the Bertin of *Ceasefire,* and finally the sudden surrender of the author in the face of so impossible a task. The most striking aspect of *Ceasefire,* applicable to all of Zweig's post - World War II novels, is the absence of a clearly discernible central plot. It is quite easy and pleasant to summarize the action of any one of the volumes in the original tetralogy. The reader of *Ceasefire,* however, asked "What happens in the book?" may stutter something about the political intransigence of the German General Staff toward the Communist peace overtures, something about Bertin's tales and the reappearance of some of their characters in Mervinsk, but in the end he has to admit that nothing really happens. The matrix of Bertin's life at Verdun, the dialectics of morality which emerge from the Kroysing case — perceptively traced in *Education* against the background of social and economic necessity — is left unresolved. Christoph is buried, but the agent and *raisonneur* of Bertin's realization, Eberhard Kroysing, never appears. Equally unsettling, the tales Bertin narrates are often left incomplete and hardly ever integrated into the time, cast of characters, or spirit of the novel's framework. How and why Zweig fails fully to merge Bertin's Verdun experience with the mood of the German army in the winter of 1917, how and why he fails to chart credibly the growth of political consciousness in Bertin, and how and why he fails to use the "education" Verdun provided to illuminate the historic and chronological framework into which he has thrust it — these are lessons Zweig never intended for young authors. His novelistic instincts, which rejected the first-person narrative in 1934 (although not necessarily for the reasons retrospectively suggested in 1953), prove superior to the sense of ideological pedagogy which rescued it two decades later.

Certainly Zweig is on solid historical ground when he praises the principles on which the young Soviet government based its peace initiative in the winter of 1917. The six-point program, which is accurately reproduced and extensively discussed in *Ceasefire,* included such proposals as the return of all occupied and annexed territories, the withdrawal of all troops from occupied areas, and the right of all nationalities to decide their political future by popular vote. Thus it corresponds in spirit and tone to the idealism expressed in Woodrow Wilson's Fourteen Points. That the Soviet proposal, "cleverly conceived, morally justified, and announced in a propagandistic manner,"[12] found a widely favorable response among the war-weary troops of all nations and political persuasions is obvious. Equally predictable is the ire which the resistance to these proposals by the statesmen of western Europe and their military advisers aroused in the armies. But Zweig does not adequately relate the drama of the long-drawn-out negotiations to the experiences of actual soldiers at Verdun, told by Bertin.

The trench recollections are always filtered through the vantage point of 1917 and the successful Russian Revolution, and events are often uneasily extended into the period of *Ceasefire:* they include material entirely omitted from *Education,* as well as events which are now retold from a new angle of vision and with a markedly different emphasis. Among the new selections is the case of Hein Jürgens and his refusal to obey an order to continue unloading ammunition from a train after twelve uninterrupted hours of such work at Verdun — a story now told by Bertin because he suddenly understands that "only types like Hein Jürgens made the Russian Revolution possible; without a multitude of Hein Jürgenses Lenin's speeches and articles would have found no echo in the land" (116). The kindest explanation for so abrupt and shallow a view of even one cause of the revolution is that Bertin, and by extension Zweig, is straining to find evidence in past experience to support present outlook, to build by individual examples a discernible path toward a new consciousness. Jürgens subsequently reappears in *Ceasefire,* in a disciplinary battalion; his punishment is all too obviously intended to contrast the victorious fate of just rebellion in the Soviet Union with its repression in Germany. Our knowledge about Verdun or the German army is not enriched by the addition of this episode, nor is our historical understanding of the Russian Revolution enlightened by it. In Zweig's other form of reworking, Bertin recalls the tragic fate of Ignaz Neumann, a story which played a minor role in *Education* and is now expanded to symbolic significance. In *Education* Neumann is touchingly depicted as one of those sweet, sickly souls utterly lost in the machinery of the army. He comprehends neither the general purpose nor the inner workings of the military. The British edition of the book lists him, rather cruelly but not altogether baselessly, as "the company fool" in the prefatory cast of characters. In *Ceasefire* this pathetic creature attempts to make contact with the Soviet peace delegation "to express his gratitude for their efforts toward an armistice and peace" (367) and is viciously beaten by a

sergeant for his "treasonous" boldness. Through the intervention of
Posnanski, acting on Bertin's urging, a military court-martial commits him to a neurological ward for treatment and thereby prepares
the way for his eventual release to factory duty. The distraught
Neumann, who confuses neurology with psychiatry and fears confinement in an asylum, commits suicide.

The stories of both Jürgens and Neumann effectively describe the
random brutality and sadism common in most armies, indeed typical
either physically or verbally wherever men have almost unlimited
power over other men. In each of these examples of man's inhumanity to man, however, Zweig blatantly attempts to draw a connection to national policy and ideological conviction, and in each
case the illogic of the attempted association is lamentably evident on
a number of levels. First, the treatment of common soldiers in the
Russian army, even after the triumph of socialism, is not shown to be
notably different from that meted out in other armies — so the intended contrast fails. More distressing than Zweig's evocation of so
naive a hope is his blending of past and personal injustice suffered
with present and public justice advocated. The critic Jürgen Rühle,
who views Zweig's socialism from a relentlessly hostile point of view,
illustrates Zweig's fallacy best by committing the same error in
reverse when he mocks the eulogistic treatment the Soviet delegation receives in *Ceasefire*.

How touching a picture we have here; the peace-loving Russian people approach to take over from the war-loving militarists, a new era in world
history is about to dawn. But let us ask ourselves, did German troops
penetrate as far into Russia in 1917 as Russian troops are stationed today
within Germany? And furthermore, what became of those who in the winter
of 1917 rode to Brest-Litovsk to make peace in the name of the Russian people, the people's commissars and revolutionaries? Where are Trotzky, Joffe,
and Sokolnikov, who led the negotiations? They were all crushed in Stalin's
grinder, by assassination, suicide, show-trial — those were their destinies.[13]

The unfairness of Rühle's argument, attempting to denigrate the
Soviet peace program of 1917 by association with the purges of the
Stalin era twenty years later, seems a viciously intentional distortion
when compared to Zweig's rather innocent twist of historical fact.
Nonetheless, the private sufferings of Jürgens and Neumann do no
more to extol the Soviet stance of 1917 than the terror of the 1930s
does to censure it. For the first time Zweig's skill in linking individual fates organically to societal forces and political events is

nowhere evident. The very quality which united the theme and content of the tetralogy with its texture and structure appears — if present at all — forced and unconvincing. The framework of Brest-Litovsk in 1917 and the memories of Verdun in 1916 touch, but they never meet.

In an effort to bring Werner Bertin up to date, Zweig resorts to the "schoolmasterly finger raised high" he had earlier warned against. By his insistence on reviving the account of Verdun in its first-person version, he limits any understanding of other characters' motivations and omits much background. Thus Bertin's gradual awareness of his changing consciousness should hold the center of attention. The tightly controlled focus of first-person narration, however, is undercut by intrusions of the 1917 framework in no distinguishable pattern, at the cost of the structural unity which such a combination might have afforded if well orchestrated. Sometimes the frame opens and closes a chapter or book, whereas at other times the Verdun recollections commence a chapter, are interruped in the middle, and never resume, and on a few occasions, either frame or flashback takes up an entire chapter or book. The randomness of Zweig's movement back and forth in time destroys the vertical momentum which Bertin's internal development could have attained. The one recurring image intended to chart Bertin's progress, that of the *Pfahlwurzel* ("taproot"), personifies some of the attributes of Bertin's growth which are demonstrated in the tetralogy but lacking in *Ceasefire*. Very early in the book Bertin explains the origin of the image:

And now I see my life developing according to the model of a taproot, about which I read in Maeterlinck's *The Intelligence of Plants*. There the Belgian writer reports that a hedge-mustard, a large, yellow weed, was found in his garden. This plant has a taproot as diffuse and strong as a carrot. But this particular specimen of taproot, in its downward growth, had pushed against the buried sole of a shoe. It could push down no farther. And now, so Maeterlinck maintains, this taproot has transformed itself into a threadlike, fibrous root, and in this manner slipped all its rootlets through the holes in the leather of the sole. Once beneath the sole it grew together into a taproot once again, according to the laws of nature. (24)

It is a charming story, and Bertin's war experience in the tetralogy supports at least its premise. It no doubt implies too that Zweig's own road to Marxism, although hindered and diffused at various stages of his growth, was just as natural and inevitable as the taproot's reversion to its proper shape. But before 1945, fortunately, such single-mindedness never exhausted either Bertin's character or Zweig's outlook. The attempt to instill such dogma into *Ceasefire* leads both to its awkward incongruities of perspective and to Zweig's ill-fated revisions of episodes from *Education*.

Within the pre - World War II volumes Bertin's character developed in reaction to external events and by adherence to his own nature; neither his ideas nor his personality approached finality. As a result, the wide panorama which Zweig spread out for him to experience, from the carefully tended opulence of the Wahl residence in 1914 to the stark poverty of Lithuanian Jews in 1917, could be presented critically but with empathy both by the omniscient narrator and, on occasion, by Bertin without violating consistency in point of view. The new, narrow angle of vision in *Ceasefire*, by assigning Bertin a predetermined outlook and eliminating the narrator from the accounts of the Verdun experience, permits no growth of character, no expansion of personality, no development of ideas — only the confirmation of a creed. In *Education* Major Jansch's anti-Semitism and Pan-Germanism were presented against his petit-bourgeois background and through it illuminated, though not excused. In *Ceasefire*, Bertin's one-sided and highly selective portrayal fails to capture the person that is Jansch or to confront his prejudices. Through Bertin's eyes we see no longer a human being but a caricature: "Jansch ate eggs and beefsteak for breakfast, food originally assigned to the company. One room in his quarters was filled with the contents of packages soldiers were to have received from their loved ones — jars of apricot marmalade, packages of socks and condensed milk, bars of chocolate, sausages, and hambones. All this and more the major hoarded with the wild passion of a demented miser" (327 - 28). There is potentially much more to Jansch than his gluttony, yet Bertin's revised description misses all but the superficial aspects. From such caricature the step to demonology is a short one. One German officer at Verdun "has a pig's head reddened by alcohol — but no, a pig shows some physiognomy. This, this was just a fat piece of meat that consumed food and drink, and emitted resounding laughter and croaking sounds from its mouth" (275). The vulgarity and flatness of the description recall, alas, Zweig's "The Beast" of 1914, in which the Belgian farmer, too, envisioned the four German soldiers as pigs before he slaughtered them (see p. 44 above). Just as in that early story, Zweig's analogy is a fallacious one. Human greed and brutality are self-created, not inspired by animals. Bertin's angle of vision has been more than narrowed, it has been blinded.

The "new" Bertin whom Zweig has hoped to create oscillates between the political naiveté of 1916 and the Marxist conviction of 1917, and each story he recalls should, by the reinterpretation he gives it, explain the gradual transformation of one into the other. The "education" of the original book, after all, was rooted in the experience of the Kroysing case, and proceeded in a carefully plotted relationship to a selection of incidents. A few of the same incidents, with the addition of several new ones, are now designed to elicit a radically advanced set of responses. But the two versions of Bertin in *Ceasefire* scarcely differ: the Bertin of 1916 already recognizes what the Bertin of 1917 later stridently proclaims, his early awareness simply becomes certainty, understanding becomes persuasion. No past history explains the growth of one into the other. In one of the episodes omitted from *Education,* Bertin recalls the occasion on which a replacement-lieutenant had dressed him down for not saluting in the ammunition park and the other soldiers had vocally supported Bertin, and he proposes that in that moment, "We were all workers. And one of us, namely me, had been insulted by this green and fresh college kid in uniform" (134). Yet incongruously, only one book earlier in *Ceasefire* Bertin's identification with the working class is nowhere in view. While speaking of a fellow soldier, he remarks that "he was a proletarian, period. He had to wend and punch his way through the bloody battleground of class-warfare. But Kroysing and I, we had been privileged children until we exchanged our civilian clothes for a uniform" (77). Bertin's conversion, based on distorted recollection of petty incidents, remains unconvincing.

In *Education* Bertin very gradually attains a socialist vision of the world because observation of the lives of others, caught in the conflict created by the forces of reaction and capitalism, leads him toward an intellectual endorsement. Thus when he declares quite similarly in *Ceasefire* that "in those days [at Verdun] the moral law was far more important in my thoughts and emotions than the fairness of our social order" (257 - 58), we believe him. However, when he protests that "power doesn't belong in the hands of people with souls of lice who look like Sergeant Glinsky, hauling his fat ass toward the railroad station over there" (91), the judgment is superficial and the tone false. For Bertin to turn to communism for his intellectual direction in accord with his character and experience seems credible, but for Zweig to transform this intellectual into a tough-talking worker is folly. The only genuinely proletarian character in *Ceasefire*, Sergeant Greulich, instinctively senses the false note. "You've always perceived things correctly, Bertin, and your reason and feelings always reacted incisively. Why have none of these decisions ever produced revolutionary actions, or at least resistance?" (403). Bertin finally admits that his impressions are converted by his imagination into creative impulses, and that the taproot, now grown together again, will not turn into a revolutionary instrument, not into "a knife or bayonet, but rather into a pencil, a pen" (412). There appear in *Ceasefire* all too often such contradictions between the Bertin whom socialist realism dictates and the Bertin whom the Grischa cycle had shaped. Even with the dynamic Bertin of the tetralogy diluted, Zweig cannot wholly satisfy the demands of dogma, for an East German study faults the manner in which he expressed the solidarity of the common German soldiers with the Soviet peace policy. It would have been better, this critic proposes, had "a markedly proletarian character"[14] made the gesture toward the Russian delegation rather than the bourgeois Ignaz Neumann, or had someone else other than Bertin whispered admiringly, after glimpsing the Soviet delegation at the railroad station, "So this is peace!" (414). Bertin's growing social consciousness is meant to heal the breach between form and content, but — as the socialist demurrer suggests — his political awareness is never earned. In *Education*, experience became part of his being and revised his thinking; in *Ceasefire* he only talks revolution, only tries to sound like a member of the proletariat. Surely "revolutionary careers are launched not by banquets and honorary titles, fascinating research and professorial salaries, but by misery, shame, resentment, prison, and an uncertainty brightened only by an almost superhuman faith,"[15] a route which neither the reflective Bertin nor his rationalist creator could pursue. Bertin's vacillation between revolutionary tone and intellectual caution reflects both the structural dichotomy of the book and Zweig's inability to adjust the old material and characters to new requirements.

One final example will demonstrate the sad decline in the subtlety of Zweig's powers. When Bertin reports to the infirmary for sick call one morning in *Education*, "there wasn't anything serious, the doctor observed, but since Bertin was an educated man, he had better spend the day in the infirmary." Bertin draws on his own conclusions about the treatment he receives from the physician. " 'Ah,' thought Bertin, as he stood at attention, 'if I had been a waiter or typesetter and were running a temperature because I experienced a shock, I would have to go out into the wet and do my job and catch my death of cold before I was sent to bed.' Health and sickness seemed to depend on the class to which a man belonged" (311). When the same scene occurs in *Ceasefire*, the doctor leaves nothing for Bertin's own interpretation: " 'I'll put you on the sick list for today,' he said. 'Take a rest. Be glad that you're a cultured person — I would have shipped a worker right back to full duty' " (323). No longer is Bertin allowed to learn through experience, he can only accept through instruction. The education at Verdun has been converted to indoctrination. Many of the incidents Bertin recalls are presented as fables, and one character is always present to spell out the moral, to dot the *i* of the ideological lesson. But the reader of *Ceasefire* waits in vain for the appearance of Eberhard Kroysing to energize and focus the recollections. Without the complication or climax of his anguish, *Ceasefire* offers no denouement or resolution either. The book fails on every formal level; more regrettably, it fails to achieve Zweig's aim of informing his readers of how progressive and revolutionary consciousness might be formed.

II *1914 Revisited: The* Time is Ripe

Conceived as early as 1929 but written at the height of the Cold War, *Die Zeit ist reif* (The Time is Ripe, 1957) covers the two years before *Young Woman of 1914* begins, from August, 1913, to the spring of 1915. If *Ceasefire* was thin in physical plot, Zweig evaded the problem in *Time is Ripe* by omitting it altogether. Bertin and Lenore, other young couples, Lenore's family, Clauss, Schieffenzahn, and Pahl go about their lives and talk, talk, talk. No narrative structure is visible. Perhaps unintentionally, some of the components of nonrealistic fiction which Zweig had always avoided have now slipped into the novel — distortion of visible reality, nonlogical or nonchronological presentation, jarring intrusion of the narrative, authorial personality. Added to all these stylistic flaws is the kind of twentieth-century Marxism that reflects a bureaucratic program rather than revolutionary fervor or theoretical speculation.

It comes as no surprise that Zweig has rewritten the character of the youthful Bertin. The Bertin of the tetralogy, self-centered and sensitive, slowly awakening to the social upheavals and injustices of his time and society through experience after experience, emerges in *Time is Ripe* already equipped with a social conscience. His view of man and society, his conception of art and the artistic process, and his manner of speech in this novel are typical of the attitudes and behavior of a socialist youth-group leader rather than of a pre - World War I aesthete. In fact, Zweig does not even make an attempt to create a transition between *Time is Ripe* and *Young Woman*. In *Young Woman* Bertin welcomes military service with thrilled delight and accepts the military as the molder of Germany's national spirit. In *Time is Ripe* — supposedly occurring a year prior to his joyful induction — he uses the occasion of the Zabern affair[16] to condemn the army for its contempt of the rights of citizens. "A green lieutenant, a bedwetter, had dared to make us Prussians look ridiculous in the eyes of the Alsatians? And his colonel, instead of calling him on the carpet for strutting about in Alsace-Lorraine as though it were enemy territory, excuses him! This sort of thing has got to be stopped! But it is a good sign that from all levels of society, from workers to the upper crust, the response was loud and clear: 'Enough! More than enough! We are free citizens, not helots'" (193).[17] That Bertin should be echoing Lenin's response to the affair — "the true order of Germany has broken out, the rule of the sword" — at the 1913 stage of his development is ludicrous in itself. Moreover, Zweig knew that the response had been anything but unanimous, that in fact "in Germany reaction to the Zabern affair was very mixed."[18] Such historical complexities, to which the tetralogy had paid careful attention by just such means as Bertin's early infatuation with the army, are now ignored to equip Bertin with a ready-made and militant political ideology. His speech to a labor union contains the essence of the new Bertin: "Somewhere on the way here I came across the words *Arbeitnehmer* ("employee," literally "taker of work") and *Arbeitgeber* ("employer," literally "giver of work"). My mind refuses to accept these terms. Just as I am drinking from this glass of water, so the entrepreneurs receive your work! Well, then, who *is* the employee? Surely not you, who offer your work — you are the employers, just as the fountain gives us the water we drink. So then something in our language has been turned upside down, right?" (198). Clever, even insightful as these remarks are, they show that it is the character of Bertin who has been turned upside down.

Bertin is not simply inconsistent with Zweig's previous incarnation of him — a discrepancy which would not in itself undermine *Time is Ripe* — but he is one-dimensional as well, lacking many other aspects and potentialities of character and opinion. In reshaping the two young lovers, Zweig paid no attention to that part of their being which is ineffable, unconscious, even unknowable. Lenore remarks in *Young Woman* that "deep inside every human being today there is a small child and a wild man" (171), but she extends no such awareness or sympathy to the intricacies of man's inner life in *Time is Ripe*. While on a trip to Italy, Bertin works on his play dealing with an Austrian bishop (a reference to *The Return*, see pp. 33 - 34 above); Lenore wrinkles her brows and remonstrates, "Are you still carrying your wild bishop around with you? You'd be better off relaxing and dropping that Catholic-Jewish soul-wrenching. I don't care for it at all" (26). Indeed, all the aspects of thought and emotion which fascinated Bertin as man and artist, and Lenore as well — the life of dreams, the ambivalence of the unconscious, conflicting desires, the symbols from the center of his being which he hoped to give artistic forms — all are thrust aside almost totally. In the tetralogy Zweig often showed how instinctive energy is modified by social influences, suggesting that Freud's discoveries and Marx's theories need not be stereotyped as alternative, adversary systems, but now Marx explains all. Although Zweig did not bow to official pressure to renounce his homage to Freud, *Time is Ripe* ignores the contributions which psychological insights make to literature and thereby reduces his characters to one-dimensional political spokesmen.

In the earlier novels, history was inhabited by and concerned with human beings, not only trends, ideologies, institutions, and diplomatic or military affairs. Prior to his return to Berlin Zweig commented on the art and aim of historical narrative: "it illuminates reality, makes the world transparent and thereby accessible to human emotions."[19] And his novels indeed had not only presented facts but created the mental and emotional climate of their time. In those books the historical facts and figures came alive because they were seen through the eyes of vividly created, three-dimensional characters. In *Time is Ripe* historical facts and events are merely discussed by characters who either commend or condemn them according to political positions, or else they are introduced by the author to guide the reader. They never become harmonious constituents of the whole work. The most striking example occurs in a description of the Fasching celebration in Munich in 1914. For a while the reader is carried along with the crowd; "only occasionally did one of the passers-by stand out froms the general frolic. One such example was a thin man in a worn overcoat, with a moistened forelock pasted over his right eye and a pencil-moustache above his

mouth. Pressed against the Arch of Victory near the Academy of Arts
this unsuccessful art student, a certain Hitler, son of an Austrian
called Schickelgruber, stared with consuming hatred at all the high
spirits and joy of life forever denied him" (218). The dime-novel
quality of authenticity produced by unnecessary details, the pom-
posity of style, and the ludicrous associations Zweig seeks to make in
this passage signal a low-point in his writing. In his best novels he
wove a historical tapestry, and all the threads were tied together in
historical phenomena experienced by all the characters. Here the
lurking Hitler neither fits into nor contrasts with the subject matter.
In place of a tapestry, Time is Ripe resembles a careless montage —
hastily put together to shock the viewer — that points at connections
rather than creates them. If such an excrescence were perhaps an
error, a lapse in taste, a snapshot which slipped into the montage unnoticed, it might be forgotten and forgiven. Unfortunately, however,
it has become a hallmark of Zweig's technique. Every right-wing
villain and left-wing hero of German, often even of French or
Czechoslovakian, history, from Dreyfus to Rosa Luxemburg, from
Masaryk to Hitler, is mentioned or discussed. And finally, the book
does not really end, it merely fades out. The last words are spoken by
Schieffenzahn: "That's life, that's our era" (600). As was shown in
Grischa, even he knew better.

III *The Last Years*

In 1963 Zweig's last novel, *Traum ist teuer* (The Price of
Dreaming), appeared in print. Marcel Reich-Ranicki opened his
review of the book in *Die Zeit* in the following manner: "It is sad and
painful, but one cannot get around it. Because this book was written
by Arnold Zweig."[20] Zweig tried to retell the case of Grischa, this
time set in World War II. The case of the Greek Sergeant
Kephalides, who slaps a Greek officer serving in the British army
because he considers him a Fascist, is told by the German-Jewish
psychiatrist Richard Karthaus. The case of the sergeant, who is
rescued from his predicament by almost miraculous means, illustrates to Karthaus that "capitalism has gone mad." His former
political ideals collapse — as his name indicates — like a house of
cards, and he becomes an ardent Communist. The book offers a few
interesting glimpses into Zweig's private life in Palestine and much
propaganda in the guise of history. Let is suffice to say that Stalin is
praised effusively.

Zweig's failure to produce successful novels under the banner of socialist realism is not surprising. He belonged to a generation of European intellectuals to whom "economic ruin, political upheaval, exile, the threat of war . . . were profoundly altering the character of their existence. In the new Europe of political terror and impending war, what place was there for the *freischwebende Intelligenz?* It might well be that the freely speculating intellectual had become no more than a useless relic of the eighteenth and nineteenth centuries."[21] Zweig's best work was created by his freely speculating intellect in rebellion against impending war and political terror, against Wilhelminian militarism and National Socialist brutality. After World War II he subjected himself to a closed system, a system which tolerated no such speculation. An old and sedentary man, he was forced by politics and circumstances to narrow the focus of his private vision so that it no longer afforded either sympathetic understanding of other viewpoints or acute criticism of his own milieu. This constraint meant the end of the broad, generous perception of reality which had infused his earlier fiction.

Zweig made headlines once more, in 1967 during the Six-Day War. West Germany's conservative press claimed that he had written a letter to a friend in Israel in which he complained that life in the German Democratic Republic was hell, and that he would be happy to crawl back to Haifa on his hands and knees.[22] Such unlikely contentions were eventually traced back to a highly suspect, fiercely anti-Communist agitprop press in West Berlin. More credible are the reports that he refused to sign an anti-Israel petition. One need not, he is reported to have said, sign everything. That he could not endorse Marxism both enthusiastically *and* critically is the tragedy of his last years. Ernst Fischer, a member of the Austrian Communist Party Central Committee, suggests that what might have been a possible stance: "After the Stalinist deformation, it is necessary to have a rebirth, a restoration of Marxism — that is, critically. Marx did not leave us a repertoire of phrases to quote, but a methodology and a quantity of scientific-philosophic notions. These essentials are 'splendid as the first dawn' [*Faust*, "Prologue"]. Others have in part been superseded by reality. Even Marxism is not a super-temporal inspiration, a divine inspiration. It is the highest consciousness of an era. In other words, it is also conditioned by time. It is not the last word of the human spirit."[23] Perhaps Zweig envisioned the possibility of such a rebirth. But for him it was too late. In 1956, when Stalin was first exposed and denounced in socialist countries, he was sixty-nine years old. He had gone through all phases of his intellectual development with a critical spirit. But after exile, after the denial of recognition and honors for works which deserved them, we should understand why he sought the peace and security of the "last word" at which he had logically and happily arrived.

CHAPTER 6

The Case of Arnold Zweig

I N an early evaluation, Lionel Trilling remarked that "Zweig is a writer considerably but not supremely endowed with novelistic skill; it was his strong intelligence playing over the confused aspects of a great theme, the problem of human justice, that made *The Case of Sergeant Grischa* so fine a book."[1] Zweig's interest in ideas, his growing and changing concern with the power that society exercises over the individual sensibility, and his tenacious search for some kind of certainty — metaphysical at first, ethical and social later — leave with the reader a much more lasting impression than aspects of form or technique in his novellas and novels. In his involvement with questions of human behavior, social conduct, national interests, and finally, class conflicts, Zweig reveals a reflective and retrospective mind, very old-fashioned and yet surprisingly prophetic, highly idealistic and yet strikingly perceptive. His uneasy but stimulating synthesis of a tragic view of human nature gleaned from Freud and an abstract humanitarianism inherited from German classical literature and philosophy mirrors the hybrid nature of German thought and the confusion of postwar intellectual life. That World War I became for Zweig the central experience and consuming theme of his life and work testifies to far more than that conflict's historic significance:

One can say that all the fundamentals of our world have been affected by the war, or more exactly, by the circumstances of the war; something deeper has been worn away than the renewable parts of the machine. You know how greatly the general economic situation has been disturbed, and the polity of states, and the very life of the individual; you are familiar with the universal discomfort, hesitation, apprehension. But among all these injured things is the Mind. The Mind has indeed been cruelly wounded; its complaint is heard in the hearts of intellectual men; it passes a mournful judgment on itself. It doubts itself profoundly.[2]

The work of Arnold Zweig chronicles the series of upheavals brought about by the war and investigates its roots in prewar society, but above all it reflects through the mind of its author the succession of intellectual commitments and doubts that characterize the fundamental development and the disarray of twentieth-century thought.

Zweig carried the political wound that Valéry speaks of, the wound of doubt and self-doubt, from one act of engagement to the next, and his writings mirror disillusion with each successive enthusiasm. His adherence to the mainstream of German intellectual development caused him repeatedly to posit an ideal, aesthetic as well as ethical, and to be repeatedly disappointed when its apotheosis was short-lived and the ideal crushed. His early stories mock the *Bürger*-artist conflict which they are intended to dramatize, while his dramas despair of a solution for the Jewish problem which they set out to reveal. But it was his tragedy that World War I destroyed the social order in which he was, however uneasily, at home and shook its foundations to the roots. His first attempts to come to terms with the war do not deal directly with brutalizing experience but seek refuge in a vague humanitarianism asserted in fables about animals. Nineteenth-century optimistic positivism, which Zweig had been schooled in at German universities and had leaned toward by personal inclination, could not survive the revolution initiated by the war. No philosophical system or critique, from Kant's to Nietzsche's, was able to resolve for him the social antinomies encountered in the postwar world. Once applied to the world of persons and objects, Zweig's beliefs — from nationalism and Kantian idealism to utopian Zionism and socialism — failed.

Zweig's literary *oeuvre*, as much as his shifting sociopolitical stance, reveals a passionate allegiance to a dying way of seeing and expressing the truth about the interconnected lives of men in society. From the beginning of his career in 1909, he groped for a unified, organic formula to order his thought and work. His fiction, like that of Stendhal and Fontane, operates within the limits of the society it criticizes; each of Zweig's characters accepts the compromises he must make in his struggle with society as victories or defeats inherent in human life. The holistic image of the taproot described by Werner Bertin is more characteristic of a Goethean or Schillerian emphasis on polarity than of the expressionist trauma, the revival of myth, and the fragmented formal experimentation so widespread among Zweig's contemporaries. As he groped toward a subject, the novellas he wrote in the early 1920s captured glimpses of a social reality which he found overwhelmingly chaotic and confusing. Both before he made the war itself his theme and again when he lived in distant exile, prewar Germany provided him with his best and most suitable subject matter. The further it receded in time — after 1935, when he moved to other material — the more repetitious he became. Zweig may not have asked existential questions or suggested universal solutions, but he recorded the complex situations which shape his novels as analogues of the German world in the early part of this century. Grischa's death and Grischa's laughter carry us beyond and above mere awareness of absurdity.

The theme which dominates Zweig's mature work, the quest for justice in both moral right and positive law, shifts gradually from the individual cases to social institutions. In the earlier volumes of the war-cycle, the psychological growth and ethical *Bildung* of a socially sensitive youth is sketched against, and interwoven into, the broad panorama of Germany's class system and Prussia's idealistic heritage. But with the death of Grischa and the apocalyptically explosive ending in *Education before Verdun* — written as the 1930s drew mercilessly on — Zweig lost faith in the preservation of individual dignity. Unwillingly but probably necessarily he renounced the legal case in which society was put on trial and looked to theories or systems to set right what other theories and systems had debased. The *Crowning of a King* and *De Vriendt Comes Home* signal the change, not from one ideal to another, but from one means for attaining it to a very different one. Until the mid-1930s, Zweig's concern with human morality had assumed that justice could transcend individual interests and class antagonisms and thereby assume some measure of universal validity or even metaphysical status. The course of current affairs and his own investigation into the nature of World War I convinced Zweig, during his exile, that Marx and Engels were right in insisting that such an absolute morality is — precisely because of its nature — never and nowhere attainable. Once Zweig acknowledged the relativity of justice, no single "case" could again signify its triumph or defeat, no one man or group of men could ever again strive to establish right. In a highly developed society, only a large administrative system, supported by a strong ideology, would be capable of responding to the infinite variety of human potentialities "from each according to his ability, to each according to his need."

Since ideas play so central a role and remain so much on the surface of Zweig's fiction, plot and structure of the novels written after his conversion to Marxism have less aesthetic independence than ever before. Beginning with *The Crowning of a King* (1937), his novels reflect the new moral relativity in a structural diffuseness. Only his revisions of earlier manuscripts dealing with Carl Steinitz resurrect once again the centrifugal plot structure and major symbols typical of his work in the Weimar period. *The Axe of Wandsbek*, with its almost rigid division between psychological dissection of the German *Bürger's* political seduction and economic analysis of the middle class's downfall, gives evidence that the synthesis of psychological probing *and* socioeconomic motivation in an artistically unified whole was no longer possible for Zweig. By 1948, he no longer viewed the weaknesses and passions which inhabited the many characters in *Grischa* or *Education* with the tolerant sympathy in which he had delineated them fifteen and twenty years earlier. But then Zweig no longer approached the course of German history with the gentle criticism of a Fontane or the cultural judgment of a Mann. After World War II, defeated by the German-Jewish tensions that inspired his work, crushed by the slide into barbarism of the German and European culture he had championed, rejected by the Zionist humanism he had hoped to rescue at last, the outsider Zweig cast the hues of gray — the subtle interplay of personal empathy and social criticism which validates his best work — in cold and harsh shades of black and white. The societal ills depicted in *Young Woman* reappear as seeds of destruction in *The Time is Ripe;* but as the latter title suggests, the vision is not now of reform but of revolution.

No author has been as successful as Arnold Zweig in translating the complexities of society into the nature of war and thereby removing from war its special aura and its last vestiges of glory. His best novels fully and openly confront the best and the worst of the world that was Germany in the first two decades of the twentieth century. They indicate an ethical direction that had already been blocked when they were published. Yet *The Case of Sergeant Grischa, Young Woman of 1914*, and *Education before Verdun* imply that it will always be worthwhile to make life better — and that to work for that goal is still possible. World War II and its consequences cast deep doubt on the effectiveness of individual efforts. But such doubt, always present yet never wholly affirmed, had its origin in the "psychological grief"[3] created by the Great War, a grief Zweig struggled valiantly to surmount. His work is a testament to that struggle.

Notes and References

Chapter One

1. Zweig so quotes Goethe in his essay "Wie ein Meisterwerk entsteht," *Beiträge zur Gegenwartsliteratur* 9 (n.d.), 8.

2. Arnold Zweig, "Wege und Umwege; Autobiographische Aufzeichnungen," *Neue Deutsche Literatur* 10 (1962), 43.

3. Kenneth Keniston, *The Uncommitted* (New York, 1965), p. 382.

4. Erich Fromm, *Beyond the Chains of Illusion* (New York, 1963), pp. 17, 28.

5. Zweig, "Wege and Umwege," p. 48.

6. Barbara Tuchman, *The Proud Tower* (New York, 1965), p. xv.

7. Marcel Reich-Ranicki, "Der preußische Jude Arnold Zweig," in *Deutsche Literatur in West und Ost* (Munich, 1963), pp. 305 - 42.

8. Lothar Kahn, "Arnold Zweig: From Zionism to Marxism," in *Mirrors of the Jewish Mind* (New York, 1968), pp. 194 - 209.

9. Hans Peter Anderle, "Arnold Zweig," in *Mitteldeutsche Erzähler* (Cologne, 1965), pp. 50 - 55.

10. Erik H. Erikson, *Childhood and Society* (New York, 1963), p. 356.

11. Henry Hatfield, *Crisis and Continuity in Modern German Fiction* (Ithaca, 1969), p. xvi.

12. Henry Hatfield, *Thomas Mann* (New York, 1962), p. 86.

13. Fritz Stern, "Money, Morals, and the Pillars of Bismarck's Society," *Central European History* 3 (1970), 72.

14. "Vorfrühling" is Zweig's first published work, printed in the journal *Gäste*, which he and a few school friends launched during their summer vacation in Kattowitz in 1909. The story was written in 1907, a year in which Zweig also completed five chapters of a *Künstlerroman* to be called *Esmonds gute Zeit* (Esmond's Good Times). The manuscript never progressed beyond its fragmentary stage and was lost during the Nazi period. Another novel, *Verklungene Tage* (Days Faded Away), was written in 1908 but published only in its revised version as *Versunkene Tage* (Days Swallowed Up) in 1938. Because the revisions betray a very different attitude toward the problem of the artist, this novel will be discussed in the chapter on Zweig's years in exile.

181

15. For a discussion of this practice, see Wolfdietrich Rasch, "Das Problem des Anfangs erzählender Dichtung; Eine Beobachtung zur Form des Erzählens um 1900," in *Zur deutschen Literatur seit der Jahrhundertwende* (Stuttgart, 1967), pp. 49 - 57.

16. Arnold Zweig, "Lebenswege mit Thomas Mann," *Neue Deutsche Literatur* 13 (1965), 167.

17. Thomas Mann, "Zu einem Kapitel aus 'Buddenbrooks,' " in *Gesammelte Werke*, XIII, 465.

18. Sigmund Freud, *A General Introduction to Psychoanalysis*, trans. Joan Riviere (New York, 1960), p. 384.

19. These words of the Viennese satirist Karl Kraus are quoted by Erich Heller in "The Modern German Mind: The Legacy of Nietzsche," *French and German Letters Today: Four Lectures*. (Washington, D.C.: Library of Congress, 1960), p. 31.

20. Heinrich von Kleist (1777 - 1811) committed suicide with his beloved, Henrietta Vogel, at the Wannsee on November 22, 1811.

21. Thus Fritz Stern entitles an essay in *The Failure of Illiberalism* (New York, 1972), pp. 3 - 25.

22. William Butler Yeats, *The Collected Poems* (New York, 1956), p. 184.

23. Granville Hicks, *The Nation* 131 (1930), 621.

24. H. G. Adler, *The Jews in Germany* (South Bend, 1969), p. 107.

25. Eva Reichmann, *Hostages of Civilisation; The Social Sources of Anti-Semitism* (London, 1950), p. 143.

26. Marie Bonaparte, *The Myths of War*, trans. John Rodker (London, 1947), p. 131.

27. Klemens Felden presents much statistical evidence to support this view in his dissertation, "Die Übernahme des antisemitischen Stereotyps als soziale Norm durch die bürgerliche Gesellschaft Deutschlands 1875 - 1900," Heidelberg, 1963.

28. Zweig had read the massive study of this affair by Paul Nathan, *Der Prozess von Tisza Eszlar; Ein antisemitisches Culturbild* (Berlin, 1892).

29. These three stories were to form the basis of a novel, a project probably interrupted by the war and never resumed.

30. The essay was printed in *Vom Judentum; Ein Sammelbuch*, Herausgegeben vom Verein Jüdischer Hochschüler Bar Kochba in Prag (Leipzig, 1914), pp. 210 - 35. All citations refer to this text.

31. Zweig, "Wege and Umwege," pp. 46, 44.

Chapter Two

1. Stefan Zweig, *The World of Yesterday; An Autobiography* (New York, 1943), p. 223.

2. Max Scheler, *Der Genius des Krieges und der deutsche Krieg* (Leipzig, 1915), p. 16.

3. Moritz Heimann, "Der Krieg I," *Die Neue Rundschau* 14 (1914), 1191.

4. Moritz Heimann, "Der Krieg II," *Die Neue Rundschau* 14 (1914), 1568.

5. Arnold Zweig, "Der Genius des Krieges," *Die Schaubühne* 11 (1915), 369.

6. All quotations from this essay appear on p. 282 of "Kriegsziele," *Süddeutsche Monatshefte*, vol. 13 (1915).

7. "Die Bestie" appeared in 1914 as part of the series *Langens Kriegsbücher; Geschichten aus Deutschlands Kämpfen*. Although most of the stories are as patriotic as the title implies, the book also contains Zweig's first antiwar story, "Der Feind" (The Enemy).

8. Werner Sombart, *Händler und Helden* (Leipzig, 1915).

9. See the quotations in Arthur Ponsonby, *Falsehoods in Wartime* (New York, 1928), p. 103.

10. For reasons not clear and no longer of great importance, Zweig's horror stories were confiscated by the German censor. It is possible that the idea of Belgian brutality seemed preposterous, even to a German military censor in 1915. For a closer examination of this curious episode, see Eva Kaufmann, *Arnold Zweigs Weg zum Roman* (Berlin, 1967), p. 313n. This major study is subsequently cited throughout as "Kaufmann."

11. Kaufmann, p. 41.

12. Zweig's interest in the writings of Martin Buber dates from his university days.

13. Zweig was enrolled in seminars on Kant at the University of Göttingen in 1912; his teachers were Edmund Husserl and Adolf Reinach.

14. *Kriegsbriefe gefallener Studenten*, ed. Philipp Witkop (Munich, 1928), p. 123.

15. Ernst Jünger, *Feuer und Blut* (Berlin, 1924), p. 151.

16. Arnold Zweig, "Wort und Blut," *Die Weltbühne* 21 (1925), 641.

17. He had been inclined to disparge the importance of Marx and Engels since "in Göttingen, as in all other universities, the historical materialism of Marx and Engels was never discussed, not even by way of suggestion," "Wege und Umwege," p. 45.

18. Nathan Ausubel, *A Treasure of Jewish Folklore* (New York, 1948), pp. 176 - 78.

19. These poems and lithographs were printed in violation of war censorship laws in 1918, but they appeared in book form in a limited edition under the title *Entrückung und Aufruhr* (Rapture and Revolution) (Frankfurt a.M., 1920).

20. The original version read "Elendgasse" ("street of misery") for "Arbeitergasse" ("street of workers").

21. Kaufmann, p. 130.

22. Thus Zweig wrote in program-notes on the origins of the play for the Halle theater, cited by Kaufmann, p. 131.

23. Peter Gay, *Weimar Culture; The Outsider as Insider* (New York, 1968), p. 152.

24. Arnold Zweig, "Abdankung," *Die Weltbühne* 15 (1919), 55.

25. A. J. Ryder, *The German Revolution 1918 - 1919* (London, 1968), p. 28.

26. Arnold Zweig, "Das Theater im Volksstaate," in *Der Geist der neuen Volksgemeinschaft* (Berlin, 1919), pp. 127 - 39.

27. Derek van Abbé, *Image of a People* (New York, 1964), p. 183.

28. For a detailed discussion of the sociopolitical objections to the expressionist protest, see Peter Uwe Hohendahl's *Das Bild der bürgerlichen Welt im expressionistischen Drama* (Heidelberg, 1967), pp. 23ff.

29. Arnold Zweig, "Journey's End," originally published in the English *Daily Express*, reprinted in the Berlin Journal *Das Tagebuch*, 36 (1929), 1484.

30. Erich von [sic] Ludendorff, *Ludendorff's Own Story* (New York, 1918), II, 408.

31. Ralph H. Lutz, *Fall of the German Empire* (Palo Alto, 1932), I, 655.

32. For an example, see Kaufmann, p. 140.

33. Germany's plans to establish along the Polish border a "frontier strip," settled with nationally or racially acceptable Germans, and the strategic origins of this policy, are documented and discussed by Immanuel Geiss, "Der polnische Grenzstreifen, 1914 - 1918. Ein Beitrag zur deutschen Kriegszielpolitik im ersten Weltkrieg," *Eberings Historische Studien*, Heft 398 (Lübeck-Hamburg, 1960).

34. Schieffenzahn's territorial ambitions for postwar Germany correspond very closely to those expressed by Ludendorff: "We must, therefore, have an increase of territory. That territory can only be found in Courland and Lithuania, which offer good agricultural opportunities. In view of the attitude of Poland, and for military reasons, we must fix the frontier of Lithuania to the South of Grodno and somewhat enlarge East and West Prussia. Only thus shall we protect Prussia," Erich Ludendorff, *The General Staff and its Problems* (New York, n.d.), II, 494.

35. Arnold Zweig, "Epoche und Theater," in *Das deutsche Theater der Gegenwart*, ed. M. Krell (Munich, 1923), p. 22.

36. Zweig, "Epoche und Theater," p. 14.

37. Yvan Goll, "Das Überdrama," in *Deutsche Dramaturgie von Gryphius bis Brecht*, ed. Margaret Dietrich and Paul Stefanek (Munich, 1965), p. 145.

38. *Sigmund Freud-Arnold Zweig Briefwechsel*, ed. Ernst L. Freud (Frankfurt a.M., 1968), p. 31. This important exchange is subsequently cited as *Briefwechsel*.

39. Georg Kaiser, *Werke*, ed. Walther Huder (Berlin, 1971), I, 515.

40. Ernst Toller, *Seven Plays*, trans. Vera Mandel (New York, 1936), p. 180.

41. *Briefwechsel*, p. 32.

42. Georg Lukacs, "Größe und Verfall des Expressionismus," in *Probleme des Realismus* (Berlin, 1955), p. 155.

43. Döblin is so quoted by Gordon Craig, "Engagement and Neutrality in

Weimar Germany," *Journal of Contemporary History* 5 (1967), 57.

44. Adrian H. Jaffe and Virgil Scott, *Studies in the Short Story* (New York, 1949), p. 219.

45. Otto Baumgarten, "Der sittliche Zustand des deutschen Volkes unter dem Einfluβ des Krieges," in *Geistige und sittliche Wirkungen des Krieges in Deutschland* (Stuttgart, 1927), p. 5.

46. Carl von Ossietzky, *The Stolen Republic* (Berlin, 1971), p. 46.

47. Fritz Stern, *The Failure of Illiberalism* (New York, 1972), pp. 199 - 200.

48. Carl E. Schorske, "Weimar and the Intellectuals," *The New York Review of Books*, May 21, 1970, p. 25.

49. Stern, p. 218.

50. Ivo Frenzel, "Utopia and Apocalypse in German Literature," *Social Research* 39 (1972), 315.

Chapter Three

1. Siegfried Sassoon, *Sherston's Progress* (New York, 1937), p. 245.

2. William Blissett, "*In Parenthesis* among the War Books," *University of Toronto Quarterly* 42 (1973), 258.

3. A study of war novels in a German journal for teachers of language and literature mistakenly but proudly praises the one attitude common to all authors, namely, that "war was recognized as necessary, indeed as a meaningful aspect of human existence," and that for the individual "war was a means to personal purification and maturation." Klaus Betzen, "Deutung und Darstellung des Krieges in der deutschen Epik das 20, Jahrhunderts," *Der Deutschunterricht* 14 (1962), 50. The most recent effort in this direction is John P. Sisk's "War Fictions," *Commentary* 56 (1973), 58 - 66. War, in Mr. Sisk's view, sounds like a private outdoor exercise with no human enemy at all: "War is a state in which the hardened self crosses over into wilderness to measure itself against elemental force," p. 63.

4. Peter Hageboldt, "Ethical and Social Problems in the German War Novel," *Journal of English and Germanic Philology* 32 (1933), 21.

5. Hageboldt, *passim*.

6. Joseph Conrad, *The Nigger of the Narcissus* (New York, 1949), p. xiii.

7. Sophus Keith Winter, *The Realistic War Novel* (Seattle, 1930), p. 31.

8. Douglas Jerrold, *The Lie About the War; A Note on Some Contemporary War Books* (London, 1930), p. 11.

9. Eugene Löhrke, "The World War in Literature," in *Armageddon*, ed. Löhrke (New York, 1930), p. 15. The German critics were less polite. Herbert Cysarz calls Latzko's description of war a "sadomasochistic witches' sabbath" in *Zur Geistesgeschichte des Weltkrieges: Die dichterischen Wandlungen des deutschen Kriegsbilds 1910 - 1930* (Halle, 1931), p. 111.

10. Löhrke, pp. 13, 16 - 17.

11. Vladimir Pozner, "Reise nach Verdun; Eine Begegnung mit Arnold Zweig," *Neue Deutsche Literatur* 11 (1963), 68.

12. Kaufmann, pp. 129 - 30.

13. Kurt Sontheimer, *Antidemokratisches Denken in der Weimarer Republik* (Munich, 1962), p. 139.

14. Carl von Ossietzky, *The Stolen Republic* (Berlin, 1941), p. 212.

15. In a speech, Joseph Joos, Reichstag deputy of the Catholic Center party and member of a commission set up by the Weimar Constituent Assembly to investigate the causes of the German collapse, remarked on October 12, 1927: "The war was regarded as a war of defense, and it was therefore a holy and just war for the masses of the population. But at the moment people began to speak of conquests, of the urge toward expansion and the lust for domination, those who had started on the assumption of a holy war found themselves at variance with themselves and this conflict developed within them." Quoted in R. H. Lutz, ed., *The Causes of the German Collapse of 1918* (Palo Alto, 1934), p. 272.

16. See the books by Emil Julius Gumbel, especially *Vier Jahre politischer Mord*, 5th ed. (Berlin, 1922), and *Verräter verfallen der Feme: Opfer, Mörder und Richter 1919 - 1920* (Berlin, 1929).

17. See Roy Pascal, *The German Novel* (Toronto, 1965), pp. 297 - 306, for a fuller discussion of this matter.

18. Arnold Zweig, "Time-Spirit in German Literature," *Library Review* 3 (1932), 221.

19. *Ibid.*, p. 219.

20. Elizabeth Bowen, *Collected Impressions* (London, 1950), p. 159.

21. All citations refer to the 1927 edition.

22. Jean-Paul Sartre, "The Republic of Silence," in *The Republic of Silence*, ed. A. J. Liebling (New York, 1947), p. 499.

23. Compare Zweig's depiction with the estimate of John W. Wheeler-Bennett: "Throughout his school years his more aristocratic contemporaries never allowed him to forget that he lacked the 'von' of nobility before his name," and of his "passionate addiction to work," "Ludendorff; The Soldier and the Politician," *The Virginia Quarterly* 14 (1938), 187 - 88.

24. Kaufmann, pp. 173 - 75.

25. Arnold Zweig, "Wie ein großes Werk entsteht," *Wochenpost*, June 14, 1958, p. 84.

26. Kaufmann, pp. 293 - 95.

27. All citations refer to the 1931 edition.

28. See the descriptions in Klaus Schröter, "Chauvinism and its Tradition: German Writers and the Outbreak of the First World War," *The Germanic Review* 43 (1968), 120 - 35.

29. Erich Fromm, *Escape from Freedom* (New York, 1941), p. 213.

30. In October, 1914, the fifty-year-old Max Weber exclaimed that "this war with all its ugliness is great and wonderful, it is worth experiencing," *Gesammelte Politische Schriften* (Munich, 1921), p. 213.

31. Nahum Goldmann, *Der Geist des Militarismus* (Stuttgart, 1915), pp. 12, 14, 20.

32. It seems certain that Lenore's words ("und sie müßten uns herrlichen Zeiten entgegenführen") are a direct parody of Kaiser Wilhelm's famous exclamation of 1913: "Ich führe Euch herrlichen Zeiten entgegen."

33. Sigmund Freud, "Why War?" in O. Nathan and H. Norden, *Einstein on Peace* (New York, 1960), p. 190.

34. Fromm, *Escape from Freedom*, pp. 267 - 68.

35. There is no adequate English translation for this term. Perhaps the best American equivalent might be "Officer of a Chamber of Commerce."

36. Eberhard Hilscher, *Arnold Zweig* (Berlin, 1968), p. 81. This study is subsequently cited as Hilscher.

37. All citations refer to the 1935 edition.

38. Ernst Jünger, *Copse 125* (London, 1925), pp. ix - x.

39. Simone Weil, "The 'Iliad,' Poem of Might," in *Intimations of Christianity*, trans. Elizabeth C. Geissbuhler (Boston, 1958), p. 41.

40. *German Students' War Letters*, trans. and arranged from the original edition of Philipp Witkop by A. F. Wedd (New York, 1929), p. 166.

41. Arnold Zweig, "Kriegsromane," *Die Weltbühne* 25 (1929), 598.

42. Sigmund Freud, *Collected Papers* (London, 1949), IV, 300.

43. Walter Gropius, *Scope of Total Architecture* (New York, 1955), p. 19.

44. Jean-Paul Sartre, *Three Plays*, trans. Lionel Abel (New York, 1949), p. 213.

45. All citations refer to the 1937 edition. Zweig planned to continue the cycle past 1918 and to show the effects of the war in the period of upheavals in 1918 - 1920. However, his project was suspended for over a decade; when he resumed it after moving to the German Democratic Republic, he set its final novels — *Die Feuerpause* (1954) and *Die Zeit ist reif* (1957) — in war and prewar periods. The following table shows the periods covered by each volume:

Book	Period covered	Written	Published
Die Zeit ist reif	August, 1913 - Spring, 1915	1955 - 56	1957
Junge Frau von 1914	Spring, 1915 - July, 1916	1928 - 30	1931
Erziehung vor Verdun	July, 1916 - March, 1917	1933 - 34	1935
Der Streit um den Sergeanten Grischa	March, 1917 - November, 1917	1926 - 27	1927
Die Feuerpause	November, 1917 - January, 1918	1952 - 53	1954
Einsetzung eines Königs	February - October, 1918	1936 - 37	1937

Among the volumes of the original tetralogy, *Grischa* — although written first — holds the climactic penultimate position in the time sequence of the plots.

46. Malcolm Cowley, "Eastern Front: 1918," *The New Republic* 95 (1938), 106.

47. For this period in Ludendorff's career, as reflected in Zweig's portrait of Schieffenzahn, see Walter Görlitz, *Der Deutsche Generalstab* (Frankfurt a.M., 1949), pp. 179 - 203.

48. The parallels between historic events and personalities and their fictional counterparts in Zweig's novels are discussed by Hans-Albert Walter, "Auf dem Wege zum Staatsroman; Arnold Zweigs Grischa-Zyklus," *Frankfurter Hefte* 23 (1968), 564 - 74.

49. Gerald Feldman, *Army, Industry, and Labor in Germany, 1914 - 1918* (Princeton, 1966), p. 519.

50. "Sneakily pulling the legs out from under a people trying to defend itself."

51. Among the books consulted were John W. Wheeler-Bennett, *The Nemesis of Power* (London, 1953); Robert J. O'Neill, *The German Army and the Nazi Party, 1933 - 1939* (London, 1966); Bernhard Vollmer, *Volksopposition im Polizeistaat 1934 - 1936* (Stuttgart, 1957); Eberhard Zeller, *The Flame of Freedom* (Coral Gables, Fla., 1969); Gert Buchheit, *Soldatentum und Rebellion. Die Tragödie der deutschen Wehrmacht* (Rastatt/Baden, 1961).

52. Maxwell Geismar, "Mankind at War," *The Nation* 146 (1938), 652.

53. Avrom Fleischman, *The English Historical Novel* (Baltimore, 1971), p. 11.

54. Helmut Gruber, "Neue Sachlichkeit and the World War," *German Life and Letters* 20 (1967), 146 - 47.

55. R. G. Collingwood, *The Idea of History* (Oxford, 1966), pp. 245 - 46.

Chapter Four

1. *Briefwechsel*, p. 74.

2. *Ibid.*, p. 123.

3. Hans Mayer, "Lion Feuchtwanger oder die Folgen des Exils," *Neue Rundschau* 76 (1965), 128.

4. *Briefwechsel*, p. 49.

5. Hilscher, p. 126, reports a conversation on this subject.

6. Among the notable exiles in this fishing village were Bertolt Brecht, Thomas Mann, Franz Werfel, Ernst Toller, Heinrich Mann, Ludwig Marcuse, and Alfred Kerr.

7. Erich Gottgetreu, "Arnold Zweigs Wanderung von Berlin nach Berlin," *Emuna* 4 (1969), 7, reports that Zweig told him so in 1934.

8. Arnold Zweig, "Heutiger Zionismus," *Die Weltbühne* 21 (1925), 126.

9. Arnold Zweig, "Die antisemitische Welle," *Die Weltbühne* 15 (1919), 443.

10. *Ibid.*, p. 444.

11. *Briefwechsel*, p. 53.

12. *Ibid.*

13. Hilscher, p. 138.

14. Ahron David Gordon, *Erlösung durch Arbeit* (Berlin, 1929), p. 243. Gordon's essays were written much earlier but were not translated from the Hebrew and published in Germany until 1929.

15. Curt D. Wormann, "German Jews in Israel: Their Cultural Situation since 1933," *Leo Baeck Institute Yearbook* 15 (1970), 90.

16. *Briefwechsel*, p. 67.

17. *Ibid.*, p. 68.

18. *Ibid.*, pp. 130 - 31. Although all of Zweig's major works have appeared in English, only one, *The Axe of Wandsbek*, in addition to the slight historical novella *The Emperor's Mirror*, was translated into Hebrew. But Zweig did have the opportunity to publish essays in English and German in various émigré journals.

19. *Ibid.*, p. 70.

20. *Ibid.*, p. 177.

21. Heinz D. Oesterle, "The Other Germany: Resistance to the Third Reich in German Literature," *The German Quarterly* 41 (1968), 11.

22. Eberhard Hilscher, "Der Dramatiker Arnold Zweig," *Weimarer Beiträge* 6 (1960), 15.

23. Hilscher, p. 141, reports this designation.

24. *Briefwechsel*, p. 33.

25. *Ibid.*, pp. 34 - 35.

26. Marcel Reich-Ranicki, "Der preußische Jude Arnold Zweig," in *Deutsche Literatur in West and Ost* (Munich, 1963), pp. 320 - 21.

27. Accounts of activities by intellectuals on behalf of socialist workers assign Zweig a less active role than the fighting stance he subsequently suggested. See *Literatur der Arbeiterklasse*, edited by the Deutsche Akademie der Künste (Berlin and Weimar, 1971), pp. 62ff. A cultural official of the German Democratic Republic clearly placed Zweig in the camp of sympathetic bourgeois, rather than convinced Marxists, in the Weimar Republic: "Our literature continued the tradition of humanist bourgeois literature, represented by such writers as Arnold Zweig," Wolfgang Joho, "Wir begannen nicht im Jahr Null," *Neue Deutsche Literatur* 13 (1965), 8.

28. See Kaufmann, pp. 14 - 16, nn. 18 - 26, for a history of the manuscript and its publication.

29. Lionel Trilling, "Manners, Morals, and the Novel," in *The Liberal Imagination* (New York, 1950), pp. 220 - 21.

30. Recent studies reveal that in the last election during the Weimar Republic the Jewish middle class gave two-thirds of its votes to left-of-center or moderate democratic parties and 25 percent to the Social Democrats, while right-wing groups barely gathered any Jewish votes at all. The most helpful work on this topic is Hans-Helmuth Knütter, *Die Juden und die deutsche Linke in der Weimarer Republik 1918 - 1933* (Düsseldorf, 1971).

31. Oesterle, p. 11.

32. *Ibid.*, p. 12.

33. *The Axe of Wandsbek* (London, 1947), p. 391.

34. The story in the *Deutsche Volkszeitung* of April 10, 1937 (cited by Heinrich Vormweg, "Gerechtigkeit über sich fühlend. Arnold Zweigs Roman *Das Beil von Wandsbek*," in *Die Deutsche Exilliteratur 1933 - 1945*, ed. Manfred Durzak [Stuttgart, 1973], p. 334) relates that a butcher named Fock executed Jonny Detmer and three other anti-Fascists. A check of studies on the resistance to Nazism in Hamburg reveals that the SS-man and

butcher Voth exeucted August Lütgens, Walter Möller, Bruno Tesch, and Karl Wolff on August 1, 1933. The four had been condemned to death for the shooting of two SA-men during the clashes between anti-Fascists and the SA on July 17, 1932, the "Bloody Sunday" of Altona, during which eighteen people lost their lives. The four were convicted, although no neutral eyewitnesses ever identified them as having fired any shots. No one was ever indicted for the deaths of the civilians during the riot. Other members of Communist and Socialist unions and organizations were sentenced and executed, among them Jonny Dettmar and three others on May 19, 1934. By 1934 the city's official executioner seems to have recovered from his indisposition sufficiently to carry out his duties; all accounts mention the butcher Voth (not Fock) only in connection with the earlier execution. See Ursel Hochmuth and Gertrud Meyer, *Streiflichter aus dem Hamburger Widerstand 1933 - 1945* (Frankfurt a.M., 1969), pp. 11 - 12, and especially Gertrud Meyer, *Nacht über Hamburg* (Frankfurt a.M., 1971), pp. 31 - 36 and 226 - 29.

35. Hilscher, p. 142, reports this insight.

36. Carrol Quigley, *Tragedy and Hope* (New York, 1966), p. 415.

37. Office of the United States Chief Counsel for Prosecution of Axis Criminality, *Nazi Conspiracy and Aggression* (Washington, D.C., 1946), IV, 1106 - 7.

38. Vormweg, p. 332.

39. Karl Bracher, *Die Deutsche Diktatur* (Cologne, 1972), p. 367.

40. Henry Ashby Turner "Big Business and the Rise of Hitler," *American Historical Review* 75 (1969), 70.

41. Hans Kohn, *The Mind of Germany* (New York, 1960), p. 11.

42. See the views expressed by Lukacs in the preface written specifically for a new, abridged version of *Die Zerstörung der Vernunft* ([The Destruction of Reason] Berlin, 1962), published as *Von Nietzsche zu Hitler oder Der deutsche Irrationalismus und die deutsche Politik* (Frankfort a.M., 1966).

Chapter Five

1. Peter Demetz, "Literature in Ulbricht's Germany," *Problems of Communism* 13 (1962), 15.

2. *Ibid.*, p. 16.

3. Harry Levin, "What is Realism?" in *Contexts of Criticism* (Cambridge, Mass., 1957), p. 75.

4. Harry Levin, *The Gates of Horn* (New York, 1963), p. 467.

5. Abram Tertz, *Socialist Realism*, trans. George Dennis (New York, 1960), p. 25.

6. Arnold Zweig, "Die wichtigste gesellschaftliche Funktion des Schriftstellers," *Aufbau* 7 (1950), 215.

7. Arnold Zweig, "Die Vermenschlichung des Menschen," *Aufbau* 6 (1949), 127.

8. *Ibid.*, p. 129. Zweig has firm Marxist support on this issue. Engels noted that "the more the intentions of the author are hidden, the better for the work of art," Karl Marx and Friedrich Engels, *Über Kunst und Literatur*, ed. Luppol (Moscow, 1937), p. 54.

9. John Flores, *Poetry in East Germany* (New Haven, 1971), p. 18.

10. Afterword to the 1953 edition of *Die Feuerpause*, p. 426. The edition in the collected works published in 1963, from which all citations are taken, omits the afterword entirely.

11. *Ibid.*

12. Gerhard Schulz, *Revolutionen und Friedensschlüsse 1917 - 1920* (Munich, 1969), p. 111.

13. Jürgen Rühle, "Die Kunst des inneren Vorbehalts," in *Literatur und Revolution* (Munich, 1963), pp. 211 - 12.

14. Hans Joachim Bernhard, "Die Entwicklung des kritischen Realismus Arnold Zweigs im Lichte der proletarischen Gestalten seines 'Grischazyklus,'" *Wissenschaftliche Zeitschrift der Universität Rostock* 9 (1959 - 1960), 65.

15. Heinrich Regius (i.e., Max Horkheimer), *Dämmerung* (Zurich, 1934), p. 74.

16. The Zabern affair began with a remark made by a German lieutenant in Zabern on October 28, 1913. Speaking to a soldier who had been charged with knifing a local civilian, he said, "if you knife an Alsatian 'Wackes' you won't get two months for each dirty 'Wackes' you bring me — you'll get 10 marks" (Wackes is a derogatory epithet equivalent to "nigger"). The incident leaked to the press and became a *cause célèbre*. The quotation comes from an excellent discussion of the entire affair in Martin Kitchen, *The German Officer Corps 1890 - 1914* (Oxford, 1968), p. 197.

17. All citations are taken from the edition of 1963 in the collected works.

18. Kitchen, p. 220.

19. Arnold Zweig, "Roman, Realismus und Form," *Das Wort* 3 (1938), 92.

20. Marcel Reich-Ranicki, *Die Zeit*, March 22, 1963, p. 11.

21. H. Stuart Hughes, *Consciousness and Society* (New York, 1958), p. 404.

22. This shabby affair is documented and discussed by Günter Grass, *Der Fall Axel C. Springer am Beispiel Arnold Zweig* (Berlin, 1967).

23. Fischer is so quoted by Edmund Demaître, "In Search of Humanism," *Problems of Communism* 14 (1965), 29.

Chapter Six

1. Lionel Trilling, "Zweig's Tetralogy; *Young Woman of 1914*," *The Nation* 136 (1933), 71.

2. Paul Valéry, *Variety*, trans. Malcolm Cowley (New York, 1927), p. 28.

3. Barbara Tuchman, *The Proud Tower* (New York, 1965), p. xv.

Selected Bibliography

Arnold Zweig's serious literary works and discussions relevant to them are listed here; his journalistic essays with only transitory interest are not included.

PRIMARY SOURCES

Ausgewählte Werke in Einzelausgaben, 16 vols. Berlin: Aufbau-Verlag, 1957 - 1967. This edition contains: I. *Die Zeit ist reif.* II. *Junge Frau von 1914.* III. *Erziehung vor Verdun.* IV. *Der Streit um den Sergeanten Grischa.* V. *Die Feuerpause.* VI. *Einsetzung eines Königs.* VII. *Novellen um Claudia. Verklungene Tage.* VIII. *De Vriendt kehrt heim.* IX. *Das Beil von Wandsbek.* X. *Traum ist teuer.* XI. *Novellen. Erster Band.* XII. *Novellen. Zweiter Band.* XIII. *Dramen.* XIV. *Jahresringe; Gedichte und Spiele.* XV. *Essays. Erster Band.* XVI. *Essays. Zweiter Band.*

1. Novels
Die Novellen um Claudia. Berlin: Kurt Wolff, 1912.
Der Streit um den Sergeanten Grischa. Potsdam: Gustav Kiepenheuer, 1927.
Junge Frau von 1914. Berlin: Gustav Kiepenheuer, 1931.
De Vriendt kehrt heim. Berlin: Gustav Kiepenheuer, 1932.
Erziehung vor Verdun. Amsterdam: Querido, 1935.
Einsetzung eines Königs. Amsterdam: Querido, 1937.
Versunkene Tage. Amsterdam: Querido, 1938. Published as *Verklungene Tage*, Munich: Kurt Desch, 1950 and Berlin: Aufbau-Verlag, 1955.
Das Beil von Wandsbek. Stockholm: Neuer Verlag, 1948.
Die Feuerpause. Berlin: Aufbau-Verlag, 1954.
Die Zeit ist reif. Berlin: Aufbau-Verlag, 1957. Vol. I of *Ausgewählte Werke.*
Traum ist teuer. Berlin: Aufbau-Verlag, 1962. Vol. X of *Ausgewählte Werke.*

2. Novellas and Short Stories
Aufzeichnungen über eine Familie Klopfer. Munich: Albert Langen, 1911.

Die Bestie. Munich: Albert Langen, 1914.
Geschichtenbuch. Munich: Albert Langen, 1916.
Bennarone. Munich: Roland Verlag, 1918.
Drei Erzählungen. (Includes *Aufzeichnungen über eine Familie Klopfer.*)
    Berlin: Welt-Verlag, 1920.
Gerufene Schatten. Berlin: Hans Heinrich Tillgner Verlag, 1923.
Söhne. Das zweite Geschichtenbuch. Munich: Albert Langen, 1923.
Frühe Fährten. Berlin: J. M. Spaeth Verlag, 1925. A slightly different an-
    thology was published under the same title, Halle/Saale: Mitteldeut-
    scher Verlag, 1949.
Regenbogen. Berlin: J. M. Spaeth Verlag, 1925. (Includes *Pont und Anna.*)
Der Spiegel des großen Kaisers. Potsdam: Gustav Kiepenheuer, 1926. Re-
    vised edition, Leipzig: Philipp Reclam jun., 1949.
Pont und Anna. Potsdam: Gustav Kiepenheuer, 1928.
Knaben und Männer. Berlin: Gustav Kiepenheuer, 1931.
Mädchen und Frauen. Berlin: Gustav Kiepenheuer, 1931.
Spielzeuge der Zeit. Amsterdam: Querido, 1933.
Allerleirauh. Berlin: Aufbau-Verlag, 1949.
Stufen. Fünf Erzählungen. Berlin: Alfred Kantorowicz Verlag, 1949.
Über den Nebeln. Halle/Saale: Mitteldeutscher Verlag, 1950.
Der Elfenbeinfächer. Ausgewählte Novellen. Erster Band. Berlin: Aufbau-
    Verlag, 1952. Republished as Vol. XI of *Ausgewählte Werke.*
Westlandsaga. Erzählung. Berlin: Rütten & Loening, 1952.
Der Regenbogen. Ausgewählte Novellen. Zweiter Band. Berlin: Aufbau-
    Verlag, 1955. Republished as Vol. XII of *Ausgewählte Werke.*

3. Dramas
Abigail und Nabal. Leipzig: Rowohlt, 1913. Revised edition published in
    Munich: Kurt Wolff Verlag, 1920.
Ritualmord in Ungarn. Berlin: Hyperion-Verlag, 1914. Revised and pub-
    lished as *Die Sendung Semaels*, Leipzig: Kurt Wolff Verlag, 1918.
Die Umkehr des Abtrünnigen. Darmstadt: Ernst Ludwig Presse, 1925. Re-
    published as *Die Umkehr*, Potsdam: Gustav Kiepenheuer, 1927.
Die Aufrichtung der Menorah. Entwurf einer Pantomine. Berlin: Aldus-
    Druck, 1930.
Laubheu und keine Bleibe. Berlin: Gustav Kiepenheuer, 1930.
Soldatenspiele. Drei dramatische Historien. Berlin: Aufbau-Verlag, 1956.
    (Contains *Austreibung 1744 oder das Weihnachtswunder, Bonaparte in
    Jaffa, Das Spiel vom Sergeanten Grischa.*)

4. Poetry
Der Englische Garten. Munich: Hyperion Verlag, 1910.
*Entrückung und Aufruhr. 12 Gedichte zu 12 Lithographien von Magnus
    Zeller 1917/18.* Frankfurt a.M.: Tiedemann, 1920.

Fünf Romanzen. Berlin: Aufbau-Verlag, 1958.

5. Non-Fiction and Collected Essays
Das ostjüdische Antlitz. Zu 50 Steinzeichnungen von Hermann Struck. Berlin: Welt-Verlag, 1920.
Das neue Kanaan. Zu 15 Steinzeichnungen von Hermann Struck. Berlin: Horodisch & Marx, 1925.
Lessing-Kleist-Büchner. Drei Versuche. Berlin: J. M. Spaeth Verlag, 1925.
Caliban oder Politik und Leidenschaft. Potsdam: Gustav Kiepenheuer, 1927.
Juden auf der deutschen Bühne. Berlin: Welt-Verlag, 1928.
Herkunft und Zukunft. Zwei Essays zum Schicksal eines Volkes. Vienna: Phaidon-Verlag, 1929. (Contains *Das ostjüdische Antlitz* and *Das neue Kanaan.*)
Bilanz der deutschen Judenheit 1933. Amsterdam: Querido, 1934.
Der Früchtekorb. Jüngste Ernte. Aufsätze. Rudolstadt: Greifenverlag, 1956.
Über Schriftsteller, edited by Heinz Kamnitzer. Berlin: Aufbau-Verlag, 1967.
Sigmund Freud - Arnold Zweig Briefwechsel, edited by Ernst L. Freud. Frankfurt a.M.: S. Fischer Verlag, 1968.

Works by Arnold Zweig in English Translation
The Case of Sergeant Grischa. Translated by Eric Sutton. New York: The Viking Press, 1928. Republished by Stackpole Books, Harrisburg (Pa.), 1969.
Claudia. Translated by Eric Sutton. New York: The Viking Press, 1930.
Young Woman of 1914. Translated by Eric Sutton. New York: The Viking Press, 1932.
Playthings of Time. Translated by Eric Sutton. New York: The Viking Press, 1935.
De Vriendt goes home. Translated by Eric Sutton. London: Heinemann, 1936.
Education before Verdun. Translated by Eric Sutton. New York: The Viking Press, 1936.
Insulted and Exiled. The Truth about German Jews (Translation of *Bilanz der deutschen Judenheit 1933*). Translated by Eden and Cedar Paul. London: John Miles, 1937.
The Crowning of a King. Translated by Eric Sutton. New York: The Viking Press, 1938.
The Axe of Wandsbek. Translated by Eric Sutton. New York: The Viking Press, 1947.
The letters of Sigmund Freud and Arnold Zweig, edited by Ernst L. Freud. Translated by Elaine and William Robson-Scott. New York: Harcourt Brace Jovanovich, 1970.

SECONDARY SOURCES

1. Books

Arnold Zweig zum Siebzigsten Geburtstag. Eine Festschrift. Presented by the Deutsche Akademie der Künste. Berlin: Aufbau-Verlag, 1957.

Arnold Zweig. Ein Almanach. Presented by the Deutsche Akademie der Künste. Berlin: Aufbau-Verlag, 1962.

HILSCHER, EBERHARD. *Arnold Zweig.* Berlin: Volk and Wissen, 1968. An earlier version appeared as *Arnold Zweig. Brückenbauer vom Gestern ins Morgen.* Halle (Saale): Verlag Sprache und Literatur, 1962. A sympathetic and valuable survey.

KAMNITZER, HEINZ. *Erkenntnis und Bekenntnis. Arnold Zweig 70 Jahre.* Berlin: Aufbau-Verlag, 1958.

KAUFMANN, EVA. *Arnold Zweigs Weg zum Roman.* Berlin: Rütten & Loening, 1967. A thorough and perceptive study of Zweig's career up to and including *The Case of Sergeant Grischa.*

RUDOLPH, JOHANNA. *Der Humanist Arnold Zweig.* Berlin: Henschelverlag, 1955.

Sinn und Form. Sonderheft Arnold Zweig. Berlin: Rütten & Loening, 1952.

TOPER, PAVEL. *Arnold Zweig.* Moscow: Soviet Pisatel, 1960. (In Russian.)

VOIGTLÄNDER, ANNIE. *Welt und Wirkung eines Romans. Zu Arnold Zweigs 'Streit um den Sergeanten Grischa.'* Berlin: Aufbau-Verlag, 1967. (Contains the most important reviews of the novel.)

2. Articles and Essays

ANDERLE, HANS PETER. "Arnold Zweig," in *Mitteldeutsche Erzähler*, Köln, 1965, pp. 50 - 55.

BERNHARD, HANS J. "Die Entwicklung des kritischen Realismus Arnold Zweigs im Lichte der proletarischen Gestalten seines Grischazyklus," *Wissenschaftliche Zeitschrift der Universität Rostock*, IX (1959 - 1960), 61 - 66.

COWLEY, MALCOLM. "Eastern Front: 1918," *The New Republic*, XCV (1938), 106.

FISHMAN, SOLOMON. "The War Novels of Arnold Zweig," *Sewanee Review*, XLIX (1941), 433 - 451.

GEISMAR, MAXWELL. "Mankind at War," *The Nation*, CXLVI (1938), 651 - 652.

GOTTGETREU, ERICH. "Arnold Zweigs Wanderung von Berlin nach Berlin," *Emuna*, IV (1969), 7 - 10.

HILSCHER, EBERHARD. "Der Dramatiker Arnold Zweig," *Weimarer Beiträge*, VI (1960), 1 - 25.

———. "Notizen zu Arnold Zweigs Biographie und Frühwerk," *Neue Deutsche Literatur*, X (1962), 10 - 15.

KAHN, LOTHAR. "Arnold Zweig: From Zionism to Marxism," in *Mirrors of the Jewish Mind*, New York, 1968, pp. 194 - 209.

KAMNITZER, HEINZ. "Arnold Zweig in War and Peace," *Mainstream*, XII (1959), 17 - 26.

———. "Arnold Zweig; Frage und Antwort 1918 - 1933," *Neue Deutsche Literatur*, XV (1967), 6 - 32.

———. "Vorkrieg," *Neue Deutsche Literatur*, XX (1972), 98 - 115.

———. "Im Fegefeuer," *Neue Deutsche Literatur*, XXI (1973), 89 - 115. The three German articles by Kamnitzer provide much biographical information.

LUKACS, GEORG. "Arnold Zweigs Romanzyklus über den imperialistischen Krieg 1914 - 1918," in *Schicksalswende*, Berlin, 1948, pp. 273 - 313.

———. "Gruβ an Arnold Zweig," in *Sinn und Form. Sonderheft Arnold Zweig*, Berlin, 1952, pp. 11 - 18.

MAYER, HANS. "Der Grischa-Zyklus," in *Sinn und Form. Sonderheft Arnold Zweig*, Berlin, 1952, pp. 203 - 219.

PFEILER, WILLIAM K. "Arnold Zweig," in *War and the German Mind*, New York, 1941, pp.. 129 - 139.

POZNER, VLADIMIR. "Reise nach Verdun. Eine Begegnung mit Arnold Zweig," *Neue Deutsche Literatur*, XI (1963), 65 - 72.

RADDATZ, FRITZ J. "Zwischen Freud und Marx: Arnold Zweig," in *Traditionen und Tendenzen; Materialien zur Literatur der DDR*, Frankfurt a.M., 1972, pp. 279 - 300.

REICH - RANICKI, MARCEL. "Der preuβische Jude Arnold Zweig," in *Deutsche Literatur in West und Ost*, München, 1963, pp. 305 - 342.

RILLA, PAUL. "Heimatliteratur oder Nationalliteratur?" in *Sinn und Form. Sonderheft Arnold Zweig*, Berlin, 1952, pp. 123 - 145.

RÜHLE, JÜRGEN. "Die Kunst des inneren Vorbehalts," in *Literatur und Revolution*, Köln, 1960, pp. 207 - 216.

SCHNEIDER, ROLF. "Das novellistische Werk Arnold Zweigs," *Aufbau*, XII (1956), 273 - 277.

TRILLING, LIONEL. "Zweig's Tetralogy; *Young Woman of 1914*," *The Nation*, CXXXVI (1933), 70 - 71.

VORMWEG, HEINRICH. "Gerechtigkeit über sich fühlend; Arnold Zweigs Roman *Das Beil von Wandsbek*," in *Die Deutsche Exilliteratur 1933 - 1945*, ed. Manfred Durzak, Stuttgart, 1973, pp. 326 - 334.

WALTER, HANS - ALBERT. "Auf dem Wege zum Staatsroman; Arnold Zweigs Grischa-Zyklus," *Frankfurter Hefte*, XXIII (1968), 564 - 574.

3. Bibliographies

RÖMER, HUBERTUS, Werner Heidrich and Ilse Lange, "Arnold-Zweig-Bibliographie," in *Sinn und Form. Sonderheft Arnold Zweig*, Berlin, 1952, pp. 280 - 301.

ZITOMIRSKAJA, ZINAIDA V. *Arnold Zweig; Ein bio-bibliographisches Handbuch*. Moscow, 1961. The most complete bibliography.

Index

Zweig's works are listed under his name.